LIFE IN AN EGYPTIAN VILLAGE IN LATE ANTIQUITY

Most ancient history studies focus on the urban elite. Papyrology explores the daily lives of the more typical men and women in antiquity. Aphrodito, a village in sixth-century AD Egypt, is antiquity's best source for micro-level social history. The archive of Dioskoros of Aphrodito introduces thousands of people going about the normal business of their lives: loans, rent contracts, work agreements, marriage, divorce. In exceptional cases, the papyri show raw conflict: theft, plunder, murder. Throughout, Dioskoros struggles to keep his family in power in Aphrodito, and to keep Aphrodito independent from the local tax collectors. The emerging picture is a different vision of Roman late antiquity than the one from the viewpoint of urban elites. It is a world of free peasants building networks of trust largely beyond the reach of the state. Aphrodito's eighth-century AD papyri show that this world died in the early years of Islamic rule.

GIOVANNI R. RUFFINI is a professor in the Department of History at Fairfield University, Connecticut. He is the co-founder of *Dotawo: A Journal of Nubian Studies* and is the author of numerous articles and several books on Byzantine Egypt and medieval Nubia. These books include *Social Networks in Byzantine Egypt* (Cambridge University Press, 2008) and *Medieval Nubia: A Social and Economic History* (2012).

LIFE IN AN EGYPTIAN VILLAGE IN LATE ANTIQUITY

Aphrodito Before and After the Islamic Conquest

GIOVANNI R. RUFFINI

Fairfield University, Connecticut

CAMBRIDGE
UNIVERSITY PRESS

University Printing House, Cambridge CB2 8BS, United Kingdom

One Liberty Plaza, 20th Floor, New York, NY 10006, USA

477 Williamstown Road, Port Melbourne, VIC 3207, Australia

314–321, 3rd Floor, Plot 3, Splendor Forum, Jasola District Centre,
New Delhi – 110025, India

79 Anson Road, #06–04/06, Singapore 079906

Cambridge University Press is part of the University of Cambridge.

It furthers the University's mission by disseminating knowledge in the pursuit of
education, learning, and research at the highest international levels of excellence.

www.cambridge.org
Information on this title: www.cambridge.org/9781107105607
DOI: 10.1017/9781316226377

© Giovanni Ruffini 2018

This publication is in copyright. Subject to statutory exception
and to the provisions of relevant collective licensing agreements,
no reproduction of any part may take place without the written
permission of Cambridge University Press.

First published 2018

Printed in the United Kingdom by TJ International Ltd. Padstow Cornwall

A catalogue record for this publication is available from the British Library.

Library of Congress Cataloging-in-Publication Data
NAMES: Ruffini, Giovanni, 1974– author.
TITLE: Life in an Egyptian village in late antiquity : Aphrodito before and after the Islamic
conquest / Giovanni R. Ruffini.
DESCRIPTION: Cambridge, United Kingdom ; New York, NY : Cambridge University Press, 2018.
| Includes bibliographical references and index.
IDENTIFIERS: LCCN 2018014719 | ISBN 9781107105607 (alk. paper)
SUBJECTS: LCSH: Aphrodito (Extinct city) – History. | Egypt – History – 30 B.C.-640 A.D. |
Egypt – History – 640–1250.
CLASSIFICATION: LCC DT73.A75 R84 2018 | DDC 932/.3–dc23
LC record available at https://lccn.loc.gov/2018014719

ISBN 978-1-107-10560-7 Hardback

Cambridge University Press has no responsibility for the persistence or accuracy of
URLs for external or third-party internet websites referred to in this publication
and does not guarantee that any content on such websites is, or will remain,
accurate or appropriate.

Contents

List of Figures		*page* vi
List of Map		vii
Cast of Characters		viii
1	Aphrodito in Egypt	1
2	A World of Violence	28
3	A World of Law	42
4	Dioskoros, Caught in Between	60
5	Working in the Fields	75
6	Town Crafts and Trades	94
7	Looking to Heaven	111
8	From Cradle to Grave	131
9	Aphrodito's Women	149
10	Big Men and Strangers	164
11	Life in the Big City	181
12	Conclusion	200
Bibliography		214
General Index		227
Index Locorum		231

Figures

1.1	An overview of the 1901 excavations in Kom Ishqaw (Aphrodito), reproduced from Quibell, J. (1902) "Kom Ishgaw." *Annales du Service des antiquités de l'Égypte* 3: 85–88	page 6
1.2	A chest found in the 1901 excavations in Kom Ishqaw (Aphrodito), reproduced from Quibell, J. (1902) "Kom Ishgaw." *Annales du Service des antiquités de l'Égypte* 3: 85–88	7
1.3	The small finds from the 1901 excavations in Kom Ishqaw (Aphrodito), reproduced from Quibell, J. (1902) "Kom Ishgaw." *Annales du Service des antiquités de l'Égypte* 3: 85–88	7
1.4	An aerial view of Egypt today, from Google Earth	14
1.5	An aerial view of Kom Ishqaw today, from Google Earth	15
1.6	An aerial view of Kom Ishqaw and its surrounding region today, from Google Earth	17
3.1	"Headman's Door," Kom Ishqaw (Egypt), Photo © 1995–2015 Clement Kuehn	48
3.2	"Rubble," Kom Ishqaw (Egypt), Photo © 1995–2015 Clement Kuehn	49
7.1	"Church Door," Kom Ishqaw (Egypt), Photo © 1995–2015 Clement Kuehn	121
7.2	"Crosses," Kom Ishqaw (Egypt), Photo © 1995–2015 Clement Kuehn	122
11.1	Antinoopolis: an illustration of the ruins, published in 1809 in the *Description de l'Égypte*	183
11.2	An illustration of charioteers from an Antinoopolis papyrus, AD c. 500	186

Map

Map 1 Map of late Roman Egypt *page* x

Cast of Characters

Ammonios the Count
An outsider to Aphrodito who appears in its records over several decades in the first half of the sixth century. He owns land in the region, some of which is managed by the town headman, Apollos. He acts as a patron of Aphrodito, or at least of the family of Apollos when that family dominates town politics.

Apollos, father of Dioskoros
Headman of Aphrodito over several decades in the first half of the sixth century. He is the father of Dioskoros of Aphrodito, and keeper of the family papyrus archives, perhaps until his death in the 540s. Founder of a local monastery in Aphrodito, he travels as far as Constantinople in defense of his family and town business.

Athanasios the Duke
An outsider to Aphrodito, a duke of the Thebaid (southern Egypt) in the 560s, and contemporary of Dioskoros. Dioskoros writes petitions to him multiple times, seeking redress both for others and for himself, particularly in the case of complaints against the pagarch, Menas.

Dioskoros, son of Apollos
Poet, headman of Aphrodito in the 550s, and the central character in his family papyrus archives. He is the son of Apollos, and husband of Sophia. His poems, petitions, and accounts record his many struggles against both internal and external rivals. He travels twice to Constantinople at least in part on business related to these rivalries.

Herakleios the Headman
Headman of Aphrodito in the 550s or 560s, and rival to Dioskoros. Count Ammonios extracts administrative favors from Herakleios for Dioskoros. Dioskoros accuses the partisans of Herakleios of damage to his property

and other attacks against him. (But this Herakleios is not the murder victim appearing at the start of Chapter 1.)

Ioulianos the Pagarch
A pagarch (regional administrator) in the 550s and colleague of Patrikia and Menas. He is a consistent target of complaints from Dioskoros, who objects to his attempts to bring Aphrodito into his administrative jurisdiction. Dioskoros also accuses him of seizing some of his family's property.

Menas the Pagarch
Patrikia's deputy in the 550s, and a pagarch in his own right in the 560s. Dioskoros writes a series of petitions accusing Menas of various misdeeds, including seizure of his land, transfer of his land to residents in a neighboring village, violence against his brother-in-law, and the arrest of his son.

Patrikia the Pagarch
A pagarch in the 550s, and thus one of the region's most influential women. She is a colleague of Ioulianos and Menas. Dioskoros writes a poem celebrating her marriage in which he compares her to the Graces and credits her with descent from the sun god Apollo.

Phoibammon, son of Triadelphos
Married to a cousin of Dioskoros and himself, like Dioskoros, a headman of Aphrodito in the 550s. He is best known as a land entrepreneur whose career stretched from the 520s to the 570s. He specializes in loans to and leases from absentee landowners and the gradual accumulation of their overleveraged assets.

Sophia, daughter of Ioannes
The "well-born" wife of Dioskoros, she appears in the Aphrodito papyri in the second half of the sixth century, particularly as an intermediary in tax receipts and a lessor in lease agreements. She is likely to have been the keeper of the family papyrus archives after her husband's death.

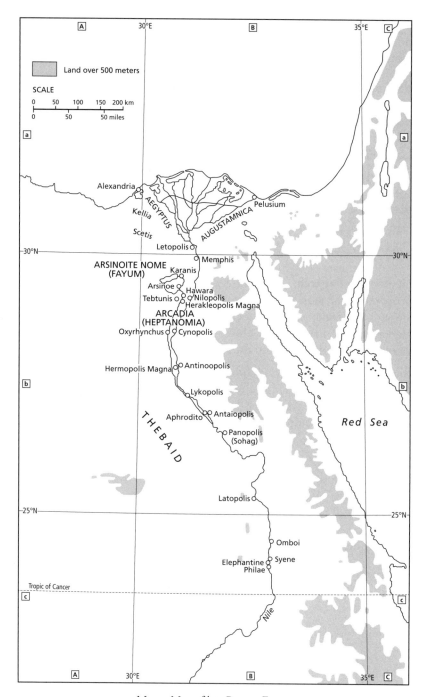

Map 1 Map of late Roman Egypt

CHAPTER I

Aphrodito in Egypt

Aphrodito, Southern Egypt, AD c. 540[*]

"The headmen of my village Aphrodito arrested my husband and put him in the watch-house of my village," Maria says to the judge.[1] "After taking wine to the watch-house, they drank with him, and when the evening came, they beat my husband Herakleios and killed him with their swords. Afterwards, they gave his remains to the fire." Maria knows who killed her husband, and she knows who put them up to it: a local nobleman, the most illustrious Sarapammon and a soldier named Menas. "When Herakleios, my wretched husband, had been killed," she continues, "and his remains had been given to the fire so that they may be burned ... they threw his bones in a basket and buried them I do not know where. I ask, therefore, that they are given to me so that I can bury them."

Earlier in the proceedings, the judge had heard further testimony against Menas from a man whose name is lost. "Menas forced my brother Victor, a priest, outside and murdered him. He threw a piece of machine wood at his left arm and beat his stomach from the fifth hour until evening of the same day ... If I shall not prove that he murdered my brother, I shall die instead of him." When Menas testifies he insists he is innocent. He claims

---

[*] Citations follow the *Checklist of Editions of Greek, Latin, Demotic and Coptic Papyri, Ostraca and Tablets* and *The Checklist of Arabic Documents*. Throughout this book, when footnotes cite only a personal name and a number (e.g., 'Dioskoros 3'), they refer to that entry in Ruffini 2011.

I am grateful to Roger Bagnall, Jean-Luc Fournet, James Keenan, and Leslie MacCoull for their ceaseless support of my study of Aphrodito, and I am particularly grateful to Roger Bagnall for his financial support of that work in its early years. I am also grateful to Clement Kuehn for permission to use his pictures of Kom Ishqaw. Two anonymous readers, Roger Bagnall, James Keenan, and Giulio Ruffini provided comments on and corrections to earlier drafts of this book and James Keenan also provided his copies of Leslie MacCoull's pictures of Kom Ishqaw. I am grateful to all of them for the resulting improvements, which have been incorporated on almost every page of this book, necessarily without further acknowledgment.

Leslie MacCoull had also agreed to read this book's first draft, but died two months before it was complete. I dedicate this book to her memory.

[1] *P.Mich.* 13.660, paraphrase of translation in ed. princ.

to have been somewhere else entirely and that Victor died from a throat abscess. As for Maria's husband Herakleios, "I was not there and I do not know."

Menas's defense does not ring true and the trial points to a larger conspiracy. Flavius Apollos, the town headman and a central figure in Aphrodito's story, suspects a setup from the beginning.[2] When he comes before the judge, his testimony hints at the truth. Imperial officials above his pay grade had instigated the killings with an eye on the kickbacks they could skim off the top of the fines levied for the murders.

It is not clear why Herakleios and Victor died or whether the plaintiffs had the right suspects. Nor is it clear whether Apollos's conspiracy theory is correct. These proceedings are exceptional: nothing else like them survives from the records of this town. Aphrodito is not awash in violent crime. But this murder mystery does record the authentic voice of the ordinary men and women of late antiquity, facing the hardships of the world around them. Moreover, it is only one story out of hundreds from the records of everyday life in Aphrodito.

These records are unique for the ancient world. No other place or time gives such an immediate glimpse of daily life for so many of the average men and women of antiquity. No other place or time lets us watch thousands of people interact with each other from cradle to grave. Almost all of these people are neighbors. Hundreds of them are demonstrably friends, family, and business partners, or in some cases the reverse – enemies and rivals. Most of the rest almost certainly know each other, or know someone else who does.[3] These ancient documents show people living their lives from the inside, the way we live our own. Regarded in this way, the ancient world starts to look quite a bit different than it does in the "big picture" histories, with their eyes on the emperors and the cultural elite.

For a modern audience, ancient Egypt may conjure up the world of the pyramids and the mask of Tutankhamen. But ancient Egyptian civilization continued after the last of the pharaohs for another thousand years under Greek and Roman rule. Although Egyptians abandoned their ancestral gods in favor of Christianity, much of their language and culture remained unchanged. The Muslims who conquered Egypt in the seventh century AD and brought an end to Greco-Roman antiquity discovered people like Maria and her husband Herakleios, who still spoke a later form

---

[2] Assuming Apollos 2 = Apollos 33 in Ruffini 2011.
[3] Hundreds connected: Ruffini 2008a, 203. Degrees of separation: Ruffini 2008a, 206–207.

of the language of the pharaohs, but also debated Christian theology and practiced Roman law.

These people lived in an intensely busy period of history. The reign of the emperor Justinian, from AD 527 to 565, is one of the most intriguing political periods in late antiquity. History remembers Justinian's reign for its architectural accomplishments, particularly the Hagia Sophia, which is still one of the dominant features of the skyline in modern Istanbul. History also remembers him for the extensive and influential codification of Roman law he initiated during his reign. His wars against Persia in the east and the barbarian kingdoms of the west show his determination to assert Roman strength after the weakness and uncertainty of previous generations.

Throughout, Justinian struggled to solve the most pressing religious issue of his time, the controversy over the Council of Chalcedon. This church council, held generations before in AD 451, had deepened an ongoing theological division in the Christian church. A debate, arcane to many modern readers, raged over the divinity and humanity of Jesus. The Council of Chalcedon declared that Jesus had both a human and a divine nature. This decision alienated many people throughout the Roman world: so-called Monophysites who believed that Jesus had only one divine nature, synthesized with his humanity. This debate would ultimately sever the Monophysite Egyptian church from the rest of orthodox Christendom. However, we must always remember as we explore Aphrodito that these pressing issues – the wars, the legislation, the theological debates of Justinian's reign – are almost nowhere to be found in the town's documentary records.

Aphrodito is a small town: it had legally been a city long ago, but probably never had more than 10,000 inhabitants.[4] Tucked away, off the beaten path in southern Egypt, it is not a center of the action. But it is not far from the Nile, and that river's regular agricultural rhythms shape its life. Like so many Egyptian towns in this period, it is dotted with Christian churches and monasteries. At the same time, its elite enjoyed a classical education, studied Roman law in Alexandria, read Homer's *Iliad* and wrote poetry inspired by it. What sets Aphrodito apart from the dozens, even hundreds of Egyptian villages like it is an accident of history: hundreds of papyri – possibly over a thousand – survive from sixth-century

---

[4] This is not a scientific estimate, merely a hunch based on the number of attestations in Ruffini 2011 and the number of apparently missing women, on which see page 158.

Aphrodito, showing the daily activities of thousands of people at a level unknown for any other site of this period.

These records paint a complicated picture, with two dominating towers of evidence. On the one hand, the forces of chaos, conflict, and struggle appear throughout the papyri. Late antique Aphrodito is a town of factions and competition for local power. Beyond the two murders, the record includes street brawls, home invasions, contested divorces, spousal abandonment, and even false enslavement. Local clans hold the reins of town power. The competition between these clans stirs up violence on the borders between Aphrodito and nearby villages. This violence is in turn part of a larger game of land grabbing and agricultural speculation played by both town elites and the more powerful but more distant provincial nobility.

On the other hand, the forces of order and control appear as well. Top officials meticulously record each theft. The town elites gather in the courthouse to settle inheritance disputes. Marriage vows include elaborate conditions for the satisfaction of both parties. Monks and nuns record the pious endowments of the local elite and guard Aphrodito from evil demons. Powerful women run local businesses and large estates. House builders, goldsmiths, ironworkers, and other tradesmen record contract after contract to order their affairs. But both parts of this picture, the order and the chaos, are ultimately exceptional. Throughout this book, we will also imagine a missing world. In this world, most events thrive on the mundane currency of face-to-face small-town trust, and need no written evidence.

Aphrodito is the best-documented place per capita in the entire ancient world. We deceive ourselves about the places we think we know better. The great cities of antiquity – Athens, Alexandria, Rome, Constantinople – have left detailed histories, literary works introducing their political and social elites, but the average resident of those cities is lost, nameless, and faceless. Pompeii, buried under ash in the first century AD, survives remarkably intact, but most of its people remain anonymous, and their affairs are largely unknown. (The papyri surviving from nearby Herculaneum only show the contents of one man's library.)

Other places in Egypt have produced papyrus finds comparable to or larger than those from Aphrodito: Karanis, Herakleopolis, Hermopolis, Oxyrhynchos, Soknopaiou Nesos, Tebtunis. These cities and towns have provided hundreds, even thousands, of papyri for our study. But these papyri cover centuries at a time. They give close-ups only rarely, of comparably few people at a time.⁵ The evidence from Aphrodito, by contrast, zooms in on just a few decades, but introduces many more people in detail. The contrast is comparable to studying a neighborhood in a modern city by looking at the passengers of a single train car stopped in a station. They are far more comprehensible than the passengers of an entire train moving past at full speed.

Because of the rich detail included in its records, Aphrodito has been compared to Montaillou.⁶ In the 1970s, Emmanuel Le Roy Ladurie published a pioneering work of microhistory on Montaillou. This French village – with a population of only a few hundred – was the subject of extensive investigation by the Inquisition. The records of that investigation allowed Le Roy Ladurie to write a detailed history of Montaillou's social life in the period from the 1290s to the 1320s. His work became one of the best-known studies of microhistory ever written. Antiquity will never produce any records so richly detailed. Aphrodito is the closest we can get.

Evidence survives from Aphrodito in part because of sheer luck. There were at least three major finds: in 1901, 1905, and in the 1930s or 1940s. In 1901, the villagers of Kom Ishqaw came across a large collection of papyri while constructing a tomb on the edge of the village's Islamic cemetery.⁷ Reporting the find the following year, the British Egyptologist James Quibell wrote:

> There was, I was assured, nearly 2 cubic metres of [papyrus]: it lay in an ancient house, with a mat above it and a mat below ... Some had been found before by *sebakh* diggers and burnt. Another pile had been found and covered up again ... But, this time ... nearly everyone in the village had a sample. Word was sent to dealers at Tema, Luxor, Ekhmim, who promptly came.⁸

After the antiquities officials were alerted, the site was guarded, and Quibell started formal excavations (Figure 1.1). He found only a few papyrus fragments, but was able to excavate parts of a series of houses, giving a sense of how the ancient residents had lived.

---

⁵ In terms of texts per period, the only real competition is Soknopaiou Nesos, which gives us 666 texts in ninety years in the second and third centuries AD: see www.trismegistos.org/fayum/fayum2/2157.php?geo_id=2157 (accessed February 28, 2016). It was a much smaller place than Aphrodito in this period, with a population around 1,000.
⁶ For the origins of the comparison, see Keenan 1984, 56 with note 44.
⁷ A tomb (Quibell 1902, 85), not a well (Bell 1908, 97; Bell 1944, 21; Keenan 1984, 52; MacCoull 1988, 2).
⁸ Quibell 1902, 85.

Figure 1.1 An overview of the 1901 excavations in Kom Ishqaw (Aphrodito), reproduced from Quibell, J. (1902) "Kom Ishgaw." *Annales du Service des antiquités de l'Égypte* 3: 85–88

The houses had been of two stories, with square winding staircases inside the building: the rooms were 3 to 5 m. long and about 1 1/2 m. wide, and often covered with barrel vaulting still complete in some cases. Every door seems to have been flanked by brick columns with capital and base of limestone... fragments of long carved beams were not rare. There were fragments too of various kinds of fine glass. The signs of a much higher degree of comfort than in modern time were unmistakable.[9]

Quibell also found a number of ostraca (sherds of broken pottery used for writing), a wooden box that he took to be a linen chest (Figure 1.2), which also held a few fragments of papyrus, and a number of other small finds, including a wooden relief of an antelope, a hammer, and some earthenware and pottery dolls (Figure 1.3).

The papyri found in 1901 sold on the open market. Over the next few years, they found their way into museum collections in Cairo, Heidelberg, Strasbourg, and London (where the largest portion of the find is housed, in

---

[9] Quibell 1902, 87.

Figure 1.2 A chest found in the 1901 excavations in Kom Ishqaw (Aphrodito), reproduced from Quibell, J. (1902) "Kom Ishgaw." *Annales du Service des antiquités de l'Égypte* 3: 85–88

Figure 1.3 The small finds from the 1901 excavations in Kom Ishqaw (Aphrodito), reproduced from Quibell, J. (1902) "Kom Ishgaw." *Annales du Service des antiquités de l'Égypte* 3: 85–88

the British Library).¹⁰ In subsequent decades, further collections came to light in the United States and the Soviet Union.¹¹ These papyri are mostly letters and accounts from the early AD 700s and represent some of the best sources for the early Muslim administration of Egypt. They include seventy-five letters from the Muslim governor, Qurra ibn Sharīk, to Aphrodito's local administrator, and some – although far fewer – addressed to the people of the region as a whole.

The local official at the receiving end of the governor's attention, Basil, is the administrator of Aphrodito. Basil's archive has over 400 texts.¹² The majority of them are in Greek, but the archive also includes over fifty texts in Arabic and over 150 in Coptic. They are an excellent source for learning about the administration and finance of early Muslim Egypt, but they are dry and impersonal compared to the earlier texts found at Kom Ishqaw.

The next major discovery came in 1905. A wall collapse in a house in Kom Ishqaw opened a crevice full of papyrus scrolls. Gustav Lefebvre, the local antiquities inspector, was able to recover some of the pieces, including fragments of a Greek comedy, but large portions of the find had already been dispersed.¹³ He took the village headman's word that he would be notified if anyone in the village made plans to demolish any of the local houses. He did not have to wait for long: the owner of the same property was soon planning to raise one of his walls as part of a house renovation.

> Hearing the news, Lefebvre launched three quick days of excavations on the site. After only one meter of digging, he uncovered ancient walls of unbaked brick. There had been a roof, of which the first few courses were still visible. The walls continued down for another two meters and demarcated three rooms. It was a medium-sized house, which had been built during the Roman period. In the corner of one small room, which had an area of no more than one and a half square meters, stood a large jar which was shattered down to its neck. It was now about .90 meter tall.¹⁴

In that jar, he found a codex (an ancient book) with fragments of the lost plays of Menander, and some 150 rolls of documentary papyri. Lefebvre went back twice in the next two years, but found nothing as spectacular as the finds from 1905.¹⁵

However, spectacular they are. This find includes 680 texts: sixty-three of them are literary papyri, preserving pieces of ancient literature; the

---

[10] Bell 1908, 98. [11] Abbott 1938, 9. [12] Fournet 2016. See also Morelli 2013, 172–175.
[13] Lefebvre 1907, ix. [14] Kuehn 1995, 43. [15] Lefebvre 1907, xi.

remaining 617 are documentary.¹⁶ Over 90 percent of these documentary texts are in Greek, forty of them in Coptic Egyptian. They include personal letters, petitions, loans, sales, rent agreements, tax lists, tax receipts, and more. A large portion of these documents relate to the business affairs of Apollos and – more importantly – his son Dioskoros, who appears in so many of these texts that for over a century they have been described as the Dioskoros archive.

This archive is a multi-headed beast. Much of its material comes directly from the town records: tax lists, police reports, court proceedings, and other official business. But this is not the town government's archive. Much of its material comes directly from Dioskoros's family affairs: rent records for family land, administration of the family monastery, personal accounts, and property lists. Apollos and Dioskoros – who both serve as village headman in Aphrodito over several decades – either conduct official business out of their own homes or take some of the town's official papers home with them when they retire. The result is an unparalleled glimpse into the public and private lives of a single town and extended family over the course of the sixth century.

According to Leslie MacCoull, "natives later carried on clandestine diggings at the Kom Ishqaw site, in 1937–38, and some papyri uncovered in these operations found their way to the Cairo Museum."¹⁷ Jean-Luc Fournet has written about clandestine digs in Kom Ishqaw taking place at the start of the 1940s.¹⁸ Both reports probably refer to the same events. One group of Aphrodito papyri purchased in 1943, and another reportedly found circa 1945, come from these clandestine digs.

Not all of the Roman-period papyri from Aphrodito came from the archive of Dioskoros. The organized excavations of 1905 and the clandestine digs of the 1930s or 1940s produced what appear to be several different late antique archives.¹⁹ The clandestine papyri, over seventy of which are known, include the Greek archive of Phoibammon, son of Triadelphos, and the later Coptic archive of Kollouthos, son of Christophoros.²⁰

These two batches of texts formed a larger single collection in antiquity. However, the exact connection between them is not clear. Kollouthos may

---

¹⁶ Totals: Fournet 2016. List: Fournet 2008a, Annexe 2.
¹⁷ MacCoull 1990a, 107, provides no source for these excavations. She argues that this dig produced the texts in P.Cair.inv. SR 37333, some of which have been published in Hanafi 1985, Hanafi 1988, and Fournet 2001. In a personal communication to me, she recalled a report of these excavations as personal information from Mirrit Boutros Ghali.
¹⁸ Fournet 2016.   ¹⁹ Gascou 1977, 361; Fournet 2001, 475, note 2.   ²⁰ Fournet 2016.

be one of Phoibammon's descendants.²¹ Furthermore, these may not be the last Aphrodito finds. A visitor to Kom Ishqaw in the 1980s could not find anyone still alive who had ever heard anything about the discovery of these papyri.²² Nevertheless, another house renovation project in Kom Ishqaw may yet outdo what we already have.

In the indigenous Egyptian language Aphrodito's name is Jkow, meaning "Emporium."²³ It must have been a market town at some point, if not for most of antiquity. The town is called Aphrodito or Aphrodite in Greek, after the goddess the Greeks believe to be the equivalent of the town's ancient Egyptian patron deity, Hathor, the goddess of love and motherhood. The spelling of the town's name changed over time from Aphrodite in late antiquity to Aphrodito in the Arab period. Although Aphrodite is the correct spelling for the period covered in this book, Aphrodito is retained throughout. The discovery of the Arab papyri came first, to some degree ensuring that Aphrodito will always remain the spelling most familiar to modern readers.

There is no real evidence concerning the town during the pharaonic period.²⁴ The first clear literary testimonies of Aphrodito come in the first century AD.²⁵ According to Pliny the Elder, Aphrodito is a *polis*, one of Egypt's celebrated cities. According to Ptolemy the geographer, writing in the second century, Aphrodito is the capital city of a *nome* or regional administrative unit called the Aphroditopolite nome. But here, Ptolemy is apparently confusing our Aphrodito with another Aphrodito farther north.²⁶ Later, in the third century, Aphrodito makes no appearance in the so-called Antonine Itinerary. This sparse collection of literary references is a fragile foundation for studying Aphrodito in earlier periods of Roman rule.²⁷

The documentary papyri give a little more information to work with. A papyrus from the 100s BC describes someone as a member of the Aphrodito bodyguard.²⁸ Aphrodito was probably never the capital of its own nome or administrative region,²⁹ but it had certainly once enjoyed the legal status of a city. A papyrus from the AD 100s mentions the city of Aphrodito and its nearby neighbor, the village of Phthla.³⁰ At this point, the city was probably under the authority of the Apollonopolite nome. When Aphrodito appears next in the papyri, in the AD 300s, the papyri specifically call it a village, not a city.³¹ For some unknown reason, it had

---

[21] Fournet 2016. [22] MacCoull 1988, 3, note 10. [23] MacCoull 1988, 6. [24] Marthot 2013, 14. [25] Marthot 2013, 19. [26] Marthot 2013, 20–22 and 30. [27] Marthot 2013, 22. [28] *PSI* 7.815; see Marthot 2013, 24–25. [29] See note 26. [30] *P.Brem.* 42; see Marthot 2013, 29. [31] *P.Col.* 8.235; *P.Kell.* 2.32; Marthot 2013, 29.

received a demotion, and so it remains legally a village, for centuries, and throughout the period covered by this book.

In the fifth and sixth centuries, it has the right to collect its own taxes through its village elites, independently of the regional officials usually responsible for doing so. As we will see, it defends this right vigorously.[32] And later, under Muslim rule, Aphrodito still maintains that independence, collecting its own taxes as a village directly accountable to the Arab central administration.[33]

The sources do not say whether the people of Aphrodito share a sense of identity. In the papyri, people consistently identify themselves as "from the village of Aphrodito," even when this is obvious from the context. But this says very little. More than once, the villagers – or at least, Dioskoros, speaking on behalf of the villagers – call themselves "small landowners."[34] In one eye-catching case, Dioskoros calls them the "wretched small-holders and inhabitants of the thoroughly wretched village of Aphrodito."[35] Elsewhere, Dioskoros calls himself a "pitiful inhabitant" of Aphrodito.[36] However, all of this is nothing more than Dioskoros trying to earn sympathy for himself and his home. In another passage, Dioskoros mentions "the splendid houses of the former great landowners" of the village.[37] This may be a note of pride, but it too comes in the middle of an attempt to earn sympathy for the village. What these people really think of their hometown is a mystery.

Similarly, the evidence says very little about Aphrodito's actual homes. One document – a division of house property – describes a home probably quite a bit bigger than most. It may even be one of the homes of those ancient great landowners. The description of the house in the original document is fragmentary, but still quite detailed. It

> had a vaulted storage room (*kamara*), a special storage room for bread (*artothêkê*) with a floor above it, a grand reception room (*andrôn*) on an upper floor, and perhaps another reception room above a gateway entrance (*pylôn*), and one or two open-air courtyards (*aithrion, exaithra*).[38]

---

[32] See page 51.
[33] But as a *dioikêsis* (a smaller administrative region under the authority of a local official), not a pagarchy (the larger fiscal jurisdiction of a pagarch, an official subordinate to the local governor): Marthot 2013, 187–196.
[34] *P.Cair.Masp.* 1.67002; *P.Lond.* 5.1674; introduction to the latter, 56–57.
[35] *P.Cair.Masp.* 1.67002.1.2.   [36] *SB* 5.8938.
[37] *P.Cair.Masp.* 1.67002.2.24; trans. MacCoull 1988, 28. Compare Banaji 2001, 10, note 29; Keenan 2007, 237.
[38] Keenan 2007, 236 on *P.Bingen* 130.

This description – borrowed directly from Aphrodito's sixth-century records – sounds like the late antique house found there in 1901: multiple floors, vaulted ceilings, doors with brick sides, and a limestone base.[39]

This impressive house makes an interesting contrast with Aphrodito's official status. Legally speaking, late antique Aphrodito is only a village. All the sources for the period call it that, but from a modern perspective, this is misleading. Villages in Roman Egypt could range in population from a few hundred to a few thousand people. Aphrodito is almost certainly at the high end of the range, and its status as a demoted city shows that it is different from the rest of the villages around it. Informally, I call Aphrodito a town throughout this book. I make an exception when quoting others who do not, or when I need to speak more formally to stay close to the official language of specific documents.

The indigenous name for Aphrodito, Jkow, survives in altered form today in the town's modern name, Kom Ishqaw: the *kom* or hill of Jkow. The modern site is small. At the beginning of the twentieth century, Kom Ishqaw was a town of 4,000 or 5,000 inhabitants.[40] A visitor at the time estimated that about a third of the population was Christian, the rest Muslim.[41] Tourists rarely visit the site today, and have little reason to.

A British visitor to the region in the first half of the twentieth century gave this unwelcoming introduction:

> If you should ever attempt to motor from Assiût southwards to Baliana and Luxor – an enterprise I do not recommend, for the roads are vile – and, after some twenty-five miles of bumping and shaking, should decide, as my companion decided, to try your luck on the opposite side of the Nile Valley, you will come, after a few miles of a straight but evil road leading west, to another which runs southward again beside a canal separated by about a hundred yards of sandy plain from the great cliffs which form the escarpment of the Libyan Desert. The road which you have reached is no better than the one you have left, the dogs of the district are of a ferocity I found nowhere else in Egypt, and the human inhabitants are surly and hostile.[42]

Kom Ishqaw itself may not have been too bad: it "makes a particularly charming effect ... on a mound above the surface of the plain ... overtopped by the one mosque and by numerous palms ... Pleasant ... on a distant view."[43] However, it was not pleasant enough for him to turn off the road to get a closer look. Harold Idris Bell, one of the greatest scholars

---

[39] See page 6. [40] Four thousand: Abbott 1938, 6. Five thousand: Lefebvre 1907, viii.
[41] Quibell 1902, 86. [42] Bell 1944, 21. [43] Bell 1944, 21.

of Aphrodito's papyri, got within minutes of the site and did not go the rest of the way.

In the early 1980s, Leslie MacCoull did visit the village with the help of a priest from the local Coptic Christian church of Saint George. MacCoull writes that "Aphrodito stands on a hill. Unusual among Egyptian sites, which more often lie below the present ground level, the modern town of Kom Ishgaw perches atop a tell that must conceal remains of the Byzantine and [Islamic-era] Umayyad city."[44] The town today sits amid a network of irrigation canals seemingly unchanged from antiquity.[45]

Modern satellite technology gives a bird's-eye view of Egypt's Nile Valley and the surrounding desert (Figure 1.4).[46] Although Kom Ishqaw is in a region called upper or southern Egypt, the town is almost in the center of the country: the Mediterranean Sea is just over 317 miles to the north, the Sudanese border just over 329 miles to the south. As we zoom in, the thin strip of the Nile is our first impression. Almost all of Egypt is desert, the fertile lands of the valley a thin green running down the middle.

As the river runs to the sea, in this region flowing from the southeast to the northwest, it irrigates only a sliver of the surrounding land. Across the river from Kom Ishqaw, farmland on the east bank of the Nile is less than a mile and a half wide. The west bank of the river is much greener, but even here, distances are small. The Nile is at its closest point less than five miles away from the town to the northeast. The western desert is just over four miles away to the southwest.

MacCoull's impression is correct: the town sits on a hill, but not a large one. The highest point in the town, just northwest of center, is only 220 feet above sea level. In fact, hardly anywhere in the town sits less than 190 feet above sea level. Furthermore, the surrounding countryside is not much lower: mile after mile of farmland is only 180 or 185 feet above sea level. This slight slope – 40 feet down from the top of the town to the fields a quarter of a mile away – gives Kom Ishqaw its life. In antiquity, the Nile's rising floodwaters filled the plains and turned Aphrodito from a hill into an island in the midst of a sea of future harvest.

Aerial views of Kom Ishqaw give a sense of the ancient town underneath. Look at the streets of the modern village (Figure 1.5): this is no classical city plan, full of right angles and straight lines. Although Kom Ishqaw is barely half a mile across at its widest point, there is no way to walk through the town in a straight line. One large street approaching from the south opens

---

[44] MacCoull 1988, 5. [45] The impression of MacCoull 1988, 6–7.
[46] Subsequent figures derive from Google Earth, accessed February 8, 2015.

Figure 1.4 An aerial view of Egypt today, from Google Earth

Figure 1.5 An aerial view of Kom Ishqaw today, from Google Earth

onto a wide public space. The rest of the streets curve in slow angles or lurch to an abrupt stop before picking up again a few houses over. It is easy to imagine ancient Aphrodito as little different, its mudbrick houses perched haphazardly on the slopes of the town rising up from the flood plains.

Look at the aerial view of modern Kom Ishqaw and the land around it (Figure 1.6). A few dozen palm trees cast short shadows across otherwise naked farmland. Long rectangular strips of rich green mark land being used for crops. Long gray strips mark the land left fallow. Heading roughly northwest, two thin canals run a crude parallel to the Nile on either side of the village. These canals – and the much smaller ones running from them – help to irrigate the modern village's land.

One ancient text shows how much of that land belonged to Aphrodito in antiquity. An important document from the AD 520s – the Aphrodito cadastre – records all Aphrodito land in the category of *astika*. This category applies to taxes on land formally registered in the accounts of the nearest big city, Antaiopolis, rather than in Aphrodito's own village accounts. It then concludes with a section explaining how that land relates to Aphrodito's total territory. According to the cadastre, that total is just under 4,000 acres of land in the Aphrodito region.[47]

The cadastre's figure leaves out non-arable parts of village land, including roads, dikes, and canals. Add estimates for these features of the land, and the overall area of the village is something like 8.3 square miles, or a circle of land with a radius of roughly 1.6 miles in each direction from Aphrodito.[48] This is more than 10 percent of the land of the Egyptian nome or region of Antaiopolis, Aphrodito's administrative home.[49]

We know ancient names for some of this land.[50] Some of the land immediately to the west and southwest of the town made up the ancient holdings of Pia Peto and Psenkour. More generally, the fields on all sides of the town are labeled by compass points: the fields of the north, south, east, and west. Within each of those divisions, we know more holdings by name. Ancient evidence refers most frequently to the southern fields, where the holdings of Nempketos and Psineiou are near each other, as are the holdings of Psilampon, Hieras, and Akanthon, with the holdings of Pherko probably bordering on land from a neighboring village.

---

[47] Gascou and MacCoull 1987, 118: 5906.375 arouras at 0.677 acres per aroura.
[48] Marthot 2013, 9–10.   [49] Marthot 2013, 10; Banaji 2001, 10; *P.Cair.Masp.* 1.67057.
[50] Marthot 2013, 3, 9–35.

Figure 1.6 An aerial view of Kom Ishqaw and its surrounding region today, from Google Earth

Look again at the aerial view of modern Kom Ishqaw (Figure 1.6). The circle over the modern fields, spreading out 1.6 miles around the village, is the rough size of the land registered in the 520s to the town's cadastre. Half a dozen much smaller modern settlements are within this area, another half a dozen comparably large ones just beyond the edge of the circle. Modern readers with little rural experience should keep this in mind. In this world, the distinction between town and country is blurred: food comes from land all around, and settlements are sprinkled throughout.[51]

Zooming still farther out, the pattern repeats throughout the small space between the river and the desert. The nearest settlement is only a third of a mile away, just a few minutes' walk to the north of the town. The nearest site larger than Kom Ishqaw, the town of al Madmar, is barely over a mile away to the southeast. Not a single place in the region is much more than a mile away from its closest neighbor: up and down the Nile Valley, hundreds of villages and small towns just like Aphrodito pack into a small space, all in walking distance from their nearest neighbors.

A later chapter shows the ongoing conflict between Aphrodito and the nearby village of Phthla.[52] Ancient Phthla may be the modern el Wa'adlah, a village five and a half miles north of Aphrodito.[53] This is more or less two hours away on foot. Tahta and Tima are the largest settlements in the immediate area today, Kom Ishqaw not quite equidistant from each of them. Tahta, just over six miles to the southeast, was the ancient Panopolite village Toetô.[54] Tima may be ancient Thmonachthe, another village often appearing in the Aphrodito papyri.[55]

To state the obvious: Aphrodito is part of a much wider geographic world. Nevertheless, the point is important, as it hints at just how normal Aphrodito might have been. Dioskoros and his neighbors do not live in a vacuum, quite the contrary. Packed so closely together with their neighbors, they live in the same world and breathe the same cultural air as countless others just like them all over Egypt. The stories in this book are stories likely to be repeated with subtle variation in many places throughout the sixth century. Aphrodito's experiences are those of Egypt's Nile Valley as a whole. This is part of what makes our journey there so valuable: what we learn there probably applies to all of Egypt, if not to large portions of the eastern Roman Empire as well.

---

[51] Marthot 2013, 31, speaks of an intermediary zone between village and countryside.
[52] See page 166.   [53] Sauneron 1983, 127, rejected as too far by Marthot 2013, 10, note 15.
[54] Marthot 2013, 11.   [55] Gascou has proposed it to be Pteme: Marthot 2013, 11.

Dioskoros, son of Apollos, is the most prominent person in Aphrodito's records. Most of the documents and all of the literature that survive from late antique Aphrodito belong to him. He serves as one of Aphrodito's village headmen, as his father Apollos served before him. During his time in office, which lasts from the 540s to the 550s, he travels to Constantinople, the imperial capital, in defense of his hometown and his own personal affairs. Later in life, he works in Antinoopolis, the capital of the Thebaid, the Roman province of southern Egypt.

Labeling Dioskoros is a tricky business. Modern authors alternately call Dioskoros a lawyer or a notary, although neither seems quite right.[56] His own records describe him as a *scholastikos* (advocate or legal adviser) only once, and never a *notarios* (notary). The one time someone calls him a *scholastikos*, the term may be mere flattery, or more generally mean that he is learned.[57] Local records call him a *ktêtôr* (landowner), a *suntelestês* (tax contributor), and a *prôtokômêtês* (headman).[58] Less technically, they call him the *eudokimôtatos* (most esteemed) and *thaumasiôtatos* (most marvelous).

At a certain point in the 540s, Dioskoros begins to call himself Flavius Dioskoros. The "Flavius" is a status designation common in the eastern Mediterranean region during this period, indicating imperial service or its honorary equivalent. Being a Flavius in late antiquity sets individuals apart and shows that they have a status and dignity superior to average Roman citizens, who are otherwise called "Aurelius" by default. Dioskoros's elevation to the status of Flavius

> is the direct result of an investment [his father] Apollos made in human capital, the consequence of the money he expended on Dioskoros' education, which opened doors into the law and civil service ... Dioskoros' social advancement owed something significant to [Aphrodito] itself, that is, to his being the product of an environment that was relatively free from aristocratic interests and demands.[59]

Put another way, even in small-town southern Egypt, a local big-man can start down the road to greater things. However, this road is full of traps. Dioskoros's records have page after page of protest and complaint about injustices he faces at the hands of everyone from shepherds to dukes.

These records – his petitions and poetry – are the most controversial parts of his legacy. Barry Baldwin called him the worst poet of

---

[56] Lawyer: e.g., MacCoull 1988, 12; Dijkstra 2004, 137. Notary: van Minnen 2003, 115; Keenan 2014, 27.
[57] *P.Cair.Masp.* 1.67064.   [58] Palme 2014, 1, prefers "foreman" to "headman."
[59] Hickey 2007, 305.

antiquity.⁶⁰ An early critic of Dioskoros's poetry damned his verses as "illustrating the morass of absurdity into which the great river of Greek poetry emptied itself."⁶¹ A generation later, not many people had changed their minds: one dissertation called Dioskoros's verses "so poor that they can hardly be called poems ... [They are] of interest to the history of literature insofar as they typify ... the kind of poetry which antiquity was capable of producing in its dying years."⁶²

More recent authors are more sympathetic. Leslie MacCoull, Dioskoros's first great champion, calls his poetry "a sensitive, living witness to the values and the preoccupations of a Mediterranean way of life."⁶³ Clement Kuehn – whose photographs of Kom Ishqaw, modern Aphrodito, appear in this book – argues that Dioskoros's poems are hard to understand because "the poet incorporated elements of Christian mysticism. These mystical elements seem to interrelate to form a deeper level of meaning."⁶⁴

Arkady Kovelman writes that Dioskoros "approached petitions as literature," that he is the "author of a masterpiece, a petition in verse."⁶⁵ Jean-Luc Fournet takes a similar attitude, arguing that Dioskoros creates a documentary poetry. His poetry is functional: taking the time to decipher his message reveals specific requests hidden behind general verses.⁶⁶ Dioskoros is a crisis poet, generating literature in direct response to his life's setbacks.

Those setbacks come more frequently over time.⁶⁷ In the 530s and 540s, some of Dioskoros's family work for a count named Ammonios, whose patronage they enjoy. Later in the 540s, Ammonios's son Theodosios is less friendly, and the villagers accuse him of appropriating their tax money for his own purposes. In the 550s, the villagers accuse Ioulianos, a pagarch (an official in charge of regional tax collection) in the nearby provincial capital of Antaiopolis, of property seizures and forcible attempts to take control of taxation in Aphrodito. In the 560s, the villagers accuse a later pagarch named Menas of still worse, including thefts, ambush, and wrongful imprisonment.

Dioskoros is in the middle of these crises, coming from one of the most important families in Aphrodito. His father holds some of the town's highest offices and like his son also travels from Aphrodito to Constantinople. Dioskoros's numerous half-brothers, cousins and in-

---

⁶⁰ Baldwin 1984.   ⁶¹ Bell and Crum 1925, 177.   ⁶² Viljamaa 1968, 33.   ⁶³ MacCoull 1988, 57.
⁶⁴ Kuehn 1995, 2.   ⁶⁵ Kovelman 1991, 146–147, referring specifically to *P.Cair.Masp.* 2.67153.
⁶⁶ Fournet 1999, 317.
⁶⁷ See the entries for Ammonios 1, Apollos 2, Dioskoros 3, Menas 13, Ioulianos 2, and Theodosios 16.

laws are among the richest landowners in town. Without his family's records, we would know hardly anything about Aphrodito, our best source for stories of town life in this period of ancient Egypt.

Knowledge of Dioskoros's family is necessary to fully understand these stories. An imperial decree issued in the early 550s calls Apollos, Dioskoros's father, the "chief of the proprietors" of the town.[68] However, this decree is something Dioskoros goes to Constantinople and requests for himself. Its words may be his own description of his father and their life back home. They do not reveal what the rest of the village thought of Apollos before he died, or where he stood in terms of wealth and power in relation to his peers. It is only certain that Apollos was one of the Aphrodito village headmen and tax contributors on and off for several decades from the 510s to the 540s.[69]

Apollos is one among many. His extended family – ancestors, descendants, relatives by blood and marriage – includes nearly forty people named in the records.[70] His brother Besarion is also one of the village headmen in the 520s. Besarion's son Victor, a priest, may be one of the village headmen in the 540s.[71] His grandsons are both prominent landowners. Dioskoros's brother Senouthes is village headman in the 540s, along with Dioskoros himself. Running the village is part of their family business, but there is more to Aphrodito than the story of Dioskoros and his family.[72] In fact, Dioskoros and his family are hardly typical of Aphrodito: they are its political and economic elite. Nevertheless, their records refer to the rest of the town's population and give an insight into the town's everyday life from the inside out.[73]

Investigation of the Aphrodito archives introduces us to thousands of the town's individual inhabitants.[74] The first thing to note is the importance of agriculture: farmers are the most common people recorded. Dozens of them appear by name – likewise, the shepherds. The town records also show beekeepers, butchers, coppersmiths, cumin sellers, doormen, fruit vendors, gardeners, goldsmiths, grain dealers, house builders, oil makers, mill masters, shoemakers – and this is only a sample.

---

[68] *P.Cair.Masp.* 1.67024.3 = *Sel.Pap.* 2.218.3: *tôn en autêi kektêmenôn prôton genomenon*. Hickey 2007, 305: "premier landowner."
[69] Ruffini 2011, *s.n.* Apollos 2.   [70] Ruffini 2011, Stemma 1.
[71] Jean-Luc Fournet (personal communication): restore his name for *tous allous* at *P.Cair.Masp.* 3.67323.5.
[72] For which, see MacCoull 1988; Kuehn 1995; Fournet 1999.
[73] Or "upside down" (Keenan 2007, 237).   [74] Prosopography: Ruffini 2011.

However, this sample is misleading. There is no way of knowing whether the surviving records show a representative part of the whole. Women are badly underrepresented. Children are almost completely missing. By way of contrast, priests are so common in the records, not because Aphrodito was particularly religious, but in part because these priests could write and, consequently, witnessed or wrote many of these texts themselves. Other people fall in our blind spots because their jobs require less paperwork, or because they take their paperwork to other people.

Despite these gaps, Aphrodito is a unique source for the social and economic history of rural life in late antiquity. Not everyone will agree, but it could plausibly substitute for hundreds of small towns throughout the entire eastern Mediterranean: evidence this detailed puts small-town Aphrodito on a bigger stage. It shows us life in Egypt more generally, and indeed life throughout the late Roman world. It gives us a chance to connect the daily life of these villagers to the larger dramas playing throughout the empire. But trying to use this evidence in such a way runs a dangerous risk. With the benefit of hindsight, historians know that Aphrodito's residents are living at the end of the ancient world – they are among the last generations to live under Roman rule in Egypt and throughout the southern Mediterranean. For this reason, Aphrodito gets pulled into a broader debate, and forced to answer questions its own residents could never imagine.

Why did Roman rule fail? Why did classical Greek culture fade away? Why did ancient fiscal and military systems falter in the face of adversity in the sixth and seventh centuries? More specifically, why did so many of the empire's eastern provinces fall so quickly, first to the Persians and later to the Arabs, in the early seventh century? Was the Roman state itself brittle to the core and if so, why? What part of its fiscal health – or its mental health – led to this failure? These debates are hard to follow, and sometimes get wrapped up in modern political concerns.

People engaging in these debates use Aphrodito and its evidence to help answer these questions because of the richness of that evidence. They seldom say so explicitly, but the town becomes a proxy for the Roman world. Aphrodito stars in a conflict over the very nature of late antiquity. For some, late antiquity is rife with class warfare and oppression of the peasants at the hands of the elite: the features apparent in the Aphrodito papyri show why the Roman world collapsed. For others, the situation is more complex: late antiquity is a vibrant time full of cultural creativity, and Aphrodito gives no answers to macro-economic questions.

Those in the first camp are most often generalists, who want to draw big-picture lessons from Aphrodito's unique details. These people study Aphrodito because of a wider interest in socioeconomics. The chief exception is the earliest: Harold Idris Bell, one of the twentieth century's first great scholars of Aphrodito. He knew the Aphrodito papyri better than almost anyone, and saw the town as typical of what he called the Byzantine servile state.[75] As he saw the late Roman world, the average peasant becomes so crushed by the Roman government's excessive taxation that he has no choice but to surrender his land and his labor to a powerful patron. The path to protection from the state is also the path to serfdom for the peasant. The patrons pay taxes directly to the imperial government on behalf of their clients, from whom they collect whatever is needed.

Some towns and villages escape this model and hold the right of *autopragia* (the ability to collect their own taxes). Aphrodito is one such town. As Bell put it, the town's records "give us the impression of a rather higher level of prosperity" than is typical for subjects of the Byzantine servile state. "But even so its lot was far from happy." Aphrodito's records tell of Roman provincial officials coming "to plunder the inhabitants, burn houses, outrage women, carry off the flocks and herds, and, in fact, reduce the village to beggary."

Bell's low opinion of late Roman society matched his opinion of Dioskoros himself. "His character," he wrote of Dioskoros, "may, for all we know to the contrary, have been infamous, his personality, as revealed in the documents he has left us, certainly does not inspire respect, and his verses indubitably merit damnation."[76] Describing Dioskoros, Bell had "the impression of a personality vain, pompous, opinionated, [and] loose in statement," calling him the wisest fool in Aphrodito.[77]

A more recent author, Jairus Banaji, shares Bell's critique of the late antique economy. Banaji's study of agrarian change relies on evidence from late antique Egypt. As he sees it, the increasing importance of gold coinage in this period dramatically alters the economy. It creates a new bureaucratic elite directing its cash income toward the creation of large agricultural estates. Inevitably, the local elite, the small landowners, and the peasants all feel the pinch. In short, the empire's mega-rich start to price out everyone else.

Aphrodito necessarily plays a part in this story. Aphrodito impresses Banaji with a "strong sense of its own autonomy" and because it is

---

[75] Bell 1917, 86–106.   [76] Presumably Bell's voice, not Crum's, in Bell and Crum 1925, 177.
[77] Bell and Crum 1925, 179.

apparently "free from the domination of the aristocracy."[78] Stronger villages can resist the worst effects of the new agrarian economy. Still, the rise of a money economy inevitably impacts peasant labor, and Aphrodito is not immune. Peasant farmers drawn to wage labor are at the mercy of their employers, in Aphrodito as much as anywhere.[79] The implication is subtle, but clear: Aphrodito is part of a larger system oppressing the lower class.

Peter Sarris, another critic of the late antique economy, makes a similar case. He sees the monetization of the sixth-century economy as an engine commodifying labor and making wage laborers dependent on their large estate employers.[80] Only competing patronage networks keep places like Aphrodito precariously independent from aristocratic expansion.[81] The main difference between Banaji and Sarris is who to blame. Sarris gives the local aristocracy considerable power, seeing them as active agents whose independence weakens the Roman Empire.[82] The great estates – dominant elsewhere in Egypt and on the horizon in Aphrodito – make it hard for the empire to collect taxes, causing its military collapse in the late sixth and early seventh centuries.[83]

Constantin Zuckerman shares with Banaji and Sarris an interest in what Aphrodito reveals about wider economic issues. His study of an Aphrodito tax register shows the town's place in the Roman imperial fiscal system.[84] Zuckerman argues that Aphrodito's "mounting money taxes" are the consequences of "an impoverished and desperate [central] government, successfully but hopelessly raising revenues, on an increasingly speeding treadmill ... trying to recover from the aftershocks of the plague."[85]

Whether we end up agreeing with Banaji, Sarris, and Zuckerman or not, their words all have the same effect: to take our eyes off Aphrodito even as we study it, and direct our attention instead to the central government. Other authors deliberately make Aphrodito the focus of their attention. They are less interested in big-picture lessons and more interested in the beauty of the particular details. Leslie MacCoull's enthusiasm for Aphrodito is nearly the opposite of Bell's disdain. Her interest in Dioskoros is a love affair both with Christian Egypt's past and its present. Coptic culture confronts the change around it "with a heartfelt affirmation of the perceived details of life," she writes. Dioskoros "sang in the noonday,

---

[78] Banaji 2001, 11.   [79] See page 91.
[80] Commodified labor: Sarris 2006, 88. Laborer dependence: Sarris 2006, 129.
[81] Sarris 2006, 114.   [82] Agency: Bjornlie 2007.   [83] Sarris 2006, 229–230.
[84] See page 91, for Zuckerman on the estates of Ioulianos.   [85] Keenan 2005, 295.

and did not ask questions."⁸⁶ His poems take wing, a vibrant example of a culture comfortable with itself and its place in the world.

James Keenan, the other American most active in studying Aphrodito, takes a different approach. He neither praises its society nor condemns it, content to show how its many complexities defy earlier expectations. He shows how conflict between Aphrodito's shepherds and its landowners reveals tensions within the town's social structure.⁸⁷ His study of Phoibammon, the son of Triadelphos, describes him as a Byzantine land entrepreneur. As new evidence has emerged, Keenan's conclusions have evolved, first seeing Phoibammon as a middle-class peasant, and now seeing him as "extraordinarily successful," "a man of means in his own village."⁸⁸

These are not the only authors to write about Aphrodito. I mention them only as examples, to show how people respond to the evidence from that town. Banaji and Sarris are not specialists in the Aphrodito material, but argue about larger questions for which that material is sometimes useful. Other Aphrodito specialists stay clear of these debates. Jean-Luc Fournet has produced the best modern editions of the town's literary papyri, and Isabelle Marthot has produced the first systematic study of the region's places.⁸⁹ Their work shows how much more we still have to learn about Aphrodito and its world.

Throughout the debates about Aphrodito, scholars rewrite the past to suit their own political and emotional biases. Bell's disdain for his subject matter suits someone with traditional training in the classics. It reflects an era still comfortable with a belief in the superiority of one culture over others. Banaji and Sarris as modern liberals quite naturally look askance at the rich as history's universal oppressing class. From this point of view, it is easy to look at Aphrodito and see evidence of governmental and aristocratic oppression.

However, the government and the aristocracy are neither the most central features of the evidence from Aphrodito nor the most interesting part of it. The men and women of Aphrodito do not share the preoccupations of modern scholars. Scholars willing to abandon these preoccupations look at Aphrodito and come to different conclusions. For my part, I do not pretend to offer a middle ground between the two sides of the debate: it will soon be obvious which side I favor. When I look at Aphrodito, I do not see a world organized by class and driven by class struggle. I see instead a world of personal relationships, a world in which

---

⁸⁶ MacCoull 1988, 159.   ⁸⁷ Keenan 1985a.   ⁸⁸ Keenan 2007, 237.   ⁸⁹ See bibliography s.n.

state superstructures matter far less than who appears at your door each morning, and who you see in the street each afternoon. Yes, rank and status matter. Titles and privileges matter. But social ties matter more.

The men and women of Aphrodito do not base their sense of self primarily on Roman imperial categories. They base their sense of self first and foremost on local realities and on local currencies of trust. They base their sense of self on membership in guilds, in local groups, in local churches. When they want to make their position at home more secure, they turn to those nearest to them with reliable information and ready cash. When they turn to these people, they care less about their rank and status than their reliability. In short, late antique Aphrodito cares more about its civil society. Civil society is the sum of all organizations and institutions other than the government itself through which people make their will known. It is the social space between the individual and the state. The late Roman state is strong, but not so strong that it pervades all aspects of village life and drives out all local options.

Only when those local options fail do the men and women of Aphrodito start to look outward and upward. Only when they fail to resolve conflicts at a local level do they need to turn to powerful patrons and engage the state apparatus. When they do, the state is not an abstract structure. For these men and women, the state has a face and a name. The state is a friend, or more likely, a friend of a friend, an introduction to a distant peer through one's patron or teacher. It is a web of connections with a place for them in it, on the fringes, pulling on the strands closest to them. In Aphrodito, patronage is only one part of a larger system of leverage. These people do look for help from those with higher status or rank, but they look first for anyone with information, with influence, with money, even if they have no status or rank to elevate them. They look horizontally before they look vertically.

The nature of the surviving evidence makes this clear. Most things never get written down. This is presumably more so of a town in Roman Egypt than it is in Western society today. When literacy is rare, people write only what they need, the documents that will help them solve problems or prevent them. These are the two kinds of surviving evidence, the two documentary towers emerging from the hidden foundations of Aphrodito society.

These two documentary groups include actions based on law and reactions to violations of it. Both types of evidence show men and women sharing the same underlying social assumptions. The lawbreakers, their victims, and all parties in a legal action behave in essentially the same way.

Regardless of the legal framework, they act to improve their social and economic position. They do so less with regard for status than with regard for influence and trust. This is clear in the visible evidence, but it also shows something about the society's hidden foundations. Underneath the evidence – in the undocumented day-to-day of everyone in Aphrodito – is a world of unwritten actions working in exactly the same way.

This is, I think, a new view of late antiquity. First, it is not the cultural late antiquity scholars have come to love over the last generation. It has no holy men[90]; it has no innovative art and architecture[91]; it has no great philosophical movements straddling the world between Christian and pagan.[92] So many of the chief characteristics of late antiquity are missing from the lives of the men and women of Aphrodito, and so they may have been missing from the lives of the silent majority in hundreds of villages throughout the Roman world.

Second, this is not the economic late antiquity some historians have recently struggled to find. On the one hand, it is not a society of grinding oppression by the government and the rich.[93] On the other hand, it is not a society of rural autonomy and peasant agency.[94] These economic phenomena are present in Aphrodito, to be sure, but it seems doubtful that the locals saw their lives in the same way we do. These late antiquities, the cultural and economic late antiquities, are not what these people would think important.

Their world – the world of the village – is a social late antiquity, uninterested in cultural and macro-economic trends. Their world is shaped solely by the push and pull of the day-to-day. For most people, most days pass in the midst of a quiet, low-level buzz: the call to a friend in the field or the haggling over rates in the market. This is a face-to-face world in which hardly anything gets written down because almost everything is mundane.

However, some people, some of the time, play with higher stakes. They rent land, borrow money, give to charity, take holy orders, raid their neighbor's houses, lie, steal, kill. This is where we come in, to watch the rare cases in this world where the story gets put into writing. The same motive drives the legal acts and the illegal ones, the desire to do better and have more. This is a face-to-face world, a world of trust, but it is not an easy world. It is a world of constant struggle, in which there is rarely a final victory.

---

[90] E.g., Brown 1971 and most recently Brown 2016.   [91] E.g., Kitzinger 1977.
[92] E.g., Watts 2006.   [93] E.g., Banaji 2001 and Sarris 2006.
[94] E.g., Grey 2011, although this study does parallel his approach to "small politics" in late antiquity.

CHAPTER 2

A World of Violence

One intriguing part of Aphrodito's evidence deals exclusively with lawbreakers and violence. Remember the murder of Herakleios and the priest named Victor, with which this book began: it is merely the best-known case. The guild leaders guilty of the crime have real grievances; they suspect Herakleios of being an informer, guilty of betraying their secrets to higher authorities. Those higher authorities in turn use the Aphrodito dispute to further their own interests.

Sometimes, the violence is personal: Matheias and Anna pillage Victor's house in an act of revenge. But sometimes it is political, as when the pagarch has Apollos's house pillaged and his grandson arrested for disobeying his orders. Also, when the party of Herakleios decides to seize Aphrodito by force their path leads straight through Dioskoros, his property, and his family.[1] These unrelated cases paint a single picture: the men and women of Aphrodito face theft and violence by appealing to higher authorities. When violence looms, social leverage and patronage are your shield and sword.

Throughout these stories, we are trapped by our evidence. Readers may wonder how common these thefts and murders actually are. Put in modern terms, they want to know Aphrodito's crime rate. There will never be an answer to this question. However, I strongly suspect that we are dealing with exceptional events, that we know about this violence at all because it is written down, and that it is written down precisely because it is so rare. The next chapter deals with legal solutions to conflict in Aphrodito, and the same argument holds there too. Legal disputes and illegal violence are both outliers, the written manifestations of moments when people turn to a higher authority because the unwritten social code does not apply.

The double murder, of Herakleios and Victor the priest, is unusual: no other court records survive from Aphrodito; and rarely does the voice of

---

[1] A case explored in more detail in later chapters: see pages 50 and 68.

a woman, a widow, a victim, come through quite so clearly. The story itself is full of eye-catching details.[2] The decision of the village's guild heads to drink with their victim before they kill him is one. Their decision to try to burn the body is another, given how hard cremation can be.[3]

It is not clear whether this job is botched or successful. The guild heads may drink with Herakleios in the hope of loosening him up, changing his mind, avoiding a conflict. Or they may drink with him to work themselves up, to prepare for their inevitable and ugly task. Maria and the other witnesses may know who the killers are because the guild heads are sloppy and make mistakes. Or they may know who the killers are because they are brazen, confident in the protection of their superiors, the soldier named Menas and the more mysterious Sarapammon. The defense that Menas offers for himself seems feeble, particularly when he blames Victor's death on a throat abscess. The beating itself could easily explain the abscess, and still leave Menas guilty as charged.[4]

One of the victims, Herakleios, may be the same Herakleios who appears as a guild head elsewhere. This means that he belongs to the same group as his killers. The records state that the guild heads kill Herakleios for being an informer or denouncer.[5] He may have alerted outsiders to some shady dealings the guild heads are engaging in on behalf of Menas and Sarapammon,[6] who may be using the guild heads to do their dirty work.[7]

Sarapammon is probably a *praes* (governor) of the Thebaid and the father of a future regional duke.[8] The governors and dukes are often blood relatives of the local pagarchs, who are the same officials whose tax collecting responsibilities make them such an ongoing nuisance to Aphrodito, with its history of tax independence. Sarapammon himself may be related to the current pagarch, or a friend of his, and is meddling in Aphrodito's business on his behalf.

If all this is true, the murders are a factional strike. The faction in control of the town, supporting its right to collect its own taxes, loyal to the local government of Dioskoros's family, wrestles with an opposing faction. If Herakleios is a guild head, then he has ties to a powerful local count named Ammonios, a patron of Flavius Apollos. Apollos in turn may have been one of the witnesses in the murder trial.[9] This puts a guild head,

---

[2] This section follows Ruffini 2008a, 180–184 and Ruffini 2008c. [3] See Keenan 1995, 59, note 8.
[4] Venticinque 2016, 95. [5] *P.Mich.* 13.661: *hôs sukophantounta*. [6] Venticinque 2016, 97.
[7] Venticinque 2016, 96. [8] Ruffini 2008c, 160, notes 13–15 for references.
[9] MacCoull 1990b, 103.

a village headman, and a count arrayed on one side, with other guild heads, a soldier, and a governor on the other.

A military officer – a *comes militum* – presides over the trial. At various points, he seems less concerned with the murder than with the money trail. Menas, one of the accused, insists, "I did not receive the gold, but the assistant did. He gave it to his headman, one and a half pounds of gold. Sarapammon received the gold from his headman."[10] Confronted with strange payments from Aphrodito, Sarapammon defends himself: "I learned that some men from the village of Aphrodito were conspiring; they wished to make the village divided so that they might again engage in murders."[11] The gold has an honest explanation: "for that reason the conspirators have been asked for one pound of gold" as a fine.[12]

Sarapammon may have encouraged the murder with an eye toward collecting the gold he could levy as a fine in punishment for the crime.[13] That money may give one motive for the murder, but it cannot explain why Herakleios himself was a target. The answer is in the court proceedings. As we have seen, "the people of the village [killed?] Herakleios as a voluntary denouncer."[14] The verb "killed" is missing in the surviving text, but the description of Herakleios is far more important. He is *hôs sukophantounta*, acting as a "voluntary denouncer" or informer. In modern slang, he is snitching.

In short, his killers may think that Herakleios had it coming. All of his killers are guild heads, representatives and enforcers of centuries of guild customs. Guild and association charters in Roman Egypt include "the threat of violence, beatings, and accosting members who had failed to follow through on their obligations to the group."[15] This violence shows the victim's degraded status and marks him as an outsider who has lost the trust of his group. At the end of the day, Aphrodito's murder mystery is not simply a crime. It is a battle between two sides, one of which must act – justifiably, in its collective mind – to protect itself and preserve its own sense of group unity.

It is surprising that we have any record of this crime. The documents themselves probably come from Antinoopolis, the capital of southern Egypt. Why they end up back in Aphrodito among Apollos's papers is unknown. However, the story is still in progress when we see it: the governor's office is putting pressure on Sarapammon to produce

---

[10] *P.Mich.* 13.660.1–3, loosely adapting trans. from ed. princ.   [11] Trans. Keenan 1995, 60–61.
[12] Trans. ed. princ.   [13] Ruffini 2008a, 182.   [14] *P.Mich.* 13.661, paraphrase of trans. in ed. princ.
[15] Venticinque 2016, 60.

Zacharias, a key player in the case.[16] Perhaps Apollos needs a copy of the records to help produce this witness, or to bring home evidence of the central government's interest in the case. In fact, records of this case may survive precisely because Apollos needs them as a weapon in an ongoing struggle.

The murder mystery of Victor and Herakleios is not Aphrodito's only violent crime. A generation later, in the 560s, a woman named Sophia writes to the duke of the Thebaid to tell her story. Her first husband has died, leaving her with a young child. She has been denied her inheritance from her first husband, but marries again. A man named Senouthes from Panopolis kills her second husband. According to Sophia, Senouthes wanted

> through perfidy to destroy my widowhood and freedom and to outrage my noble feelings. When I refused to yield to his persuasions and his unbridled craving for delights, he threw me into his private prison and ordered me to be beaten with sticks all day through, my legs to be lashed and me to be hung up without mercy.[17]

Throughout this ordeal, Sophia struggles to get a higher power on her side. The pagarch Kollouthos orders Senouthes to free her, but Senouthes ignores him. This is why she turns to the duke to find a more powerful patron, one more likely to succeed.

At first glance, this is a crime of passion: Senouthes kills to remove a rival for the woman he wants. Sophia wants it to seem this way: she cites her resistance to his hedonism as the reason for her imprisonment.[18] But as with the first murder mystery, we have to follow the money. This is murder for profit, or at the very least, murder to recoup a loss.

Note the repeated role of village officials. When Sophia cannot claim the inheritance from her first husband, she blames "the injustice of the public tax-collectors and my dead husband's brother."[19] When Senouthes finally releases Sophia and goes back to Panopolis, he turns her over to the village assistant, "the foolish Ieremias who is ruining the whole village."[20] Ieremias is only involved in the first place because Sophia's husband had provided him with a guarantee of surety.[21]

This is all very murky, but we can make an educated guess. Sophia's first husband was in debt. The land she thought would be her inheritance had guarantees against it, and has to be seized. Not all of the creditors are

---

[16] Keenan 1995, 62. [17] *P.Cair.Masp.* 1.67005.17–18; trans. from Kovelman 1991, 141.
[18] *P.Cair.Masp.* 1.67005.18: [a]*kolastôi êdo*[n]*êi*, Kovelman's "unbridled craving for delights."
[19] *P.Cair.Masp.* 1.67005.12–13. [20] *P.Cair.Masp.* 1.67005.21. [21] *P.Cair.Masp.* 1.67005.15.

satisfied. One of them, Senouthes, comes from Panopolis and confronts her second husband, hoping for some of the money he is owed. The confrontation turns violent, and her new husband dies. Senouthes – now desperate – seizes Sophia herself. When Senouthes finally goes back home, he gives her to Ieremias, who holds a guarantee from her dead husband, and is in a better position than Senouthes to recover some of the bad debt.

The search for a patron is central to this story. Kollouthos the pagarch is not powerful enough to help Sophia, but Athanasios the duke may be. However, we should also note who involves Kollouthos in the first place, when Sophia is locked in a dungeon. Dioskoros himself writes Sophia's petition, when he is in Antinoopolis. He must have known that she had been seized and turns to Kollouthos on his own initiative. When that fails, he may be the one who suggests going to the next level, writing to the duke Athanasios. In these same years, Dioskoros writes two poems to Kollouthos and three poems and several petitions to Athanasios. In short, he is a broker, trying to connect his people in Aphrodito to more powerful people in the wider world.

Dioskoros may not be the best choice, and Sophia has much to lose. All this happens when Dioskoros is away from Aphrodito, when his family is no longer in power. Indeed, Sophia's swipe at Aphrodito's village assistant, "who is ruining the whole village," is probably Dioskoros editorializing, frustrated at the current village government and his inability to handle things back home himself.

When Senouthes had control over Sophia, he left her holdings uncultivated.[22] When Ieremias has control over her, he hands her over to a local military unit, "utterly in debt."[23] Her husband's murder may seem like the most dramatic moment to modern eyes, but in her plea to the duke it is only the second or third step in Sophia's prolonged struggle for economic security and independence.

Sophia's struggle includes prolonged beatings. She is not alone. An undated papyrus has a fragmentary petition from two men, named Ioannes and Panechates.[24] The address is lost, but they probably intended their complaint to go to the town *riparios* (policeman). As they put it, they have been beaten in violation of the laws: "The persons mentioned below, in defiance of the considerable laws, have dared to beat us without reason.

---

[22] *P.Cair.Masp.* 1.67005.20. [23] *P.Cair.Masp.* 1.67005.23.
[24] Papyrus: *SB* 16.12371. Panechates: Ruffini 2011, 52. Translation: Hassanein 1981. Revision of the text (Panechates for Apa Nechatos) removes the motive for the attack proposed in the ed. princ.

Wherefore, we present to you this our petition, begging you to keep it in a safe place, until the judgment of trial, and for our safety, we make this petition to you."

Two things stand out from this complaint. First, that Ioannes and Panechates still fear for their safety. Second, that the beating took place "in defiance of laws" and "without reason." These men can imagine being beaten legally, with reason. With the birth of universal citizenship under the emperor Caracalla in AD 212, the old privileges of Roman citizenship began to disappear. The famous claim of Saint Paul – that he should not face corporal punishment as a Roman citizen – no longer had any meaning.

Romans had long seen the distinction between upper and lower classes – the so-called *honestiores* and *humiliores* – in terms of how each class could be punished. In late antique legal culture, the *honestiores*, the better men, the ones with greater honor, are immune from corporal punishment. The *humiliores*, the lesser men or more humble ones, face it as a matter of course. This is not a new trend in late antiquity, but one deeply rooted in Roman legal culture.[25] Inequality or legal discrimination had always been part of the Roman system of legal privilege. This in turn came from the dignity and honor that were the natural consequences of power and wealth. Even within the *honestiores*, men had greater or lesser honor and greater or lesser access to the tools of justice protecting them.

We cannot be sure just what Ioannes and Panechates are complaining about. Perhaps they are simply the victims of assault. Or maybe they have been punished for some legal offense, and are complaining that they received a corporal punishment that violates their legal dignity. The petition refers to two assailants. The name of one is damaged, but his title, *diakônos*, stands out. Giving this deacon the benefit of the doubt, we might assume he has a legitimate complaint against Ioannes and Panechates, and is not simply prone to random violence. He tries to collect a debt or enforce a guarantee, or is somehow, himself, doling out punishment for a crime.

Ioannes and Panechates's appeal to the state may not be a mere legal claim reporting an assault. It may also be a social claim: those men who beat us – and specifically this deacon who beat us – are not our betters. One of the victims, whose own handwriting appears in the text, is a slow writer: his letters are large and clumsy on the page. But he must be better than the other, who does not write at all. This slow writing seems almost defiant, as

---

[25] Garnsey 1970, 277–280.

if to insist: we are not *humiliores*, we cannot face corporal punishment and we demand recognition of this fact.

Aphrodito's records also include many cases of pillaging and theft. A handful of these cases are political. A badly damaged petition – probably sent to someone in the office of the local duke – from the late 560s tells one such story. Menas, the pagarch of Antaiopolis and villain in many of our stories, secures the appointment of Dioskoros's brother-in-law Apollos as village headman in Aphrodito. At some point later, "by evil and by force," Menas "plundered his house."[26]

Menas justifies his acts – including the seizure of some of Apollos's land – by claiming that he has failed to pay the taxes he owes on behalf of the village in his capacity as village headman. Apollos's brother-in-law, Dioskoros, says that Apollos had indeed made the payments: "if, when his house was pillaged, the receipts were taken ... I do not know."[27] Dioskoros's own son is implicated: he is the Aphrodito village assistant, and Menas arrests him on the premise that he is therefore responsible for the village debts his uncle, the headman, has failed to pay.[28]

It is easy to imagine the other side of the story. Perhaps Menas has an official guarantee from Apollos, or at any rate claims that he does. The guarantee spells out exactly which pieces of property, including movables in his own house, Apollos offers as surety against his payment of Aphrodito's tax burden. Menas waves these papers like a search warrant as he enters the house. In his mind, he is neither pillaging nor plundering, but seizing what he can claim by right. Nevertheless, the suggestion that Apollos had paid the debt and that the receipts were stolen raises questions. Menas may be doing his job, but he may also be lining his own pockets. As with Aphrodito's murders, its thefts have a money trail, and victims respond by looking around for a more powerful patron.

Dioskoros's complaints against Ioulianos have the same feel to them. Dioskoros has two cousins: another Dioskoros and his sister, a woman named Anastasia.[29] Years before, when their parents died, their uncle Apollos – Dioskoros's father and headman of Aphrodito – took care of them, and managed their maternal inheritance. When Apollos dies in the late 540s, Ioulianos, the pagarch of Antaiopolis and another major villain for Aphrodito, sends his men to town. They, "saying that the aforementioned

---

[26] *P.Lond.* 5.1677.26–27, if Apollos in line 23 is the antecedent of *autou* in line 26; damage intervenes.
[27] *P.Lond.* 5.1677.52–53, trans. Bell, introduction to ed. princ.
[28] See Bell at *P.Lond.* 5, pages 69–70.
[29] Dioskoros 31 and Anastasia 1 (*hê kai Tekrompia*), the wife of Phoibammon, son of Triadelphos.

Apollos died under liability to them," seize some of the maternal inheritance left to Dioskoros and Anastasia.[30]

Again, it is easy to imagine the other side of the story. Ioulianos may indeed have a legitimate claim to some of Apollos's property. What he does not realize is that Dioskoros and Anastasia do not have that property, only their maternal inheritance. Seizing their property as a claim against Apollos's debt is a non sequitur, a mistake. Maybe the "precise composition of Dioscorus's family eluded the authorities just as it has eluded us."[31]

This story survives only because Dioskoros goes looking for help. He finds it in Constantinople, the imperial capital, where he gets a rescript ordering that justice be done in this case. Throughout the rescript, the imperial authorities describe Dioskoros and his relatives as suppliants: they are clients, and the emperor the ultimate patron. These stories of property seizure may look like abuses of state power. However, assuming the best of the antagonists in these stories – that they have legitimate property claims as surety against debts they are owed – then they are no different from a creditor pushing a private claim.

In any case, this list of thefts is only part of the picture, and emphasis on the local pagarch's pillaging draws too much attention to the state. The little people do their share of pillaging as well. In the late 520s, a soldier named Victor writes to the town *riparios* to complain about a husband and wife team, Matheias and Anna.[32] According to Victor, these two

> from our village were robbing my house in a piratical way, and they dragged off the things they found in that house of mine. Through this, I deliver to your industriousness my petition to order those named in order below to be carefully guarded and to act as guarantor until the lawsuit, the trial and the judgment.

As always, there is a concern that defendants will disappear before the day of trial, unless someone else pledges their good faith.

But the quirk in this case is the status of its main characters. Victor is a soldier in the unit of the most noble Moors, a Flavius by right. Although he is originally from Aphrodito, he serves in Hermopolis, some distance to the north. He describes Matheias as "my farmer."[33] We sense a crime of opportunity here. A local boy in military service is prosperous enough to have his own land and his own tenants, but when he is called away on duty

---

[30] *P.Cair.Masp.* 1.67026.9–10.   [31] van Minnen 2003, 130.
[32] *P.Cair.Masp.* 1.67091: AD 528 (?).   [33] If *P.Cair.Masp.* 1.67091.25 is correctly restored.

these tenants know exactly what to take and when. This is not the only story we will see of soldiers losing out to locals.[34]

Aphrodito's crime victims have one common road to justice, through local law enforcement. It is not clear why Victor suspects his farmer Matheias and his wife Anna or whether he will be able to win his case. Because the records are not complete, we are never sure whether we are catching a story at its beginning, or walking in halfway through. But there is always this standard step, to petition the town police. Ioannes and Panechates complain to the *riparios* about being illegally beaten. Victor takes the same step when Matheias and Anna pillage his house. In a later chapter a failed marriage leads the prospective bride, Eirene, to petition Victor the *riparios* to imprison her fiancé until she can bring a case against him for outrage and oathbreaking.[35] In the 550s, a farm laborer named Victor petitions the same *riparios* in a case for which we have lost the details.[36]

All of these petitions ask the police to intervene, to hold the defendant in prison or at least guarantee his presence until the day of trial. It is the equivalent of a modern victim filing a police report and pressing charges in a single text. The constant requests for a guarantee suggest what can happen next. Prison is not the end of the line for our defendants, as many of these records show. A letter to Aphrodito's headmen includes an order "to release Herakleianos son of the most blessed Gesios from Psinomounis, who is under guard."[37] The order is damaged, but whoever gives it is worried that the headmen will neglect it, and cause public harm as a result. They want Herakleianos to get back home to Psinomounis in time to attend to his harvest. This is important enough that Herakleianos's freedom comes with "the guarantee of the free men of the same village of Psinomounis or at least the shepherds of the same."

It is not clear what got Herakleianos into this situation, but a few guesses are possible. He does something to get in trouble in Aphrodito: theft, perhaps assault, or slander against a jilted fiancée, as we will see in the case of Eirene. Someone petitions the local *riparios* to have him thrown in jail. The *riparios* complies, and Herakleianos awaits trial. But someone higher up the hierarchy now orders the headmen to set him free. The explicit reference to his harvest shows why: Herakleianos is too big a man with too much land for the local provincial officials to see his harvest go bad. The tax

---

[34] Samuel and Phoibammon: see page 75.   [35] See page 138.
[36] *P.Cair.Masp.* 1.67093; contra the DDBDP, I reject identifying Biktor 197 with Biktor 132, whose appearances are a quarter of a century or even more earlier.
[37] *P.Cair.Masp.* 1.67078.

money will matter too much. Maybe the shepherds are clients or employees of his, pledging themselves to secure their patron's freedom. I do not suggest that justice is bought in this case, but this is something similar: once Herakleianos is gone, back to Psinomounis, his accusers will be much worse off. The road to justice – whether he is guilty or not – no longer goes through the heart of town, but runs instead past imperial officials with one eye on the health of the harvest and another eye on the social status of the accused.

However, another prison-release letter raises doubts about how often the higher officials get their way. This letter, addressed to Apollos or his son Dioskoros, complains that earlier release orders in a different case have been in vain.[38] In this instance the prisoner is a woman: the most magnificent count and the *scholastikos* Hermogenes have "made quite a few complaints concerning the woman's arrest." The letter writer, someone else entirely, notes that the count "wrote to your brotherliness on the spot with the most wise *scholastikos*'s judgment entrusting you to fetch her out at once." We know nothing about the woman or why she is in jail, but we have a subtle reminder of the power of the village against the state. Travel takes time, letters get lost, and delay is never quite the same thing as disobedience. The count and his men can complain all they want, but unless they come to Aphrodito themselves, there are limits to their power.

When Dioskoros complains about the abuses of Menas the pagarch, he writes that "those accompanying him to help him deflowered the virgins and tore the nuns apart, pillaging and driving off the whole village and its borders as booty."[39] In another petition, Dioskoros complains about officials trying "to ruin the maidens and the virgin nuns and to take away our animals and to devour with troubles the sowing for their feeding pastures."[40]

After beatings and murders, rape might not be surprising. However, these accusations do not quite ring true. They are vague, nebulous, and come too close to the main point of these petitions: frustration over real economic loss. In fact, they are stock accusations, without names attached. They show only that this society recognizes the rape of a virgin or nun to be a serious offense. In the end, we have no strong evidence for rape in Aphrodito, and no evidence at all for rape of women who were not virgins or nuns.

---

[38] *P.Cair.Masp.* 2.67202.
[39] *P.Cair.Masp.* 1.67002.3.2–3. For Dioskoros's emotional strategies in describing the conflict with Menas, see Palme 2014.
[40] *P.Lond.* 5.1674.62–64.

needs to look higher up – above Florentius – for patrons with power to reach down and clean up the mess.

Few of these stories are clear-cut. Every beating may be a legal act against a social inferior. Every theft by a government agent may be a legitimate claim to property offered as a guarantee. Only the murders give the sense that something has gone wrong. But even then, we can never quite tell exactly what. This murkiness may seem like a flaw of fragmented evidence, but it is not. It is a fundamental feature of the system.

This is a world in which everyone pushes as far as they can, to find out just where the boundaries lie. Part of that push manifests itself through writing, using words to shape how people see the past. Ancient petitioners use powerful rhetorical devices to protect their dignity and to improve their position in the eyes of their peers.[50] Every victim in this chapter is doing the same thing. They may reach too far and exaggerate the harm they face. The actual facts of violence are sometimes vastly different – improvised, confused, disorderly – from the stories surviving in the text.[51]

Here and throughout this book, we are at the mercy of our evidence. Violence leaves a bigger paper trail than peace and quiet. We must not take these stories as typical. Indeed, we can assume that they are outliers. However, for every conflict ending in violence there must be many more that threaten it, or stop just shy of it. Aphrodito is not a very big place: no one is more than two degrees of separation away from anyone else.[52]

Everyone there knows someone who knows one of these victims of violence. It must loom in the background as a constant possibility. The violence we see in Aphrodito – as limited and rare as it may be – is probably happening everywhere in Egypt. It may in fact be happening everywhere throughout the Roman Empire in the sixth century. But we have to be cautious before we make sweeping generalizations. We have no reliable methods to measure the absolute or relative levels of violence in this society, or even any good way to define what violence actually means.[53]

The reign of Justinian can seem rife with corrupt tax collection; lawless behavior; theft by the local elites; armed resistance to central authority; indeed, pervasive anarchy.[54] One interpretation of this period sees class conflict as a central part of the story.[55] In this version, the oppressed classes are tossed into a world of lawlessness in which they are deprived of the protection of the state. Imperial legislation speaks of "large, free villages, who often are in revolt against the imposition of taxes ... and are full of

---

[50] Bryen 2013, 7. [51] Bryen 2013, 90. [52] Ruffini 2008a, 205, Table 19.
[53] Frier 1989, 223–225. [54] Bell 2013, 103–106. [55] Bell 2013, explicitly at 88.

murders and brigandage."⁵⁶ Banditry and widespread violence in this period take place in the shadows or under the umbrella of patronage, in "the quasi-symbiotic relationship of landowner and 'bandit'," in which landowners (patrons) use violence both to protect and to control their clients.⁵⁷

If late antiquity is interpreted in this way, then there is a direct connection between violence and patronage. A patron's private armies, or bandits, depending on one's point of view:

> were employed partly to keep tenants and labourers in their place, subject to their traditional masters, but also to prevent their being "stolen" by other local notables who might "protect" them more effectively from the tax collector, as well as extend their own masters' lands and patronage.
> ... On balance, the institution of patronage also added to the centrifugal forces operating in the empire in that it reduced the power of the centre, the imperial administration, over its subjects. And, while it may have mediated some conflicts, it exacerbated others. On balance, we should regard it as exploitative.⁵⁸

This view of the sixth century as a sea of anarchy caused by class conflict rests on modern political assumptions, not least the beneficence of the state.

However, such a vision of patronage and violence does not seem to fit the evidence from Aphrodito. Indeed, I doubt very much that they would recognize this description of their world. If the men and women of Aphrodito feel exploited by their patrons, if they suffer from the weakened power of the central state, it is not at all obvious from the evidence. That evidence shows that state officials are chief among those instigating murders and pillaging private property. But these are exceptional moments, during which the victims turn to their patrons for protection to balance the power of the state. The institution of patronage and its response to violence – far from spinning the empire into fragmentary pieces – is a vital part of civil society's response when conflict turns to violence.

---

⁵⁶ Bell 2013, 108, discussing *Novel* 24 (about Pisidia) and quoting Patlagean. ⁵⁷ Bell 2013, 110.
⁵⁸ Bell 2013, 109 and 111.

CHAPTER 3

A World of Law

Against these murders and beatings, against the pillage and plunder, stand the forces of law and order. These two aspects of society – the forces of violence and the forces of law, the forces of chaos and control – are visible when the otherwise normal, humdrum endeavors and social tensions of everyday life reach unusual levels of complexity. Just as the moments of violence discussed in the previous chapter are exceptional, so too are the legal actions described in this chapter. These are moments just a little bit more important than the rest of daily life, moments when reliance on casual trust gives way to reliance on the law.

The forces of law work on two different levels. On the one hand are the village headmen, the forces of local government, natives who collect the village taxes and enforce local order. On the other hand are the distant forces of the Roman Empire, the imperial court and its legislation, the law of the land. Any legal action in late antique Aphrodito must confront or avoid these government structures. This is when law becomes personal, a soft and fuzzy web of connections entangling friends and enemies. Aphrodito's men and women present formal cases directly to the highest authorities. They also sit cautiously on the sidelines, hoping to do better outside court than inside it. How and whether they apply the law depends more on who is in and who is out than on the facts at hand.

These men and women negotiate a complex hierarchy, connecting the center to the periphery.[1] The Romans divided the diocese of Egypt into six provinces. One, the province of the Thebaid, included Aphrodito and all of southern Egypt. The civil authority in each province rested with a *praeses* or governor. The military authority in the Thebaid rested with a *comes* or count of the Thebaid. A reform under the emperor Justinian in 539 subordinated the province's civilian *praeses* to the authority of a military

---

[1] For what follows, see Palme 2007, 244–248.

dux or duke. These officials appear most typically in the Thebaid's provincial capital, Antinoopolis.

The Thebaid itself was divided into smaller organizational units called nomes. At the heart of each nome was a *polis*, a large town with the legal status of a city. Aphrodito was in the Antaiopolite nome, the region with Antaiopolis as its administrative center. These nome units were largely for tax-collecting purposes. Officials called pagarchs, stationed in Antaiopolis and the other nome capitals, oversaw tax collection for their nomes.

Aphrodito is an exception to this system. It is outside the purview of the pagarch of Antaiopolis and, as a result, is allowed to collect its own taxes. This frustrates the pagarchs enormously, and to some degree empowers the town headmen. Among Aphrodito's leading men are village headmen ultimately responsible for ensuring that Aphrodito makes its tax payments to the central government. The sources also describe some men as tax contributors or collective taxpayers, but their role is less clear. Presumably they are part of a group ensuring that Aphrodito's public treasury has enough revenue to make its tax payments and meet its other expenses at a local level.[2]

Tax collection follows a long-held pattern. Some dates in this book appear as indiction years, for example, "in the (year of the) 10th indiction." This means that local records follow a fifteen-year tax assessment cycle, standard since the reign of Constantine, with the count going back to one at the end of every fifteen years. The Roman state collects a gold tax aimed directly at financing its military. It also collects a land tax in grain or some other kind, often then converted to gold as well. The amounts payable for both taxes are fixed per unit of agricultural land.[3]

This description makes the Roman tax system sound quite organized. However, the closer we look the fuzzier things get. Many late antique and early medieval states are complex blends of public and private control over resources, "of centralized and decentralized political and fiscal authority."[4] The state assesses taxes on each province, on each region in a province, and in each city's territory in a region. But at that point, how to assess things further becomes a matter for the locals to work out on their own, without central oversight from the state.

The struggle for control over this system between regional authorities and village authorities is a central part of the story of sixth-century Aphrodito. Before early November of AD 547, some of Aphrodito's

---

[2] See Ruffini 2011, Index *s.v. prôtokômêtês* and *suntelestês*.   [3] Bransbourg 2015, 267.
[4] Haldon 2015, 381.

leading men write a petition to the empress Theodora in Constantinople. In it, they complain that the provincial authorities in Antaiopolis are illegally plotting to absorb Aphrodito into their administrative jurisdiction, and they ask for imperial assistance to stop them.

Their ultimate goal is to deliver the petition in person, to Theodora herself. Only a few of Aphrodito's elite would make the trip, but the petition makes a point of listing as many local notables as possible. Over fifty of Aphrodito's leading men attach their names, either by signing themselves or having someone else sign for them. In addition to this long list of signatures, the petition itself has two different sections. The first section, quoted here in heavily restored form, describes the exact complaint:

> [(We report to our most august mistress that his brilliance Ioulianos (?) wishes), against] custom, to drag us into the pagarchy of the (city) of the Antaiopolites, of which he has gained control [... although we are] under the authority of the *dux* and our mistress' agents. And we are at a loss to imagine the grounds [(of this attack on our independence?) ... For] the competent local office knows that we have never been in arrears.[5]

Ioulianos disagrees, and attempts to take his own collections, which, to the people of Aphrodito, looks like an invasion. The second section of the petition is more colorful: the petitioners accuse Ioulianos of

> plundering our property more than the places ravaged by barbarians ... [so that we are not able] to pay our [customary] contributions to the public dues, or to live a modest life in possession of our animals ... they have left us [nothing] and in the village absolutely none of the furnishings of a decent life for us ... foul killings ... have occurred as part of this plague, which has struck and brought shrieking.[6]

We are torn between horror at the tax collectors and doubt over whether the locals have exaggerated. Their claim to have never fallen into arrears seems doubtful, when they admit at the same time that they are so devastated by these collections that they are unable to pay. At a very basic level, the locals are asking for the right to collect their own taxes, free from outside interference. But more is going on here than meets the eye.

It is not clear how this petition first comes about. Some see it as a "unique snapshot of the adult male élite of Aphrodito" and imagine a "general

---

[5] *P.Cair.Masp.* 3.67283, trans. Rowlandson 1998, 45 ("Ioulianos" for "Julianus").
[6] *P.Cair.Masp.* 3.67283, trans. Rowlandson 1998, 45–46.

A World of Law 45

meeting of the adult male inhabitants of Aphrodito to discuss the petition, followed by a signing ceremony" in which the "social hierarchy of Aphrodito was dramatically confirmed by the order observed in the act of appending the signatures."[7] In this portrayal, the petition is a "display of an ancient civic virtue," a "show of power."[8]

I have my doubts about this modern interpretation of civic unity.[9] The first doubt comes from the fact that the bulk of the signatures appear "in more or less random order."[10] This does not seem like the way status-conscious Romans would behave. The second doubt creeps in when considering how many people have been left out. The occupations of the people who sign the petition are revealing. The boat makers sign, while the beekeepers do not, even though the records show more town beekeepers than boat makers.[11] The head coppersmith signs, but the head goldsmith does not. The guild of hunters and the guild of oil men – both known from town records – are also left out, for no clear reason.[12]

These petitioners may be the town elite, but if so, some of them are noticeably absent.[13] We do not see Apollos, son of Isakios, who is the town assistant in the 520s and one of its headmen in the 550s. We do not see Flavius Anouphis, an Aphrodito official active in the 530s. We do not see Menas and Pesalous, two liturgy-holding tax collectors active in the early 550s. Any one of these people may be out of town. However, some of them may be uninterested, or even actively opposed. Furthermore, if these petitioners are the town's elite, they – especially those described as landowners – should be among the town's richest people. There is no way of discovering whether this is true, but the town's cadastre and its fiscal register from twenty years earlier raise doubts. None of the signatories to the petition appear in the town's fiscal records, and we do not know why. The town's fiscal records may somehow miss the town's richest people.

More likely, however, is that the petition is too much later in time, the two decades from the 520s to the 540s having brought a new elite to the head of the town. Egyptian demographic data indicate an annual male death rate of 24 per 1,000 for males over the age of five and 123 per 1,000 for males over the age of sixty-five.[14] The petitioners in the 540s include fifty-one men.[15] A group this size will lose at least one person on average per year through normal death rates, and as many as half a dozen if they are all over sixty-five. A group the size of these petitioners, alive in the

---

[7] Gagos and van Minnen 1994, 10 and 13.   [8] Gagos and van Minnen 1994, 14.
[9] Ruffini 2008a, 177–179 and Ruffini 2008c, 163–165.   [10] Gagos and van Minnen 1994, 12.
[11] Ruffini 2008c, 159–160.   [12] Ruffini 2008c, 165.   [13] Ruffini 2008c, 163–164.
[14] Bagnall and Frier 1994, 102.   [15] Gagos and van Minnen 1994, 10.

520s, could have been almost entirely replaced by the 540s. Equally, the younger generation in the petition may be missing from earlier records because the older generation still controls the wealth. In several cases, we find someone in the town's fiscal records in the 520s and his son signing the petition to the empress in the 540s. This is true for Victor, Dioskoros's cousin; Kornelios, the grandfather of Dioskoros's wife; and Apollos, Dioskoros's own father.

However, this is not particularly satisfying. At least seven of the petitioners – probably more – were active adults during the 520s, and are still missing from the town's fiscal records.[16] This group includes Dioskoros's father-in-law, brother, and one of his second cousins. This leaves the impression that the men petitioning the empress did not in fact control a large proportion, still less a majority, of the town's wealth. They may have been only one town faction, claiming to speak for the town as a whole.

In the late 540s, Aphrodito's residents say that they are accountable only to the local duke and functionaries of the empress Theodora.[17] This may have meant only that imperial estates in the area had been assigned to the empress personally.[18] In roughly the same period but in another text, an anonymous petitioner to the imperial court writes that Aphrodito's locals are "self-taxing [autopract] and enjoy the privileges of collecting their own taxes since the time of their fathers and forefathers, holding their privilege from an imperial rescript of the emperor Leo."[19]

In about 551, a rescript from the court of Justinian says that Apollos, "being chief of the proprietors [in Aphrodito], used to collect the contributions for the whole place and deliver them to the agents of the local *officium*."[20] This is how Aphrodito's autopract status works, but "being subjected to some flagrant injustices by the governors of the day they betook themselves to our divine house and had recourse to its protection."[21] This is a complicated picture, and is often made more confusing than it needs to be. Some people have said that Aphrodito – under pressure from local officials – gives up its *autopragia* for the safety of direct patronage from the imperial family.[22] Others have taken a more extreme position, claiming that Aphrodito became the personal property of the empress Theodora before it ultimately "surrendered itself" to her husband Justinian.[23]

---

[16] Abraam 3; Enoch 7; Ioannes 31; Isakios 40; Kallinikos 6; Senouthes 1; Theoteknos 1.
[17] *P.Cair.Masp.* 3.67283.1.3.   [18] Rowlandson 1998, 45.   [19] *P.Cair.Masp.* 1.67019.3–6.
[20] *P.Cair.Masp.* 1.67024, trans. *Sel.Pap.* 2.218.   [21] *P.Cair.Masp.* 1.67024, trans. *Sel.Pap.* 2.218.
[22] Gagos and van Minnen 1994, 10.   [23] Hanafi 1988, 94.

This is all a little breathless. The empress's personal estates have functionaries in the region,[24] but this does not mean that Aphrodito gives up its self-collecting tax status, still less that it becomes the private property of the imperial family. It means only that the town of Aphrodito – or some of its leading representatives – turns to informal imperial patronage to protect their existing legal status. Theodora's patronage of Aphrodito is a sign of her widely known role in public affairs during this period.[25] Petitioning the imperial court more generally is not a sign of surrender, but an attempt to leverage a distant but greater power against a closer but lesser one. If we are right, not everyone in the town supports this move.

Some of this is guesswork. But it does raise the question of who is in charge in Aphrodito. The family of Dioskoros provides several Aphrodito headmen in the sixth century. The records show many more. Daueid, son of a man named Victor, is already a former Aphrodito headman in the AD 510s. His family, including prosperous farmers and town tax collectors, may have been the leading power in Aphrodito in a previous generation.[26] Two of the best-known headmen, Bottos and Charisios, serve as a pair in the 530s, before Charisios dies.

How this town government works and who becomes headman are complicated issues. The explanation seems to depend on the circumstances. In AD 540, Count Ammonios sends a letter through one of his officials to Apollos and Senouthes, two of Aphrodito's headmen.[27] He writes, "I am telling Bottos and his son and those around him to retire and rest themselves, to see to their own affairs." This sounds like a relaxing way to end a career, but there may be more to it.

That same year, Ammonios writes to the village headmen telling them to regulate the gold in their tax collection more carefully.[28] A change of management at the top may be connected to this problem with tax payments controlled by the headmen. In his letter to Apollos and Senouthes, Ammonios arranges to have all business papers belonging to Bottos and his son handed over to Apollos and Senouthes. He concludes with an order that the two men work with the arrears collectors to settle the town's affairs: "do not turn away from the matter" and "in all ways be guided by the orders."

An Aphrodito headman named Apollos appears in the previous chapter.[29] His brother-in-law Dioskoros writes that the pagarch, Menas, "being

---

[24] For the *domus divina* in Egypt, see Azzarello 2012. For Theodora's estates, the role of local patrons, and Aphrodito's conflict with local authorities in the 540s, see particularly Azzarello 2012, 78–90.
[25] Brubaker 2005, 438.   [26] *P.Flor.* 3.280; Daueid 4; Ruffini 2008b; Ruffini 2011, Stemma 2.
[27] *P.Cair.Masp.* 3.67323.   [28] Fournet 2001, 481–482; P.Cair.inv. SR 3733 (2).   [29] See page 34.

Figure 3.1 "Headman's Door," Kom Ishqaw (Egypt), Photo © 1995–2015 Clement Kuehn

Figure 3.2 "Rubble," Kom Ishqaw (Egypt), Photo © 1995–2015 Clement Kuehn

a soul-deceiver ... wanted to make Aphrodito village headman ... my sister's husband Apollos."[30] Some of the words are missing, and this is really a complaint against Menas, not a summary of Aphrodito's constitution. But still, we get the impression – thanks to both Ammonios in one case and Menas in another – that town governance was a top-down affair, the headmen being appointed from outside.

But another letter gives a different impression. At some point, someone whose name is lost writes to Apollos, during his time as one of the village headmen, to inform

> your office and bureau that Senouthes, the recently appointed village headman ... [has been acting?] towards the village in an unjust fashion, plundering ... and [we request?] that your marvelous esteemed person remove him from affairs and appoint to his place someone to be responsible for this job.[31]

Here again, we are plagued by damaged papyri. It is not clear who was writing to complain about Senouthes, or what exactly Senouthes had done.

The letter asks that Apollos get rid of his fellow headman and replace him with another one. This may imply a hierarchy, in which the senior

---

[30] P.Lond. 5.1677.23–25. [31] P.Lond. 5.1681.

headmen have the right to appoint their junior members. It may also mean that the headmen work as part of a collective bureau, a group responsible for its own membership. One village headman named Senouthes is probably Apollos's own son.³² If this is the same Senouthes, the anonymous letter writer is trying to get the ranking local leader to fire his own son. If so, we may reasonably doubt his chances of success. When Bottos and his son are in power, they come as a package deal, and only resign together. The anonymous letter writer may have no recourse, if the town government is a family business.

But it is not always this way. Sometimes the top positions in the town are indeed handled by committee. In the mid-550s, after Apollos is dead and his sons are apparently no longer in office, Aphrodito has no fewer than five village headmen at once: Enoch son of Hermaos, Phoibammon son of Triadelphos, Ioannes son of Hermeias, Ioannes son of Promaos, and Psan.³³ Only one of these five has any connection to the previous ruling family – Phoibammon, who had married Dioskoros's cousin Anastasia.

When Ammonios fires the headman Bottos and his son, the family of Dioskoros rises to prominence. But in the 550s and 560s that prominence fades, and Aphrodito's power shifts. A man named Herakleios, son of Psaios, is the man with the most to gain.³⁴ Early in the 550s, Dioskoros complains about "our adversaries, the party of Herakleios son of Psaios and other people of our village."³⁵ The records also include a list of pasture land belonging to Dioskoros, destroyed "through the former headmen, the party of Herakleios and Ioannes."³⁶

Herakleios is probably the same man in both places, a rival to Dioskoros. In another administrative letter, an official apologizes to the local count for adding Dioskoros's name back onto a taxpayer list after the count had already removed him, explaining that Herakleios himself had explicitly ordered Dioskoros's name restored to the list.³⁷ This is a little murky but it leaves a distinct impression. The rise and fall of village headmen is not a passive accident: it comes from competition, an aggressive ambition to hold something worth fighting for.

In Aphrodito, a particular family might have power in one decade, another family in the next. But generally speaking, everyone faces the same set of responsibilities as headmen. First, the external responsibilities: the *autopragia* so important to some of them, the right to collect their own

---

³² See Senouthes 1; Senouthes 4; Senouthes 17.   ³³ *SB* 20.15018.
³⁴ Ruffini 2008c, arguing that Herakl(e)ios 2 = Herakl(e)ios 34 = Herakl(e)ios 35.
³⁵ *P.Cair.Masp.* 1.67032.23–25 with trans. at *Sel.Pap.* 2.363.
³⁶ *P.Cair.Masp.* 3.67319.3, 4, 5, 7, and 16.   ³⁷ *P.Cair.Masp.* 2.67200.

taxes, and the accompanying responsibility of dealing with the Roman state's fiscal system. Second, the internal responsibilities: the maintenance of the legal system at the local level, handling the town's crime, complaints, disputes, petitions, and paperwork of all kinds.

First, *autopragia*. It cannot be easy for the village headmen to oversee tax collection for thousands of people, and they must fight to keep the right in the first place. We may well wonder why they bother. *Autopragia* must have perks, if they fight so hard to maintain it. We can guess that it is to avoid Constantinople's impinging bureaucracy, but it may be more complicated than that. We should always ask, who gains?

So much of the violence in the previous chapter comes down to money. Aphrodito's insistence on the law, and on its legal right of *autopragia*, also comes down to money. The fight for *autopragia* is not just a struggle against the state or in favor of some abstract ideal of independence. It is a struggle for control over local resources – in other words, it is rent-seeking.

The same point holds in late antique Egypt more generally.[38] Late antiquity's fiscal system comes with a heavy transaction cost: landowners enrich themselves through rent-seeking when they handle the empire's tax collecting. People are rent-seeking when they attempt "to increase their personal wealth while at the same time making a negative contribution to the net wealth of their community."[39] This is precisely what Dioskoros and his family are fighting for the right to do.

An anonymous complaint addressed to Apollos the headman claims that Senouthes, another village headman, is "plundering," and uses a Greek word that could equally mean seizing, overpowering, or grasping.[40] This may be a small-town mayor and his thugs running amok, going from farm to farm, rustling cattle and stealing cheese. However, it does not appear to be a likely picture: it may not be genuine theft, but instead something inherent in the job of a village headman that leads men to file this sort of complaint. Put another way, one man's plunder is another man's tax collection.

This is what *autopragia* looks like on the ground: plunder by a local instead of plunder by an outsider. The little villagers of Aphrodito want big government off their backs, but mostly so that they can keep doing to each other what big government wants to do to them. With this in mind, who signs the petition to Theodora and who does not may show the

---

[38] Kehoe 2003, 718–719, with Eggertsson quote in note 23.   [39] Eggertsson: see previous note.
[40] *P.Lond.* 5.1681.2: *arpazón*.

money trail – who is in Dioskoros's rent-seeking network and who is not? Those who sign look at the current town government and see friends and patrons. Those who do not sign wonder whether someone else might offer a better deal come tax time.

After tax collection, the local government's other major responsibility is the local legal system. Apollos, the father of Dioskoros and headman in the 520s to the 540s, has his hands full with legal proceedings. We have already seen Apollos receive complaints about Senouthes plundering the town while in office.[41] Apollos also receives a letter – possibly from the office of the provincial governor – saying that high officials are unhappy at his failure to curb the abuses of another man, named Eudoxios.[42] As headman, Apollos takes part in a debate held before Flavius Paulos, a *defensor* overseeing small claims cases in the regional capital, Antaiopolis, over how to handle a land transfer case between Aphrodito and the village of Thmonachthe.[43]

An Aphrodito headman named Apollos – it is probably the same man, but in this case we cannot be sure – receives an order about a butcher named George.[44] "Do not impose this man's financial requirements on George the butcher." We do not know who "this man" is, but everyone in Aphrodito probably does. "If you are ready to put an agreement to him, you should give six gold pieces." The end of the letter seems threatening. "If you cannot settle the matter," Apollos is told, "I will put an agreement to them myself, so do not be negligent." Some higher authority is telling the village headman to find a settlement between two opposing litigants: a considerable sum of money is at stake.[45]

These examples show how local government acts when something goes wrong, when private citizens cannot settle disputes on their own. When everything goes well, local officials are hardly ever in sight and no evidence is generated to tell the tale. When tensions arise, Aphrodito's social machinery uses a legal framework to channel life's nervous energies into a happy ending for everyone involved. That framework has deep roots in the legal anthropology of the ancient Mediterranean region.

Contracts are the backbone of this legal framework. Many of the Aphrodito contracts are fragmentary and many of those that survive are mundane. The records include contracts for teachers educating children;

---

[41] See page 49.
[42] *P.Cair.Masp.* 3.67290, if the Apollos there, whose name is restored, is Apollos 2.
[43] *P.Cair.Masp.* 3.67329.
[44] Following the French translation in Boud'hors 2008, 69 (and correcting Ruffini 2011, George 1).
[45] Boud'hors 2008, 74.

rent contracts; contracts to guard agricultural land; contracts of agreement to work together; harvest contracts; and many more.[46] Throughout late antique Egypt, whenever men and women meet to draft these documents, they bring witnesses along to sign their names, numbering from one to as many as half a dozen.[47] Usually, these witnesses are deacons or priests.[48]

In Aphrodito, priests are the most common witnesses. They bring a special prestige to the table because of their relationship with the divine.[49] Their presence is not necessary to fulfill a legal requirement: if it were, the number of witnesses would not vary so widely.[50] Rather, they serve as social glue, to build trust between two sides. When that trust is broken, disputants may take the formal route and approach local government with a petition. Disputants may also take the informal route, and seek arbitration. In fact, this informal route to dispute settlement is so much a part of daily life it is even referred to in the period's pleasure reading.

Menander's play, *Epitrepontes* ("The Arbitrants" or "Men at Arbitration"), is famous for its depiction of men settling a dispute. It is "one of the most favorite plays by Menander, read throughout the Roman world precisely because of the arbitration scene."[51] Dioskoros owns a copy of the play, a copy which – as luck would have it – is the only copy of the arbitration scene to survive today.[52]

These lines between two of the disputants and their arbitrator, written eight centuries before Dioskoros read them, reflect a dramatized version of many scenes from his own life.[53]

DAOS: You blackmail me.
SYRISKOS: You have no right to what's not yours.
DAOS: Let's leave the case to some third person.
SYRISKOS: I agree.
DAOS: Let's arbitrate . . .
SYRISKOS [INDICATING SMIKRINES]: Will you take him as judge?
DAOS: Luck help me, yes!
SYRISKOS [TO SMIKRINES]: We've a question in dispute . . . Some impartial judge for this we're seeking now, and so, if nothing hinders you, adjust our quarrel . . .

---

[46] Respectively, e.g., *P.Lond.* 5.1706, *SB* 22.15522, *P.Cair.Masp.* 1.67001, *P.Cair.Masp.* 2.67159, and MacCoull 1993, 30 (a letter mentioning such a contract, not the contract itself).
[47] Worp 2008, 151–153.
[48] Worp 2008, 150, where soldiers also figure prominently as witnesses because of the evidence from Syene.
[49] Worp 2008, 150.   [50] For the widely varying number of witnesses, see Worp 2008, 146–150.
[51] Gagos and van Minnen 1994, 33–34.   [52] Gagos and van Minnen 1994, 33.
[53] Trans. adapted from Allinson 1964, 27–31.

SMIKRINES: Will you abide by my decision? Say.
SYRISKOS AND DAOS: Of course.

Menander's fictional arbitration repeats itself in real life several times in sixth-century Aphrodito.

The best example is the Nikantinoos dispute. The story of Nikantinoos appears on a single papyrus roll a foot wide and nearly six feet long. This long roll survives in two pieces. One piece had been left to the University of Michigan by a classical studies professor, and the other is now in the Vatican library. The two fragments combine to form one of the largest surviving texts from Aphrodito, over 110 lines long.[54] The contents reveal one of the most complicated cases in the Aphrodito records.

The backstory is unclear. A man named Nikantinoos, otherwise unknown, speaks in his own voice in this text, describing the situation. It is easy to get lost in the tangle of words as Nikantinoos tells the story, explaining that he has paid

> for the redemption of a deed of security drawn up in favor of Iosephios, on the initiative of his parents concerning the estate that was put up as security to him by my parents and that was sold to . . . Phoibammon and Anastasia, his wife, by my nephew and nieces a short while ago.[55]

Put more simply, Nikantinoos pays a debt that was not really his in the first place.

His parents had borrowed money from the parents of another man named Iosephios. Both sets of parents are now dead. Nikantinoos has inherited an obligation to pay the debt, and Iosephios has inherited a lien against an estate, most likely a vineyard called Mounlakon, which Nikantinoos's parents put up as security against the debt. In the meantime, Nikantinoos's nieces and nephew had sold the estate to Phoibammon and Anastasia, Dioskoros's cousin. The result is a mess: the sale of property still serving as security in a loan is illegal under Roman law. Phoibammon and Anastasia have tainted property, and Nikantinoos has a debt, but no security with which to back it.

When the action starts, the main characters are not in Aphrodito, but in Antinoopolis, the capital of southern Egypt, which we will explore more closely in a later chapter. Nikantinoos is from Aphrodito, but describes himself as living at Antinoopolis. His name itself "suggests that the connection of his family with Antinoopolis is of long standing – maybe an

---

[54] Gagos and van Minnen 1994, 3.   [55] *P.Mich.Aphrod.* trans. in ed. princ.

ancestor won a victory in the games that were held there."⁵⁶ Phoibammon and Anastasia are not present – they are probably back home in Aphrodito – but Anastasia's uncle is. Apollos, father of Dioskoros the poet, the same headman of Aphrodito we see throughout this book, represents Phoibammon and Anastasia while in Antinoopolis. He and a series of other men gather to help solve the mess caused by this illegal sale.

Nikantinoos, Phoibammon, and these others ultimately come to an agreement in the local courthouse at Antinoopolis. The words of Nikantinoos give a sense of how complex that process is:

> And after many words have been said and many moves have been made here between me, Nikantinoos, and Apollos, village chief and the one who represents you, the aforementioned, finally, before a lawsuit and before cognition trials took place, good friends mediated between us by taking up the case.⁵⁷

Nikantinoos agrees to accept a payment from Phoibammon and Anastasia of slightly less than seven gold pieces and 776 liters of wheat, "roughly the equivalent of four years' income for an ordinary worker."⁵⁸ (The wheat alone is the equivalent of the "annual food supply for two adults."⁵⁹) In exchange, he agrees to pay the debt owed to Iosephios. In return, Phoibammon and his wife walk away with property no longer encumbered by someone else's debt. Nikantinoos describes this settlement as "what has been agreed upon to be given to me in accordance with the fair judgment of the mediating friends." He agrees to these terms with an oath to the Holy Trinity and the Roman Emperor, and a series of witness signatures finalize the agreement.

The text describes Nikantinoos and Apollos as "content and pleased." This seems unlikely when we consider the "good friends" we are dealing with in this case. The list of witnesses who sign the agreement is revealing.⁶⁰ Nikantinoos does not bring any of his own friends to the table. Apollos, representing his niece and her husband, packs the room with his own supporters. The witnesses include Apollos, son of Besios, who worked with Apollos on a debt agreement in AD 514; Mouses and Hermaos, who both worked on contracts between Aphrodito and its shepherd communities in previous decades; and Apollos's own son Senouthes. In short, when Nikantinoos goes to the courthouse to settle the dispute, he finds himself surrounded by Apollos's own men and those close to Aphrodito's center of power.

---

⁵⁶ Gagos and van Minnen 1994, 75. ⁵⁷ P.Mich.Aphrod. ⁵⁸ Bagnall 1995a.
⁵⁹ Gagos and van Minnen 1994, 93. ⁶⁰ Ruffini 2008a, 170–171.

It is not clear who initiates this settlement. If the buyers had known about the lien against the land, the sale would never have taken place. They would have wanted a clean sale, and never thrown away money on a speculation. Nikantinoos, who inherited the debt, no doubt wants the problem to go away. It is possible that he and some brother or sister both inherited the land, and that his sibling's heirs sell their share of the land, leaving him with co-owners he does not want.[61] But the right time for him to act is before the sale, when the land is still in his family. Iosephios, whose parents lent the money in his name, is the one who benefits here. He may have heard about the sale, and pushes for a settlement in the hope of getting his money. Either way, Nikantinoos may be the real loser. He is the one who has to concede defeat to Phoibammon and Anastasia and who must admit in writing that "from now on no legal action whatsoever is left for me ... I am not able at any moment or time to proceed against you or your heirs in courts of law."

We never hear the amount of the original loan, only that Nikantinoos pays it back having received his settlement payment from Phoibammon and Anastasia. However, Iosephios has no reason to settle for anything less than the full amount, and is in a position of strength. Phoibammon and Anastasia are too closely allied with the mediator and witnesses to have come away with a bad deal. We are left guessing that Nikantinoos himself has to make up the difference between the settlement and the loan, out of his own pocket, bowing to social pressure from the friends and neighbors around him.

Behind all this social pressure is the ever-present threat of legal action. The mediation itself takes place in the Antinoopolis courthouse. The parties might have been on the verge of taking the matter to court in that very building before the potential risk and expense brought them back to the negotiating table.[62] This case is the most complicated we know of, but several similar stories survive.

A dispute involving a priest and monk named Ioannes gives one of the most colorful pictures of Aphrodito life. The plaintiffs are a man named Psaios and his wife Talous, who bring a case against Ioannes's heirs at some point in the late 530s or early 540s.[63] The settlement shows an almost theatrical seriousness to the business at hand. The participants are called "to swear a bodily oath" on their testimony. Only "after many things had

---

[61] Bagnall 1995a.   [62] Gagos and van Minnen 1994, 82.
[63] *P.Mich.* 13.659 with references to discussion of dating at Psai(o)s 37, contra the dating proposed at Gagos and van Minnen 1994, 38, note 80. Trans. from ed. princ.

been said and pleaded in these matters by the people of both parties" do those parties at last agree "in accordance with an arbitration and a friendly arrangement and judgment and examination by a common arbiter."

The case has several parts. The two central parts are the plaintiffs' claim to have a deed of security against Ioannes worth eighteen gold pieces, and a claim that a thirty-six gold piece land sale to Ioannes had never been fully paid. Psaios presents a deed of security he made for the defendants against property belonging to a third party, Theodosios of Pakerke. Psaios and Talous also allege "fraud or deceit of the notary" to explain some ambiguities in the paperwork.

But the particulars of the dispute are not the most interesting part of this case. More revealing is how Psaios and Talous go about solving the dispute once it has gone too far. The settlement notes that:

> The people of the prosecuting party [that is, the plaintiffs] proved that they had often used loud complaints in the Holy Church against Ioannes . . . and that they also often had approached the *praeses* of the province regarding this reason but that after there had been much cajolery by the opponents the discussion about that inquiry had been closed.

In other words, the plaintiffs see two paths forward.

They try the official option, going through the provincial government, but that gets them nowhere: their opponents are too well connected, their "cajolery" too convincing. But they can also try the social option, trying the case in the court of public opinion, in church on Sunday. Ioannes "must have been embarrassed when he was booed in his own church," but "he was able to hush up the issue through his connections with those in power."[64]

This simplifies the power dynamics at work. Another text calls Victor, one of those representing the defense, "a priest of the church situated in Aphrodito."[65] It is probably the town's main church. This means that Victor is representing the heirs of the man who was priest in his own church before him.[66] This is a cozy arrangement, and it gets cozier: Victor is Dioskoros's cousin, and the other man representing the defendants in this party is Dioskoros's brother Senouthes. In other words, Psaios and his wife Talous are in conflict with a family at Aphrodito's center of power.

The land at the heart of one part of the dispute is in Aphrodito territory but belongs to Theodosius of Pakerke. Pakerke may have been Aphrodito's immediate neighbor to the south, even though it was in a different nome or administrative district.[67] Part of the settlement stipulates that Psaios and

---

[64] Gagos and van Minnen 1994, 39.　[65] *P.Cair.Masp.* 2.67126.1–2.
[66] See Gagos and van Minnen 1994, 39, note 84.　[67] Marthot 2013, 10.

Talous have no responsibility for handling any future eviction actions against Theodosius. The defendants "or the persons who undertake business for them" – namely, Victor and Senouthes – agree to handle Theodosius themselves.

This short story, confusing as it is, shows how legal action involves so much more than just the law. The case crawls with micropolitical meaning: an outcome that satisfies the prosecution also secures the prestige of the town's main church; strengthens the influence of the town's ruling family; and hands to that family control over a situation impacting relations with a neighboring town. This case also shows that legal action never separates from social action: who you are; who your opponents are; and what you are willing to do to them in public matter just as much as the nature of the case itself.

These cases might not be very common. There is no way of knowing how much evidence is lost, and arguing from silence is dangerous. But a careful discussion can clarify. If disputes over control of village government were common, we might expect many more examples than we have. If property disputes were common, we might expect more of them to end with "loud complaints" in church. We know thousands of people from Aphrodito. If everyone as lowly as George the butcher could end up at the receiving end of a forced settlement, we might expect to see hundreds of them, but we do not.

The presumption here – and throughout this book – should be that through the written evidence we are studying the exceptions, not the rule. Underneath this evidence, out of sight, are the implicitly quiet lives of those thousands of people not appearing in such conflicts. We should suppose that their lives look quiet not because evidence for their conflicts has been lost, but because their lives are quiet. We do not see hundreds of these cases in Aphrodito's archives because most of its people, most of the time, do not need the law.

This is quite different from claiming that the courts are no more. Previous generations of scholars said just that, arguing that Egyptian hostility toward the central state stemming from the period's raging theological controversies led that province to abandon any meaningful engagement with civil courts. A generation of new evidence has finally buried that thesis.[68] Egyptians of late antiquity are more than happy to use the courts when it suits their purposes. Enough people do so to keep those courts occupied.

---

[68] Beaucamp 2007.

The law creates a framework to gain – and regain – control over what we believe is ours by right. The government enforces the law and strengthens our ability to claim what is ours. Time and again, this boils down to money. Access to the law and control over the government gives us more financial security. Some of Aphrodito's elite petition the Roman empress, not in the name of an abstract independence, but to keep outsiders out of their finances. They seek the patronage of local counts for the same reason.

But it is not enough to keep outsiders out of the finances. They have to keep the wrong insiders out as well. This is why Dioskoros and Herakleios jab at each other, adding the wrong names onto tax lists, destroying pasture land, and complaining about it all the way to the imperial capital. Village power matters to these people – the right to become village headman – because with power and position comes patronage and protection. When you have protection, you preserve your *autopragia* and the rents that come to you along with it.

Going to law may be a last resort for Egyptians under Roman rule, if they prefer more informal ways of settling their disputes. But we cannot be so sure that Egyptians feel this way. Petitions and litigation ensure social control and ensure that those around you conform to social norms.[69] Petitions may not be a last resort, but a first resort, a trigger to force a private resolution. At the very least, legal action can take place in parallel with other ways of solving a dispute: two groups in conflict can grope their way forward to a solution "in the shadow of the law."[70]

Aphrodito makes more sense with this model in mind: the formal and the informal working side by side. This is why Nikantinoos settles his dispute in the courthouse, but not actually in court. It is also why Psaios and Talous make a little noise in church at the same time as they take their case to the regional government. This model of parallel tracks, of private and public approaches to power, explains much more than these two cases. The local headmen have formal power, but use it to order informal settlements. Higher regional officials have formal power over the headmen, but face informal limitations, local realities curbing that power. Higher still, the imperial government gives Aphrodito formal fiscal rights, and Aphrodito seeks to protect them through informal appeals to the protection of the empress. The formal and the informal, the legal and the social intimately intertwine.

---

[69] Kelly 2011; Ruffini 2013.   [70] Kelly 2011, 245 borrows the phrase from modern legal sociology.

CHAPTER 4

Dioskoros, Caught in Between

If we believe everything Dioskoros writes, half the town is out to get him. But he is not always believable. The two previous chapters have shown Aphrodito's evidence of violence and order. In this chapter, Dioskoros himself reveals the gray area between these two extremes. Setting aside tax disputes – these will return in later chapters[1] – Dioskoros mostly complains of two kinds of damage: trespass and theft.

These may seem to be clear categories: either someone steals, or they do not; either someone trespasses, or they do not. But looking closer, things seem a little less certain, a little less black and white. The accusations people bring to Dioskoros and the accusations he aims at others have a fuzzy logic defying simple categorization. These accusations are currency with a value, both social and legal, which is not fully realized until it is time to cash them in. Dioskoros holds onto his information, knowing when to use the law and when to avoid it, guided by a social instinct about his world's legal boundaries and how he should employ them.

The first case comes in an affidavit written in December AD 543 by Kollouthos, a public official from Antaiopolis, the regional capital, and addressed as a letter to Dioskoros himself.[2] "I arrived at the village of Aphrodito on public business," Kollouthos says to Dioskoros, "and was asked by Your Excellency to come and inspect the crops of the field subject to you belonging to the holy monastery" named after Sourous, referred to as Apa, the honorific for a monk or priest meaning "father." When he goes to carry out the inspection, he finds crops that "had been utterly ruined," some that "had been trampled down and trampled in the mud," and others "thrust aside and uprooted."

Kollouthos is obviously not an eyewitness to the actual events. We do not even know whether Dioskoros is an eyewitness to what has happened. But Dioskoros gives his side of the story anyway, and Kollouthos repeats it

---

[1] See page 165. [2] *P.Cair.Masp.* 1.67087, adapting the translation in Keenan 1985a, 247.

on paper. Someone – his name is lost – came to Dioskoros "intent on driving his sheep to the field of Makarios, his brother, just below my field, for pasturing." Dioskoros denies permission, but the shepherd proceeds anyway, "steadfast in his tyrannical behavior, driving his aforesaid sheep and as many lambs as he had through my crops." He later claims that the field is "in a category of thoroughfares for lambs 'in our times and that of our ancestors'." In other words, the shepherd asks Dioskoros for permission to pass, to be polite, but tradition lets him cross Dioskoros's land anyway.

This is either trespass pure and simple, or a perfectly legal use of land under easement. Other alternatives include a traditional right to cross this land, but not at this time of year, or only in years when the land is fallow. The lambs might be allowed to cross but not the sheep.[3] The right to cross might include an expectation of speed and efficiency that the shepherd fails to meet. We may be looking at "the outlines of a deeper and wider social tension" between the town's herders and its landholding elite.[4]

However, something else may also be at work. This is not Dioskoros's land. He is only leasing it from the Apa Sourous monastery. In 543, Dioskoros's father is still alive and Dioskoros himself has as yet done little with his life: this is the first time we see him in a text with a definite date.[5] We may have caught him in the middle of a mistake. He leases land not knowing it has an easement on it. He bungles the face-to-face meeting with the shepherd and fumbles for a solution once the damage becomes clear.

It is possible, looking at the tension between shepherds and landholders, to see the landholders as the "moving forces in village life," as "the exploiters, not the exploited."[6] But if Dioskoros is the exploiter in this story, he has not yet perfected his technique. The shepherd, whoever he is, does not seem threatened by Dioskoros or scared of exploitation. Put another way, Dioskoros needs to turn to an outsider for legal support because he does not have the upper hand.

A quarter of a century later, Dioskoros still does not have the upper hand. A well-known set of texts describes Dioskoros's struggle against the pagarch Menas and the shepherds of Phthla, the neighboring village. Much of this story is described in later chapters.[7] For now, the main point is trespass, once again. In AD 567, Dioskoros petitions the duke of the Thebaid province in southern Egypt, complaining that the shepherds of

---

[3] Keenan 1985a, 252.   [4] Keenan 1985a, 253.   [5] Ruffini 2011, 160.   [6] Keenan 1985a, 253.
[7] See page 166.

Phthla have occupied the land he owns in that village and are enjoying its produce.[8]

Menas, "the most illustrious *scriniarius* [secretary] and pagarch of Antaiopolis," since taking over the pagarchy,

> reaps the profits of the acres of … the miserable slave … Dioskoros, a man utterly needy, who has young children scarcely knowing as yet their right hand from their left, and needing heavy expenses for their maintenance.

The same man

> scrupled not to bestow on the Assistant of the village of Phthla and on its shepherds free of rent and taxes, to appropriate to themselves, his acres, which they enjoy without rent and taxes, leaving to him, to his utter destruction, the tax quota on them, assigned to his charge.[9]

We can imagine Dioskoros's frustration, seeing his land in the hands of these shepherds – uncouth, unclean men he compares to savages and barbarians.[10] Again, it may seem a clear-cut case of trespass: either these men have occupied land they do not own, or they have not. But this is more than a legal question. It is a social and political question as well. Dioskoros's difficulty here comes from the fact that these shepherds are in Phthla, not in Aphrodito: it is harder for him to impose his will on outsiders.[11] To do so he needs to build his case, collect his evidence. Whether he uses that evidence to reach a legal solution to his problem, or a political one, is ultimately not important.

These two episodes are not isolated. They are part of a recurring problem for Dioskoros, a problem so severe that he starts keeping a list of all of the pasture land that his enemies destroy – more on which later.[12] For now, the important point is how widespread this damage seems to be. The list names no fewer than twenty places (*topoi*) in which Dioskoros's pasture land has been damaged by the same sort of trespass he has faced in earlier examples.[13]

Several of these places are in Aphrodito's south field, others in the fields of nearby Phthla, to the east of Aphrodito. These sample entries include the names of the places, the year the damage is done, and who reports the episode.

> The place of Isakios son of Beskouis in Nepke, through Phoibammon and Menas, from the report of Iakkubios the farmer, from the 14th to the 15th indiction …

---

[8] *P.Cair.Masp.* 1.67002.1.14 (*oikeiôsasthai*) and *P.Lond.* 5.1677.13 (*karpountai*).
[9] The introduction to *P.Cair.Masp.* 1.67002, trans. in Bell 1944, 33. [10] See page 169.
[11] Keenan 1985a, 258. [12] See page 66.
[13] *P.Cair.Masp.* 3.67319. For discussion of each place, see Marthot 2013, Volume II *s.n.*

> The place of Horion son of Eulogios . . .
> The place of Karkaros through Biktor son of Tachumia, a shepherd, from the 14th indiction to the present 1st indiction . . .
> The place of Apa Onophrios through the son of Martha from Phthla, from the 15th indiction.

Some of the places are not well known, and could be anywhere in the town's territory. When Dioskoros stands on Aphrodito's elevated heights and looks down at the town, he sees enemies encroaching on his land from all sides, and knows that he has to begin collecting evidence.

In earlier periods of Roman Egypt, the legal system can be a weapon for litigants.[14] It can be another stage in a feud or an ongoing quest for vengeance. Trespass is "often used for vexatious suits" in these earlier periods because of "its elastic nature."[15] Dioskoros and his complaints about trespass come quickly to mind.[16] When Dioskoros gets Kollouthos to record his complaint against the shepherd, we remember that Dioskoros will have ongoing problems with shepherds at other points in his life.[17] When the shepherd himself claims to have an ancestral right to passage through the land, there is something believable about it. We leave the story wondering whether Dioskoros is collecting evidence for a larger case, preparing what some would consider a vexatious lawsuit. The suit itself is a weapon, to use to a legal end if necessary, or to turn into social pressure when the moment is right.

Dioskoros collects evidence against thieves just as carefully as he does against trespassers. Several of these lists survive, naming the thieves and what Dioskoros thinks they have stolen from him. One list, from the 530s or 540s, goes on for over fifty lines.[18] Most of his attention dwells on the animals he has lost (sheep and goats) and the occasional bit of food.

> By Georgios son of Plasaik, 4 sheep, by the report of the son of Sapah, son of Phoibammon, also called the shepherd.
> By Agnaton son of Kaliarios, 5 sheep, by the report of the same.
> By Pathn, also called Anouphios, son of Psaios son of Patermouthos, 5 sheep, by the report of the same . . .
> By Herakleios, son of Papas son of Psimon, 1 goat and cheese.

However, in some cases the thefts are more impressive: two olive presses, a fruit press, a resin or pitch press. Olive presses are neither light nor easy to use. Dioskoros may be simplifying, referring to the wooden axles of these

---

[14] Kelly 2011, 287.   [15] Kelly 2011, 288.   [16] Ruffini 2013, 609.   [17] See page 166.
[18] P.Cair.Masp. 2.67143.

machines. Even so, this is a relatively serious degree of effort on the part of the thieves.

Few scholars have paid much attention to this list of thefts. The thefts could be a caper, the list itself the product of a single episode.[19] The presence of craftsmen in this text – shipwrights, builders, clothes menders – men who are certainly members of their respective craft guilds, may show that the thefts in this list are guild-related. Something like this happens in the Aphrodito murder mystery, in which the town guild leaders get together to kill Herakleios.[20] Something similar also happens elsewhere in Egypt in the sixth century, with a headman from the village of Spania who faces a massive theft by a "cross-section of the community."[21]

Imagine this: Dioskoros wakes up one day to find himself facing a coordinated strike, dozens of men from all walks of life stealing dozens of his animals and several pieces of heavy machinery in one swoop. But it may happen another way, the thefts coming in dribs and drabs, over weeks, months, years, with Dioskoros collecting his evidence and biding his time. The difference is real. One scenario is a sudden crisis, a specific conflict with a hidden but powerful cause and a laser-focused and detailed response. The other scenario is an ongoing nuisance, a pervasive and never-ending problem, another reason for Dioskoros to look out at the world around him and see an array of enemies.

The second picture probably makes more sense from the way Dioskoros collects his information. His lists use two specific terms to describe this information. First, his entries repeatedly describe theft reports coming from the *hupobolê* – suggestion or reminder – of a third-party informant. Second, in several cases, Dioskoros refers to the *gnôrisma* available to him, the mark by which something is known, the evidence, or in legal terms, the *corpus delicti* – the proof that a crime has actually been committed.[22]

These two terms contrast sharply with another word used in the Aphrodito archives to describe how people tell their stories and pass information. In the Aphrodito murder mystery, the victim's offense is his decision to be a *sukophantês*, an informer or denouncer.[23] The Greek term is a reminder of its modern derivative: a sycophant's information is tarnished, tainted, not the sort of thing we want as proof of a real crime.

The difference between the people reporting for Dioskoros and Herakleios himself – whose denunciations get him killed – is in the eye

---

[19] Venticinque 2016, 93. [20] See page 28.
[21] Interpretation of *P.Oxy.* 16.2058 in Venticinque 2016, 94.
[22] *LSJ* cites only *P.Cair.Masp.* 2.67143 for the latter legal sense of the term. [23] *SB* 16.12542.7.

of the beholder, the threshold a matter of perspective. Herakleios may commit a more severe breach of social protocol than Dioskoros's informants, who, in his mind, are merely giving him suggestions or reminders. Here Dioskoros is a paranoid artist at work, crafting his evidence with just the right choice of words. As he collects his evidence for retaliation against his enemies, he paints the right social picture: his allies are not sycophants, but give him real, solid *gnôrismata* to provide proof in a court of law.

These are fascinating lists. It is strange that Dioskoros should be the victim of so many thefts. It is even stranger that he knows the thieves in so many of the cases. (Many more thefts against him may go unrecorded in his notes because he did not know the perpetrators.) The plot thickens when we look at the informants themselves. Some of them are repeat informants. Some of them inform for Dioskoros while stealing from him elsewhere in the same texts. (This is arguably the proof that these thefts are not a single strike, but spread out over time.) Both informing for and stealing from the same man is bizarre behavior, begging an explanation.

We have three texts in Dioskoros's own hand, thanks to his own meticulous recordkeeping. Two of them record damages against him and members of his family, and probably date to the late AD 530s or 540s.[24] The third is a little later, most likely from AD 552/553.[25] Four cases in particular from these three texts are worth closer attention. The first text includes an "account of people to be accused." One entry in this account accuses "Kollouthos son of Kuriakos, the goldsmith, for Serakoutios the coppersmith." Lower down on the same page, another account appears under the heading: "Account of thefts of my animals, from whom we see the proof of the crime." One entry in this account of thefts, a few lines lower down, reads, "By Mesmouis, 25 sheep and 30 goats, through the report of Kollouthos the goldsmith."

Kollouthos is the same man in both entries. The same Kollouthos the goldsmith appears in another text from AD 535, the subject of a guarantee from the priest Iosephios to Apollos the policeman, stating that Kollouthos will stay in Aphrodito.[26] The very fact that Apollos needs such a guarantee suggests that Kollouthos is a flight risk, and had been in trouble with the law in the past. This may be due to previous debts, or a history of tax

---

[24] *P.Cair.Masp.* 2.67143 and *P.Cair.Masp.* 2.67144.
[25] *P.Cair.Masp.* 3.67319 and Fournet unpublished. The Papyrological Navigator (www.papyri.info) dates the text to 567/568, following Maspero's lead in the ed. princ. and connecting the events in this text to those of *P.Cair.Masp.* 1.67002. I prefer 552/553 because of the appearance of the party of Herakleios, for which see page 66.
[26] *P.Cair.Masp.* 3.67297 + *P.Flor.* 3.287.

evasion. The curiosity is clear: Kollouthos is a thief in one of Dioskoros's lists, an informer in another, and appears elsewhere as a flight risk in need of a guarantee. In short, he is a prototype of the thief/informant, a model repeated throughout these lists. We do not know the chronological relationship between these events in Kollouthos's life. If the entries in the theft list appear in the order they take place, then Kollouthos turns informant after being reported for theft.

The same text has a separate section, an "Account of thefts of my lambs, from their visible marks" or brands. One entry in this section reads: "By the shepherd Pathelpe, 2 sheep of Mesmouis." In a separate text, in an account without any descriptive heading, we find an entry for a theft recorded "through the report of Ieremias, son of the shepherd Pathelpe."[27] Pathelpe is probably the same man in both texts.[28] Pathelpe's family presents another variation of the thief/informant. Pathelpe steals from Dioskoros, and Pathelpe's son informs on someone else stealing from Dioskoros. Again, we do not know if the order of the entries reflects the order of events in real life, but if they do, the family become informants after being reported for theft.

The third case appears in an account we have discussed earlier, under the heading, "A list of my pastures destroyed by various men, as arranged in order."[29] The most interesting entry records damage to:

> The place of Isak son of Beskouis in Nepkê, by Phoibammon and Menas, through the report of Iakob the farmer, from the 14th to the 15th indiction, and Biklos also called Phôt Megme, through the report of the same [Iakob].

This case is different from the first two. Instead of an accused thief or thief's relative turning informant, we have a recurring informant. Iakob, about whom we know nothing else, informs for Dioskoros about damage and trespass committed over the course of two consecutive years.

A final case appears in the same text. This portion of Dioskoros's list also records damage to specific places, probably pastures, along with the names of the informants and the identity of the suspects:

> The place ... through the report of Patermouthis and Enoch from the 14th indiction to the 15th indiction, and the same under the party of Herakleios and Ioannes. The place Pasikorios by the same village chiefs through the report of the same guild heads. The place Piah Sachô likewise by the same.

---

[27] *P.Cair.Masp.* 2.67144.
[28] The name is extremely rare in Aphrodito, both men are described as shepherds, and both men appear in Dioskoros's records of thefts and informants.
[29] *P.Cair.Masp.* 3.67319.r.1.

The place Nilamon and the arouras [or "acres"] of Tasneouos from the 14th indiction through Ioannes son of Tanoure the farmer, through the report of Abraam son of Victor the shepherd, also known as Soul, from the 15th indiction, through the aforementioned village chiefs Ioannes and Herakleios ... The place Pallos, by the guild head Patermouthes, through the report of Mousaios son of Kallinikos, the deacon and farmer, from the 14th and 15th indictions ... The place Exactor, by the former village chiefs, the party of Herakleios and Ioannes, through the report of my brother Menas.

Dioskoros begins by writing the names of the informants (Patermouthis and Enoch) and the suspects (Herakleios and Ioannes). He realizes as he goes further that he has to be more specific. So, the accused party of Herakleios and Ioannes (or, alternatively, "those around Herakleios and Ioannes") appear later as "the same village chiefs" and later still, and even more specifically, as "the former village chiefs, the party of Herakleios and Ioannes." Similarly, Patermouthis and Enoch first appear with no particular label, and later appear as "the same guild heads." They must be "the same guild heads," since they are informing on the same group of people, and no other guild heads have appeared in the text previously. Yet Patermouthis the guild head appears in the same text as the accused in a report against him.[30]

This is a bizarre collection of accusers and accused, and a fascinating glimpse into local politics. Herakleios, Ioannes, and their faction are accused of trespass and destruction. In one case, the accuser is Menas, a blood relative of Dioskoros. In other cases, they are accused by Patermouthis and Enoch, two guild heads who are cooperating with each other and Dioskoros for unknown reasons. In the final twist, Patermouthis himself is accused to Dioskoros by Mousaios, a deacon in debt to Dioskoros at one point in the 550s.[31] Dioskoros may lend money to Mousaios as a reward for his services as an informant.[32]

Patermouthis is a version of the thief-turned-informant from earlier cases. But if Dioskoros records the entries in chronological order, Patermouthis is accused of destruction to Pallos after he has already twice served as an informant in his own right. This distinguishes Patermouthis from the thief/informants in the other cases, in which

---

[30] Patermouthis is a rare name in Aphrodito: Ruffini 2011 records half a dozen examples; he is the only *kephalaiôtês*.
[31] *P.Cair.Masp.* 2.67130 and Ruffini 2011, Mousaios 48.
[32] If *P.Cair.Masp.* 3.67319 dates to the 550s. The alternative, dating it to 567/568, could suggest that Mousaios turned informant for Dioskoros out of continued obligation to him following his loans in the previous decade.

Dioskoros receives information from a source only after being wronged by that source. The explanation for Patermouthis's behavior may be the very identity of the people he accused in the first place, "those around Herakleios and Ioannes."

The party or faction of Herakleios (*tôn peri Herakleion*) appears elsewhere: in AD 551, Dioskoros travels to Constantinople and receives an imperial rescript against the party of Herakleios and other enemies back home in Aphrodito.[33] These two appearances of Herakleios's faction might explain Patermouthis's behavior. In 551, armed with a letter against Herakleios, Dioskoros is ascendant in Aphrodito, leading Patermouthis and others to inform against Herakleios the following year. But Patermouthis's subsequent decision to turn on Dioskoros may be evidence that, behind the scenes, Herakleios is later triumphant in his factional struggle with Dioskoros.

Some of these men are trying to buy favor, but there may be other motives.[34] These men may be responding to social tensions around them. If two people have a good relationship but hold different opinions about a third party, it causes tension. Put more simply, the enemy of my enemy is my friend, and if not, something has to change in these relationships for my social life to find balance. A thief becoming an informant is doing exactly that. Informing on one enemy to another enemy is a way to make your enemy's enemy into your friend. This may be what is happening in Aphrodito. If so, Dioskoros's thief lists may be a play-by-play account of town factions fighting with each other, stealing and turning each other in as people fight for social position.

Examples from other places in the Mediterranean region provide more information about these cases of animal theft. The Italian island of Sardinia can help explain what we see in Aphrodito. There, the state saw informing as a way of restoring one's good name. In Sardinia, until 1872, being labeled a bandit was not a permanent problem from the state's perspective: "any bandit who consigned to the authorities another bandit with a sentence at least as severe as his own earned the right to a pardon."[35]

The case of Pathelpe and his son becomes clearer in this context: "The pardon could also be extended" to the family "of the captor who might themselves be bandits ... the law permitted those who had chosen to step beyond its boundaries a means of resuming their full membership of

---

[33] *P.Cair.Masp.* 1.67032 = *Sel.Pap.* 2.363. See Ruffini 2008c, 166 for the argument that Ruffini 2011's Herakleios 34 and Herakleios 35 are the same individual.

[34] What follows is informed by balance theory: see Cartwright and Harary 1956.

[35] Moss 1979, 481.

society."[36] So Ieremias also informs for Dioskoros to restore his father Pathelpe's position with Dioskoros. The Sardinian parallels also help explain the motives of the thieves.

> A theft can also be the appropriate response to any instance of uncompensated damage caused by a shepherd, and the deliberate attempt to make the value of the animals taken roughly equivalent to the debt to be redeemed explains why whole flocks are very rarely stolen.[37]

This also looks like the story in Aphrodito, where so many of the thefts are small scale. Consider that we only have Dioskoros's side of the story. Many of these thieves may think they are being righteous in some way, and only taking back what ought to be theirs.

These Sardinian examples show why so many unrelated people appear in Aphrodito's animal theft cases, or, put another way, why someone knows who is guilty in so many cases. "The livestock-rustler is in any case secure against betrayal to the victim so that he can claim knowledge of, and elliptically suggest his participation in, a theft without direct danger. Indeed a young shepherd of proven reliability in handling these exploits may expect to be recruited for further displays of prowess, thus improving his own rate of accumulation of animal capital."[38] In this way, Iakob, Dioskoros's serial informant, builds his own reputation, his own social capital, and perhaps his own livestock.

So we understand the thieves and informants, but not Dioskoros. It is not clear what he thinks he is doing when he writes these entries. He may be saving evidence in anticipation of his day in court. On the one hand, there is evidence that Dioskoros is familiar with imperial law: he can quote the exact language of the law in a given case[39] and he can imitate the style of imperial legislation.[40] Dioskoros's allusion to the emperor Justinian's inheritance law shows that he was "juridically up to date."[41] On the other hand, there is reason to be skeptical: Dioskoros is guilty of the occasional "imprecise, popular use of a technical term."[42] Even so, Dioskoros clearly has "legal expertise" based on notes he had taken "from the lectures he had attended,"[43] which allowed him to use the law with "great skill."[44]

---

[36] Moss 1979, 481.   [37] Moss 1979, 490.   [38] Moss 1979, 492.
[39] Citing legislation by the emperor Leo: van Minnen 2003, 123–125 on *P.Cair.Masp.* 1.67028.
[40] van Minnen 2003, 126.   [41] van Minnen 2003, 129 on *P.Cair.Masp.* 3.67353.
[42] Urbanik 2008, 141.   [43] Urbanik 2008, 140.   [44] Urbanik 2008, 135.

Roman law has precise guidelines on whether an animal theft is merely *furtum* (theft) or constitutes the graver offense of *abigeatus* (rustling).[45] If the total number of sheep stolen at once or in aggregate over separate occasions is less than ten, only theft has been committed. But if ten or more sheep are taken at once or over time, rustling has been committed instead. The following shows every case from Dioskoros's lists, giving the number of sheep or goats involved in a theft, along with the alleged thief.

Agnaton	5 sheep
Enoch	1 sheep
Herakleios	1 goat and some cheese
Hermauos	2 sheep
Hermauos	1 goat
Georgios	4 sheep
Makarios	1 goat
Mesmouis	25 sheep and 30 goats
Mouis	2 goats and some cheese
Pathelpe	2 sheep
The gravediggers	3 sheep
Pathn	5 sheep
The son of Patkax	5 sheep
Pelish	1 sheep

What leaps out almost at once is the trivial nature of the cases: thirteen of the fourteen list five animals or fewer. The unspecified amounts of cheese make a good punchline: Mesmouis has the skill to make off with fifty-five animals, but Herakleios shows a sense of humor, taking one goat and stopping on the way out to grab some cheese. Meanwhile, only one of the fourteen cases rises to the level of *abigeatus* or animal rustling.

If Dioskoros does have a legal education, he knows full well the distinction between Agnaton's theft of five sheep on the one hand and Mesmouis's twenty-five sheep and thirty goats on the other. This second case is clearly rustling. Mesmouis is likely to be one of the *humiliores*, society's lesser men, those who can be beaten under the law. He faces very severe penalties. Again, Dioskoros may know this, but his informant may not. This case has already been discussed: Kollouthos, the informant, tells on Mesmouis for his *abigeatus* only after being himself accused in another case. The accusation against Kollouthos is unspecified. We do not know whether it was *abigeatus* or mere *furtum*. But either way, his value to Dioskoros is clear: Kollouthos's information on *abigeatus* is more valuable

---

[45] Shaw 1984, 32, note 81.

than it would be for a lesser crime, and could go farther toward wiping away his own debt to Dioskoros for his earlier crime.

This distinction between rustling and theft is important: Aphrodito's society might seem ripe for the outbreak of full-scale banditry. In the early modern and modern worlds, bandits require a weak state and "undeveloped electoral processes in which politicians ... utilize strongarm tactics ... by coopting ex-bandits as retainers."[46] This co-optation of bandits as retainers sounds rather like the co-optation of shepherds by local elites in Aphrodito, a development central to the dispute over Aphrodito's fiscal independence.

However, banditry is not widespread in Aphrodito. The words of an army officer in Sicily in 1871 may explain why. "If the peasants know that the group in question is under the protection of (a bandit) they don't harm the shepherds, but are friendly to them, because they fear them. Otherwise the shepherds are unable to pass: their animals destroy everything."[47] This is exactly what happens when Dioskoros denies the son of Mousaios's ancestral right to cross his land. Dioskoros does not fear Mousaios, and his list of informants shows why: he has people he can trust.

Bandits in the Roman world "had wide links with parts of society that were considered legitimate."[48] This is true both for Rome's bandits and Aphrodito's sheep thieves, connected to Dioskoros and other local elites. The Theodosian Code, the great codification of Roman law enacted a century before Dioskoros's life, contained explicit warnings to the lords or *domini* who give material aid to bandits, understood to be their own shepherds.[49] Roman law recognizes a "nexus of power networks" connecting lower-status thieves and higher-status landowners and receivers, the fences for stolen property.[50]

This "nexus of power networks" seriously complicates law enforcement in the face of elite collaboration. In the context of Roman law, "An exception then had to be made [to the more harsh forms of punishment laid down by law] in the case of those receivers who were none other than members of the landowning elite. If culpable middlemen were of higher social status (*honestiores*) they were only to be relegated (a lesser form of exile) or suffer loss of their status and/or property."[51] In short, this means that when it comes to animal theft, the severity of the accusation had different implications based on the social status of the accused. Dioskoros

---

[46] Sant Cassia 1993, 783.   [47] Sant Cassia 1993, 781.   [48] Shaw 1984, 31.
[49] Shaw 1984, 32 citing *C.Th.* 9.30.2.   [50] Shaw 1984, 31.   [51] Shaw 1984, 32.

would know this, and may well limit his accusations with an eye toward their social implications.

Some modern scholars believe in a kind of "social bandit," an outlaw who remains a criminal in the eyes of the law and the local lord but is a hero to the peasants around him.[52] Banditry in general seems to be a ubiquitous threat in the Roman world.[53] And that image of a social bandit, a just figure resisting the oppression of an unjust ruler, is undoubtedly common in Roman literature.[54] But real historical evidence supporting the existence of social bandits in the Roman world is thin, and probably imitates the great stories in Roman fiction.[55] Aphrodito's thieves, even filtered through Dioskoros's biased lens, are no social bandits. If they were, Dioskoros would not be so blessed with informants, and Aphrodito's peasants would cheer for the thieves and turn their backs on Dioskoros.

I have said nothing about whether or not Aphrodito's informants were telling the truth: I would like to know, but it really matters very little. Legal justice is not the main point – it is to turn your enemy's enemies into friends. Despite Dioskoros's background, and despite the relevant laws on banditry, these thieves and vandals and their informants exist outside the world of law. We hear nothing of the concepts of crime and punishment.

Instead, we have a local big man who is wronged – repeatedly – and his would-be clients who aim to make it right. Those who wrong him have information of their own through which they find absolution and recruit a powerful friend. Dioskoros's careful records are not an attempt to bring the force of the state into play against those who wrong him. He knows full well that the piece of cheese he records is legally irrelevant, but it is socially relevant, for two reasons. First, it is an insult to his dignity that he clearly intends to remember. Second, it is leverage: accusations used against thieves may compel the thieves to repay him in the future with information.

It is not clear whether Dioskoros ever does anything about these thefts, or whether he ever tries to take meaningful legal action. In the 570s, Dioskoros writes a letter complaining about Enoch, the steward of his father's monastery.[56] Some of the monastery's animals have been stolen, and the "worthless, impious, and most lazy field-guards of our village jeered at Enoch daily."

In the face of this frustration, Enoch is ready to retire, and plans to "leave the holy place without supervision." Dioskoros has to "embarrass him and

---

[52] Hobsbawm 1969, 13.   [53] Shaw 1984, 8–12.   [54] Shaw 1984, 50–51.   [55] Grünewald 2004, 7–8.
[56] *SB* 20.14626, adapting the trans. in Hanafi 1988, 98–99. See page 118.

persuade him to remain and did so until I was able to persuade him to be sent with one of the two monks to the upper districts on account of these same animals." Clearly, Enoch faces social pressure that makes him think that dealing with these thefts is not worth the trouble.

Hidden social pressure may also explain the case of Hermauos, son of Laborios.[57] In Dioskoros's account of "thefts of my animals," Hermauos stands accused of stealing two sheep from the flock of the heirs of Pasois. We can only guess at the exact arrangement here. Dioskoros may take care of the flock of the heirs of Pasois on their behalf, or he may be one of those heirs himself. Either way, Dioskoros thinks Hermauos is a thief. Hermauos appears again in a much more official document, an order from the provincial government at Antinoopolis complaining that the people of Aphrodito "have not sent him to court even up to now," despite his "wickedness," and urging the anonymous recipient to "give all of your help to the police in this place" to bring Hermauos to court.

This may only be a coincidence. The regional government is not likely to issue a warrant over the theft of two sheep. Still, we have an explicit statement that official arrest orders are being ignored at a more local level, something we have already seen on previous occasions.[58] Anybody facing the jeers of the field-guards may be willing to let Hermauos get away with his wickedness. If any legal action takes place in the wake of either of these two cases, we never see any evidence. Local social pressures may trump the relevance of the law.

Dioskoros and his town do not exist in a vacuum. They are subject to a legal system coming all the way from Constantinople.[59] Clearly, knowledge of the law in this period varies, based on social status, and on which fields of law matter for any given question.[60] Social status matters in Aphrodito, and it helps to explain Dioskoros's continual problems with thieves and trespassers. He knows the law and how to use it. We doubt that the shepherds and house builders stealing from him know the law nearly as well. This should give him a distinct advantage. However, the small number of cases in which Dioskoros seeks a legal solution – compared to the long list of wrongs he suffers – once again raises questions about our evidence.

Dioskoros faces considerable lawbreaking and collects legal evidence in response, but does not need to use the law to be effective. Legal remedies

---

[57] Ruffini 2011, Herma(o)(u)os 13.   [58] See page 37.
[59] For the following discussion of imperial law, see Beaucamp 2007.
[60] Beaucamp 2007, 274–275.

exist alongside social ones, and social remedies leave fewer traces in our records. Dioskoros collects information from his friends about his enemies. Outside of the written record, hidden from the world of formal petitions, this information probably produces invisible results. Simply knowing that Dioskoros has informants arrayed against them may make the thieves and trespassers more cooperative, or at least more cautious, in the future. As in other places throughout this book, the visible legal weapons suggest that quite a bit more conflict, tension, and resolution remain invisible, beneath the surface.

Again and again in Aphrodito, we see crowds fighting for position. We see it in the murders, with one victim killed for informing on his colleagues to their rivals. We see it in the ongoing turnover of the village headmen, and the constant accusations of evil deeds they face. We see it in these thefts, over which so many people are willing to turn each other in. This is village factionalism.[61] From the point of view of Dioskoros and his family, there is an enemy faction lurking in the village.

Essentially, these thieves and their informants do not care about Constantinople's legal system, which only impinges so far. They are shopping for patrons. The thieves do not need Dioskoros: they see him as weak, or they see the people who oppose him as strong. The informants do need Dioskoros: they are willing to bet that his family's strength is not yet spent, that their information can purchase his patronage, that he is still strong enough to repay that debt when it comes due.

---

[61] Ruffini 2008c.

CHAPTER 5

Working in the Fields

In the late 540s, when Dioskoros's father Apollos dies, he leaves two-thirds of his estate to Dioskoros, and the remaining third to a man named Phoibammon, son of Triadelphos.[1] Phoibammon's wife Anastasia is Dioskoros's cousin, and her mother is a sister of Dioskoros's father Apollos. But Phoibammon is less interesting for his family connections than for his business sense.[2] Phoibammon is an energetic businessman, an entrepreneur, a speculator, the type of character once unimagined in the modern vision of late antiquity.[3] Phoibammon's entrepreneurial career lasts nearly fifty years. He first appears in AD 526, and last appears in 572. His career in the Aphrodito papyri is longer than that of Dioskoros himself, whose securely dated appearances span the period from 543 to 573.[4]

Whether Phoibammon is a success story, and whether he is rich, depends on "what exactly is meant by 'rich'." Maybe he is more than an entrepreneur, perhaps one of the town's ancient great landowners. Or maybe he is something less, "still a peasant but an extraordinarily successful one," a well-off farmer.[5] If our categories fail, we should let his actions speak for themselves, starting with his relationship with Samuel.

Samuel is a soldier from the village of Tanuaithis in the Apollinopolite nome.[6] He has daughters whose names are unknown. He can write, but not easily: the papyri describe him as a "slow writer." We know him from four published texts. The first one to give any detail is a lease he makes in June 526. He has almost nineteen acres that he leases to Phoibammon for eight years. But it is really family land he leases. When he describes "the farm belonging to us," the antecedent is missing. Lost from the lease's left

---

[1] Keenan 2007, 236, summarizing Fournet 2000.
[2] See originally Keenan 1980, now with Keenan 2007, 233–237. [3] Keenan 2007, 237.
[4] See the summary of evidence at Phoibammon 1 and Dioskoros 3. [5] Keenan 2007, 237.
[6] Subsequent discussion follows Keenan 1980.

margin are the names of his children, and Samuel "also does business for them."

Phoibammon agrees to pay all the farming expenses, and pay Samuel a rent of 291 liters of grain per acre. This is the baseline: his rent also includes fifty cheeses and half of the fruit he gets from the farm's fruit trees, which "would surely have provided, beginning with the next harvest, a more than satisfactory basis for subsistence for Samuel and his daughters. Samuel's problem, however, seems to have been the immediacy of his need for cash and grain."[7]

Against the same nineteen acres he just leased to Phoibammon, Samuel then borrows from Phoibammon eighteen gold coins and 2,249 liters of grain. Instead of paying interest on the loan, he gives Phoibammon a discount on the terms of his lease. Early the next year, in 527, Samuel takes another loan from Phoibammon, and writes, "I now acknowledge that … there has been measured out to me by you for my urgent need the sum-total" of 1,163 liters of grain, "and I am willing to repay you at the time of the harvest."[8] Later that same year, in July, Samuel borrows another 698 liters of grain from Phoibammon, and "resigns any right to dislodge Phoibammon from the farm until this and the other debts have been repaid."[9]

At each point, Samuel specifies whose measure he will use to repay the grain: at first, he offers a measure belonging to his own former tenant, a man named Ioannes; later, he offers a measure belonging to a neutral local official; finally, he offers a measure belonging to Phoibammon himself. Obviously, he is losing leverage to Phoibammon at each step of the way.[10] The total amount he owes to Phoibammon gives the latter what amounts to a free year's rent on Samuel's family farm.[11] Samuel, who is not working his own land, is probably an absentee landlord, risking his children's property.[12]

This is all part of a pattern for Phoibammon. A large part of his life's work is renting land from absentee landlords. In many cases, he handles land belonging to distant religious organizations. In this way, he fills a void as a middleman: churches and monasteries will have no expertise in working their land, but Phoibammon can connect them through subleases to people who do.

Phoibammon's work also includes the direct ownership and renting out of his own land. One sort of work can lead directly to the other: owners

---

[7] Keenan 1980, 146.   [8] *P.Mich.* 13.670.   [9] Keenan 1980, 148.   [10] Keenan 1980, 148.
[11] Keenan 1980, 149.   [12] Keenan 1980, 150.

who fall deeper in debt to their tenants soon turn the tenants into owners themselves. Phoibammon is already on his way to taking over Samuel's land. When he buys land from two brothers, the shepherds Victor and Kollouthos, in the summer of 540, it is easy to imagine that they too had fallen into his debt and now lose their land to pay themselves clear.[13]

Throughout this book, I draw attention to points at which our evidence is probably exceptional.[14] This may well be true of Phoibammon as well. There are unlikely to be many people in Aphrodito like him, well positioned to benefit from the declining fortunes of an outsider. But his career is still instructive. Careers like his are not possible in a lawless, chaotic society. Nor are they possible if the weight of the state and the aristocracy rests too oppressively on the shoulders of free men. Investing in the way he does demands confidence in the future. If we trust his judgment, we should probably conclude that his world is one of reasonable certainty, that it is not rife with interference at the hands of the state or oppression at the hands of ultra-rich aristocrats.

The best-known large estate of late antique Egypt – the obvious home to one such aristocrat – is the "glorious house" of Flavius Apion in the Oxyrhynchite region, far to the north of Aphrodito.[15] The records from this estate dominate the surviving sixth-century evidence. These records seem to show a protofeudal family of high-ranking imperial officials owning and operating as much as 75,000 acres of agricultural land throughout the region. But it is more likely that the family is so prominent in the area because it collects taxes throughout the region, without in fact owning all the land in its records.[16]

At the same time as we argue over the large estates of Oxyrhynchos, it is natural to wonder whether they are typical of the rest of Egypt. When we look at Aphrodito, we never see a large, dominant estate in the hands of a single family. We have already met Count Ammonios, a high-ranking official active in southern Egypt in the first half of the sixth century.[17] While Ammonios is not a resident of Aphrodito, he is the most noticeable aristocratic landowner in the area. He owns only forty-six acres of land. More than 10 percent of his holdings are vineyards and gardens.[18]

Substantial portions of the count's account books survive covering the years AD 541 to 546.[19] In some cases, the books reveal professional contractors such as the house builder Jeremias, whom Ammonios pays a fixed

---

[13] *P.Michael.* 45.   [14] See, e.g., page 2.   [15] See most recently Hickey 2012.
[16] Following McConnell 2016 and McConnell forthcoming.   [17] See page 47.
[18] Hickey 2007, 300.   [19] *P.Cair.Masp.* 2.67138 and 67139.

annual salary as a sort of retainer.[20] More frequently, the books focus on taxes, a rigorous recording of payments in cash and kind. Peasants make payments to Ammonios and Ammonios makes payments to higher officials. Most of these records are mundane, little more than lists of names and amounts.

But in some sections of the accounts, the estates of Ammonios come alive. One section is an account of barley from the properties of the count, in AD 543/544.[21] Here, the list splits in two, recording people paying grain to the estate and the people who buy the same grain from it. Enoch pays 320 liters of barley to Ammonios, who resells it to Phanes the butcher. Agnaton also pays barley to Ammonios, who resells it to Kostantios the grain dealer. This part of the account goes on for twenty-five lines.

All told, in this section of the accounts Ammonios receives over 3,800 liters of grain. Small amounts go to pay a tax in kind and as a gift to a local monastery. As for the rest, Ammonios sells the vast majority of it.[22] Aphrodito's largest estate is a marketplace in miniature. Peasants living or working near estate holdings or already doing business with Ammonios can buy grain from him in preference to using the open markets.

At first glance, the names in these accounts might seem like the closest we can get to meeting the faceless peasants oppressed by the great aristocrats. Indeed, these men – and in a few cases, women – are tenants, which is probably typical of most Egyptian peasantry. But as the career of Phoibammon makes clear, being a tenant does not always make you a subordinate. Note these entries for payments in and out of the Ammonios estates.[23]

> Herakleios, son of Balantios and Talous: one gold coin less two and a half carats.[24]
> To Talous, daughter of Balantios: six and a half carats.
> From Herakleios, son of Balantios: 1629 liters of grain.

Balantios is a rare name, unique in Aphrodito. We have already met his granddaughter, Talous, daughter of Herakleios, and her husband Psaios: they are the ones who "used loud complaints" against a priest in his own church to settle a case for no fewer than thirty-six gold pieces.[25] This is real money: some of Ammonios's tenants clearly have means, or will soon produce them.

---

[20] Thomas 1987, 62–63. [21] *P.Cair.Masp.* 2.67139.4.v.
[22] *P.Cair.Masp.* 2.67139 introduction, 44. [23] *P.Cair.Masp.* 2.67139.
[24] A carat is 1/24th of a "gold coin," what this book calls the late antique solidus.
[25] See pages 57–58, if Ruffini 2011 Herakl(e)ios 22 is correct.

Ammonios is not someone deeply engraved in Aphrodito's landscape. In fact, he is a relative newcomer. The Aphrodito cadastre records his local landholdings in 524. Every entry with his name includes a note explaining who used to own that part of his land.[26] This is only helpful for record-keeping purposes, to compare the new cadastre with an old one, or to cross-check against other documents. In other words, every piece of land Ammonios has, he has taken over recently enough that the old owners still appear in the records.

I do not mean to downplay Ammonios – he is an important man, active in regional politics, giving orders to Aphrodito's headmen, and expecting obedience.[27] However, he is neither economically dominant nor indispensable. His presence in Aphrodito is an opportunity. The local monks and village headmen who manage his estates do so for a profit.[28] The more well-to-do tenant farmers – the family of Balantios, for example – no doubt have the same motive in mind. This particular large estate is not a protofeudal monolith but simply another player in the local landscape.

The family of Dioskoros also owns and manages its own property. We have a series of pages from an account book describing this activity in the late 530s or the mid-550s.[29] These pages are a gold mine of little details. Parts of the book keep track of flocks of goats and sheep, and their shearing. Other sections record names and days, possibly the amount of time worked by each of the estate's workers. Two other parts of the account describe the daily activities of the estate over the course of a calendar year.

A quick glance shows his workflow. Dioskoros makes nine payments in the month of Thoth and five payments on two different days in Phaophi. He is busier next month, making at least eleven payments on five different days in Hathur.[30] He makes three payments involving the same person on the 21st of Choiak, one on the 25th, two on the 26th, and three involving the same person on the 30th.[31] He pays for camel food, dog food, and "for the mixing of animal seed."[32]

From here, we can start to imagine the outlines of a full year.[33] The stretch from Thoth to Choiak – mid-September to mid-January – is the peak and end of flood season, and the start of sowing. Cultivation and preparation for the harvest begins in the spring months (Tubi, Mecheir,

---

[26] *SB* 20.14669–14670, with discussion of the *onomatos* entries at Gascou and MacCoull 1987, 109.
[27] See page 47.
[28] Presumably the implication of the instruction to Apollos to subtract four carats from his collection for Ammonios at *P.Cair.Masp.* 1.67062.8.
[29] *P.Cair.Masp.* 2.67141. [30] *P.Cair.Masp.* 2.67141.1.v. [31] *P.Cair.Masp.* 2.67141.2.r.
[32] *P.Cair.Masp.* 2.67141.1.v.13–15. [33] See related remarks in Keenan 1984, 62, note 43.

Phamenoth, and Pharmouthi), and harvest and threshing continue in earnest in the summer months (Pachon, Pauni, Epeiph, and Mesore), when the Nile waters begin to rise again. Dioskoros is not really much busier in these months.[34] He makes at least six payments in Phamenoth, eleven in Pharmouthi, and only a handful of payments in Pachon, Pauni, and Epeiph. These excerpts show an interesting mix:

> Phamenoth
> To the camel drivers, 19 liters.
> Pharmouthi
> For the wages of the gathering, to the workers, 194 liters of lentils.
> Pauni
> To my sister Rachel, lentils.

Some of these payments are work-related. Others are more like a family allowance system.[35]

On the one hand, if this is a typical year, it does not seem like much of an operation. Someone doing no more than making a few payments a month is not working very hard. On the other hand, this account covers only one part of Dioskoros's day-to-day existence. It says nothing about estate income, taxes, or rents. We are missing the evidence for many other activities.

Once in a while, these other parts of his business appear in extreme detail. We even have paperwork for a single wagon in AD 553.[36] Dioskoros rents the wagon to a tenant farmer named Menas, originally from the village of Tanuaithis in the Lesser Apollinopolite nome. This simple transaction generates twenty-six lines of text. Dioskoros does not let his wagon go easily: two carpenters have to provide a guarantee of the rental. Dioskoros may be paranoid, but a wagon is the sort of item that is easy to make off with. Over seventy-five years later, a similar transaction – in which Tsura sells her wagon to a man named Colluthus – requires a similar amount of paperwork.[37]

The papyri never reveal the size of Dioskoros's estates, but the estates of Ammonios are exceptional in Aphrodito. He has eleven separate plots in the town cadastre, more than double any other living individual.[38] Ammonios's aggregate holdings are over seven times larger than the average aggregate holding of living individuals, and over twenty-three

---

[34] *P.Cair.Masp.* 2.67141.5.r.   [35] See also page 159.   [36] *P.Cair.Masp.* 3.67303 and page 110.
[37] *P.Vat.Copti Doresse* 1, with trans. in MacCoull 2009, 26–28.
[38] *SB* 20.14699. The heirs of Theodosios *scholastikos* also hold eleven plots between them. See page 87, for discussion of income inequality and the Gini coefficient.

times larger than the mean. Smaller collections of land are more normal. The average living individual in the cadastre has only one or two plots of land in Aphrodito, of less than seven acres in total.[39]

However, this is not simply a world of small farmers working their own land. The rental market flourishes in Aphrodito and rents come in all shapes and sizes. Ioannes, son of Hermeias, is a good example.[40] In August AD 530, he leases a vineyard in Aphrodito from a woman whose name is lost, the daughter of a most magnificent and most glorious count.[41] The terms of his lease are interesting.[42] In exchange for the security of a ten-year lease, Ioannes agrees to pay a rent in kind of a fixed amount of wine per acre.

On top of this rent, he also agrees to pay with his own labor: irrigation work, vineyard work at his own expense, farm labor on adjacent plots, and improvements to a nearby piece of dry vineyard land. When he describes some of the payments due on these additional plots, he adds, "I will make the payment according to the force of the previous farmer's lease" and describes some of these payments as "the other usual things."[43] This is an interesting touch: lease terms are not fixed, but vary in relation to custom and past precedent.[44] The decisions your peers make when they rent land today will impact the quality of the lease you can get when you rent the same land tomorrow.

Ioannes is no exception. Records show the custom of sprinkling rents with a "grab bag of extras" thrown in.[45] When Samuel leases land to Phoibammon, the latter agrees to pay – on top of the base rent – an additional fifty cheeses, four *koloba* of *lapsane*, an unknown number of chickens, and half the produce of the fruit trees.[46] Many decades later, in 598, when a man named Theodoros leases land to Psais, he agrees to pay "75 dry pieces of landlord's cheese, 6 mustard vessels and 3 holiday gifts of cheese and vegetables annually."[47]

These are not minor details, but represent part of a larger picture. We can easily imagine a more rigid rent system, in which any given amount of

---

[39] Mean number of holdings: 1.775. Mean aggregate size of living individuals' holdings: 9.55025 arouras. Median aggregate size: 2.875 arouras. Figures in this paragraph utilize an MS Excel spreadsheet of the Aphrodito cadastre. I am grateful to Roger Bagnall for providing this spreadsheet.
[40] Ioannes 123, with note at Herm(e)ias 11. The identifications taken as certain in Hickey 2012, 71, note 55 are plausible, relying on a common patronymic, but unsubstantiated.
[41] Ioannes 124, for whom see Ruffini 2008a, 190.   [42] See Hickey 2012, 70–71.
[43] P.Cair.Masp. 1.67104.13–14.   [44] Hickey 2012, 71.
[45] Keenan 1985a, 256, note 27 (calling the custom "peculiarly Aphroditan"), quoting Bagnall ("grab bag of extras").
[46] P.Michael. 43.   [47] P.Vat.Aphrod. 1.35–37.

land has a known market value in cash or kind, and tenants take those terms or leave them. A more flexible system, one relying on custom and ad hoc extras, may put more power into the hands of the peasant. A good negotiator may angle for forty pieces of cheese instead of fifty, or claim that ancestral practice on a nearby plot is really not what the landowner says it is.

Rents are not always simple arrangements between owner and tenant. Sublets are also common, the business domain of a "cadre of local worthies" in Aphrodito who serve as "middlemen for absentee landowners and for landowning churches and monasteries."[48] Phoibammon is one representative of this group, Dioskoros's uncle Besarion is another.[49] He leases land from Aphrodito's Holy New Church and sublets it to two tenant farmers who agree to split the crop yield evenly with him. The following year, Besarion leases the same land again, but takes on a partner in the project, a man named Victor. At some point, Besarion drops out of the arrangement altogether and his younger brother Apollos takes over. Apollos in his turn handles the land for several years in a row.

Here too, these details are part of a larger picture. The so-called cadre of worthies seems a little unstable in this example: the Holy New Church goes through three arrangements with its tenants in as many years before Apollos stays for several years: this shows economic natural selection in action. Besarion, Victor, their subletters, Apollos, and the Holy New Church are shopping around, moving their assets and energy in an endless attempt to find the most successful arrangement.

While this process was repeated on a much wider scale throughout the history of Greco-Roman Egypt, one form of lease, the *antimisthosis* or reverse lease, is known only from the Aphrodito papyri.[50] It appears nowhere else in Egypt. Legally, it works just like a normal lease, except that it turns the lease language on its head. "I rent out to you," the landowners declare to the tenants, instead of the usual declaration by the tenant, "I rent from you." This form of reverse lease is "reserved for the local elite,"[51] while regular leases are for "tenants belonging to a lower order of the village society."[52]

These reverse leases may be one way that status-consciousness shows itself in Aphrodito. The better man, the richer man, has the power and the resources, but the lesser man must come to him and say, "I rent out to you." The better man need not lift a finger to finalize his transaction with

---

[48] Keenan 1985b, 137. [49] Besarion 1; *P.Lond.* 5.1694 and 5.1705; Keenan 1985b, 161–168.
[50] Lemaire 2010, 400. [51] Lemaire 2010, 404. [52] Lemaire 2010, 404.

the lesser man, still less speak to him. The better men in Aphrodito's reverse leases are nearly all relatives of Dioskoros by blood or marriage.[53] By making landowners come to them to offer their land for rent in this way, they declare their greater status in a legal form so far unique to their own town.

Of course, leased property does not run itself. Dioskoros cannot sit back and wait for the rents to come pouring in. In some cases, the decision to rent land can be worse than doing nothing with it. A Coptic arbitration shows "the sort of last-straw frustrations [Dioskoros] had to endure in the business of estate management."[54] Dioskoros has leased land to Joseph, but the land has not been productive. Dioskoros is stuck with paying tax on it anyway, and accuses Joseph of negligence: "He made my portion into rust and blight."[55]

The arbitrator agrees with Dioskoros, that Joseph has been negligent, but admits that Joseph may not have known he was being negligent. With agreements relying on previous leases and "the other usual things," landowners and tenants face ambiguity at every turn. Cases in which the legalese seems to outweigh the importance of the business itself – the twenty-six lines for the lease of a wagon – are reasonable insurance policies against any claim of ignorance, and the loss that results.

Hidden behind this paperwork are the fundamentals of life. First and foremost, these people eat what they grow. Second, some of their product has to go back to the land itself, as seed and food for animals. Finally, they go to market, but not yet to make a pure profit. If they pay their rents in cash, they need to sell their crops to get that cash. Likewise, with the tax collector: with assessments on arable land collected in coin, anyone not already sitting on a pile of gold will need to take crops to market just to pay their taxes. By one calculation, the "gross marketed surplus" of their food grain – that is, what they sell at market – must have been somewhere between 10 and 25 percent of their total harvest just to pay taxes.[56] Only then do they start to see any profits.

Tax rates are clearly one case where external factors impact people at the local level. Under the emperor Justinian, Aphrodito's total tax burden payable in gold increased threefold in forty years.[57] Around 570, Dioskoros writes a petition complaining about some of these increases.[58] Aphrodito

---

[53] By my count, seven of the ten tenants collected in Lemaire 2010.
[54] MacCoull 1988, 22 regarding P.Berol. 11349.   [55] MacCoull 1988, 23.
[56] Banaji 2001, 27. See van Minnen 2000, 208–210 for a discussion of surplus and tax rates from earlier in the Roman period.
[57] Banaji 2001, 59; Zuckerman 2004a, 213–219.   [58] P.Lond. 5.1674 with introduction, 57–58.

had previously been assessed at a rate of four carats for every two-thirds of an acre of its arable land, but the pagarch Ioulianos doubles that rate. Despite promises to make no further increases, higher rates soon come, with government troops right on their heels to enforce the measure.

Nevertheless, even here we cannot be sure that the state weighs oppressively on Aphrodito. Some of this increase may be attributable to the state's growing preference for payment in gold instead of kind.[59] This is nothing more than the transfer of the same burden from one form to another. In any case, high taxes are not always crushing: rural communities in Syria and Palestine produce crops for local markets and remain prosperous in late antiquity, even with relatively high tax rates.[60] Moreover, if taxes are crushing, we cannot be sure that the peasantry in Aphrodito understands this in the same way we do. Quite the opposite, in fact: Dioskoros, the only voice the peasantry has in this situation, sees taxes in purely personal terms. A good duke in the past had granted a remission, and now a bad pagarch today revokes that same remission.[61] No abstract forces are at work here, only patrons and villains.

We have seen in a previous chapter that the right to collect their own taxes is very important to at least some of the people in Aphrodito. Next we will look more closely at how that actually works: who pays, how much, and based on what set of records. Obviously, we start with the pagarchs.[62] They do not set the assessments for their district as a whole, but they are responsible for determining the rates needed to reach those totals. When Aphrodito collects its own taxes, the pagarchs have to be sure that they pay what they actually owe.

In other villages, the pagarch will be involved more directly, collecting taxes himself, or arranging with village officials to do it for him. Those village officials can then subcontract out to get help with the process. A copy of one of these contracts survives – a rough draft of an agreement from around AD 553 to collect a portion of the taxes due for the nearby village of Phthla.[63] It seems likely that it is only a draft: while it names the pagarchs Ioulianos, Patrikia, and Menas, the village official and his tax collector are anonymous, their names to be added in the final copy.

It is curious that this document survives with Dioskoros's papers. Note that Ioulianos and Menas are two of the chief villains in Dioskoros's complaints against the regional authorities. They are the evil-doers in his stories, time and time again. If this agreement to collect the taxes for Phthla

---

[59] Gascou 1985, 11. [60] Haldon 2015, 362. [61] *P.Lond.* 5.1674 introduction, 57–58.
[62] *P.Lond.* 5.1674 introduction, 58. [63] *P.Lond.* 5.1660.

is a draft, Dioskoros is either helping to draft it for someone working with these evil-doers, or he himself is that person, planning to work hand in hand with them. Remember this: as we follow the tax collecting process, the people responsible for collecting the taxes are the very people complaining about them the most loudly.

The Aphrodito papyri include records of people paying taxes for someone else. Usually, this is a tenant paying taxes for a landlord, because the tenant has the produce. But there are other reasons to pay someone else's taxes. Someone buying land might agree to pay the seller's taxes on some other piece of land, the taxes transferred in a contract, or through some other transaction.[64] Paying someone's taxes can also be a favor, an act of patronage, or prestige. Count Ammonios is responsible for almost half of the cases in the cadastre in which someone pays taxes for someone else.[65] He might buy land from time to time, and agree to pay in this fashion. But a man of his stature is just as likely to be buying power and favor as he is buying any tangible, legal commodity.

The collecting all of these taxes generates an enormous amount of paperwork. Two major documents still survive. We have discussed one, the Aphrodito cadastre, several times: it records Aphrodito land registered to nearby urban residents. Another text, the Aphrodito register, records taxes on Aphrodito land registered specifically to the village's own tax account. These documents have a lengthy prehistory.

Sometime before June or July of 524, Ioannes the *scholastikos* (advocate) and *kensitor* (author of land registers) reforms the fiscal apparatus in Antaiopolis, the local capital. He takes a land survey of the region and records the results in a codex. This land survey, in use in Aphrodito from its creation in the 520s, is still in use as late as the 560s. An extract from that survey, covering Aphrodito itself, still survives: this is the document known as the Aphrodito cadastre.[66] The register, a closely related document from the following year, records hundreds of tax payments on land in Aphrodito.[67] These are a few examples.

> The monastery of Smin through Palos the farmer, one gold coin less 6.25 carats.
> Ieremias son of Kuros through Komasios, one gold coin less 5.5 carats.
> Apa Biktor son of Apollos through Charisios, one gold coin less 5 carats.
> The heirs of Promaos son of Mousaios through the son Biktor, one gold coin less 5.25 carats.

---

[64] Mirković 2010, 569. [65] Mirković 2010.
[66] Gascou and MacCoull 1987, 104–105; see Ioannes 66. [67] Zuckerman 2004a.

The heirs of Ermeios son of Biktor through Psatos, one gold coin less 5.75 carats.

The carat or more subtracted in these entries is standard, a "margin retained to cover the costs of collection and unanticipated budgetary needs on the part of the village."[68]

This small clue is a reminder – yet again – of the importance of Aphrodito's fiscal independence to the town elites. Add up all of these tiny amounts subtracted from the full payments, and the result is real money. This "margin" may be the profit from their rent-seeking.[69] More likely, it is insurance against inferior coinage, "an advance, safe-side surcharge" in case the coins are underweight.[70] Alternatively, the "minus carat" system reflects different weight standards in different places.[71] The extra value collected would go to administrative costs or a budgetary reserve. Administrative costs include hiring staff to collect the cash and security to guard it, a reminder of the never-ending logistical difficulties inherent in tax collection.

One phrase appearing repeatedly in the cadastre marks land in the hands of "so and so after the removal of so and so." This probably indicates that someone new is renting the land after the old tenant's lease has expired. If so, the cadastre shows how often land changes hands in Aphrodito, at least at the level of the tenant: Aphrodito's rental market must be very active.[72]

The cadastre creates a neat and tidy picture: this land belongs to Aphrodito and other land does not. But the satellite views of the Aphrodito countryside and the smaller villages in close orbit around the larger towns tell a different story (see page 17). There are no borders between any of these places, no easy way to tell which land belongs to which village, and this leads to ongoing disputes. Aphrodito's conflict with the neighboring village of Phthla – which appears in more detail in later chapters – includes shepherd raids from Phthla's territory and a complaint that some of Aphrodito's territory has been transferred to Phthla's jurisdiction.[73]

This is not an isolated event. When Ioannes drafts his land survey of the entire region, he transfers certain plots of land from the fields of Aphrodito

---

[68] *P.Lond.Herm.* introduction, 29; see the comparison by the editors of the Aphrodito cadastre to the Temseu Skordon codex.
[69] See page 51. This opinion does not represent a consensus.
[70] Keenan 2005, 289–290 describing Zuckerman 2004a, 66–68.
[71] Most recently Harper 2016, 812, following Banaji 1998.
[72] See Banaji 2001, 195, taking *apo ekb(olēs)* as "following the expiry of the lease held by."
[73] See pages 61 and 166.

to the fields of neighboring Thmonachthe. In 524, a *defensor* or public advocate in Antaiopolis orders the land transferred back to Aphrodito. Dioskoros's father, Apollos, takes part in the proceedings and probably deserves credit for getting the land back on Aphrodito's registers.[74]

On the one hand, this is not major turmoil. A short note accompanying the proceedings lists the land in question: approximately twenty-nine acres in half a dozen plots, most under 3.5 acres and only two any larger than seven acres.[75] On the other hand, enough of this sort of whittling around the edges can start to destroy a town from the inside out. This is good arable land, 1 percent of the arable land registered to Aphrodito's accounts and a comparable hit to the town's tax base.[76] This is Aphrodito's *autopragia* at the micro level: some unknown farmer works Eutropia's 0.8 acres and sells his gross market surplus to pay taxes that go either to Apollos, the headman back home, or to a local assistant of the pagarch working in Thmonachthe next door.

After he pays the tax collector, in this town or the next, it is not clear how much he will have left. We hear a great deal in the modern age about the consequences of income inequality. It is a common complaint that the rich are getting richer and the poor are getting poorer. We think we know instinctively what this means, but economists have also developed a number of ways to measure it in practice. They also debate extensively about the impact of income and wealth inequality in modern societies.

Some economists argue that a certain level of inequality promotes investment. More commonly, economists criticize high levels of inequality in modern societies in part because the rich effectively crowd out the poor. Unable to compete with the buying power of the rich, the poor eventually lose access to such basic resources as housing or quality health care. The same factors potentially impacted the poor in antiquity as well. The lower end of Aphrodito's rural peasantry could find itself squeezed by the unequal power of the rich. Economic opportunity for the poor could be limited by the purchasing power of the rich. The quantitative measurements of modern economists show one way to calculate whether this is likely to be true. The Aphrodito cadastre and the Aphrodito tax register give the raw data for these calculations.

The starting point is the Gini index, a number between 0 and 1 measuring the degree of income or wealth inequality in a society: the lower the number, the lower the level of inequality; the higher the number,

---

[74] *P.Cair.Masp.* 3.67329. [75] *P.Cair.Masp.* 1.67150 and Gascou and MacCoull 1987, 105.
[76] *SB* 20.14669.305–307: just over 3,824 arouras of arable land according to village accounts.

the greater the level of inequality, and more wealth or income is concentrated in the hands of the few. Aphrodito's Gini index is 0.473 if we only count villagers or 0.508 if we count both villagers and outsiders owning village land.[77] We can compare Aphrodito's figures to those of other Egyptian villages, both in late antiquity and in earlier centuries. Aphrodito's numbers are neither too high nor too low: Egyptian villages from the AD 200s to the 500s record Gini indices both higher and lower. Comparisons between the tax yields from the Aphrodito register and the tax codex from the sixth-century village of Temseu Skordon "suggest that wealth was on average slightly more concentrated in Aphrodito."[78]

We can also compare Aphrodito's figures to some from the modern world, although this is admittedly a tricky business.[79] Village land in Aphrodito is – for example – more equally distributed than income in modern Honduras. However, village land in Aphrodito is less equally distributed than land in mid-nineteenth-century Wisconsin. Aphrodito's land is far more equally distributed than land in modern Egypt before the agrarian reforms of the 1950s.

This evidently presents a mixed picture. Obviously, there is a gap between Aphrodito's rich and its poor. But nothing suggests that income inequality is a runaway train, crushing the town's poor beneath it. If the numbers do not answer everything, the papyri also give qualitative ways to look at wealth and the distance between rich and poor. To begin with, we can look at economic mobility and estimate the likelihood (or cost) of moving up the social ladder.

We have already seen how Phoibammon, son of Triadelphos, earned his reputation as a land entrepreneur. One way to think about upward mobility is to ask how hard it might be to become Phoibammon. Think about renting new land: Phoibammon commits to paying only a few hundred liters of grain per acre of land he rents. In one case, he pays 194 liters of wheat and 155 liters of barley for every acre on a nineteen-acre farm, 6,631 liters in total per year.[80]

Other examples complete the picture of the task ahead. You might get a yield as low as 580 liters to the acre.[81] But the bulk of the data from the early Roman Empire suggests a yield ranging from 580 to 1,160 liters per acre, and even as high as 1,450 liters.[82] You would lose seventy-eight liters or

---

[77] Bagnall 2008, 186–187. [78] Bagnall 2008, 183. [79] See the figures in Bagnall 1992, 139–143.
[80] Keenan 1980, 146. This rate is comparable to others in the sixth century, perhaps even on the high side: see the data assembled for Harper 2016.
[81] Banaji 2001, 27. [82] Rowlandson 1996, 251, Figure 6.

slightly more to taxes.[83] Then, like Phoibammon, you might pay something like 350 liters per acre in rent. This leaves you with at least 100 liters per acre for subsistence and profit, but with larger yields as many as 500 liters. If you have only yourself to feed, you might need to work three or four acres to harvest enough grain with low-end yields.[84] If you work six or seven acres and got high-end yields, you might walk away with 1,500 liters of profit.

It then remains to turn that profit into cash for investment. The price of wheat in Aphrodito varies quite a bit, based on now invisible variables. In a seller's market, with wheat getting a good price, you might receive half a gold coin for 150 liters.[85] In sixth-century Aphrodito, half a gold coin is enough for Apa Victor to buy fifteen acres of land.[86] This rate is a steal, but it gives you a sense of what is possible at the cheap end. At the high end of yields, profits on six or seven acres might leave you with five gold coins, certainly enough to buy an acre of your own.[87]

Remember how many entries in the cadastre show the removal of previous tenants, and how many entries show new owners for land still listed under old names.[88]

This is not something unique to Aphrodito. Over a third of the land in the Hermopolite nome changes hands over the course of a decade in an earlier period of late antiquity.[89] This turnover means that there is plenty of room for an aspiring Phoibammon to wiggle his way in,[90] and our rough calculations show that it would not take him long to do so.

Earlier, I asked whether Phoibammon was rich. We should ask the same of Dioskoros. At first, the question may seem strange. Both he and his father Apollos serve as village headmen, so we expect them to be at the top of the economic pyramid. But the evidence of the town's cadastre and tax register is complicated. Dioskoros would have been too young to appear in the Aphrodito cadastre and register. His father Apollos is missing from the cadastre altogether, and appears in the register only once, making a payment through an intermediary of 6.25 carats in November 525.

---

[83] Bagnall 1993, 157. For the "gross marketed surplus" see page 83.
[84] Scheidel 2009, 7: "Bare bones subsistence" at 172 kilograms of wheat per year, an artaba being 30 kg. We may imagine other parts of the "bare bones" basket being supplied through other arrangements.
[85] Compare the wheat prices in Aphrodito listed at Johnson and West 1949, 177–178 and more recently the data on wheat prices assembled for Harper 2016.
[86] *P.Herm.* 32.   [87] Johnson and West 1949, 78–79, e.g., *SB* 1.4661 or *P.Cair.Masp.* 2.67169.
[88] See pages 86 and 79.
[89] Grey 2012, 633 contextualizes Bowman's earlier analysis of the Hermopolite data.
[90] Although it might have become more difficult after the Justinianic Plague. Harper 2016 shows a dramatic drop in the price of wheat after 541, with variability in rent prices and no demonstrable decrease in the price of land.

This is an unimpressive sum.[91] The median payment in the register – the halfway point between the largest payments and the smallest – is three times that much. The average individual in the Aphrodito tax register pays five times that much. The largest individual payer in the register, a man named Promaos, son of Isakios, pays forty times more than Apollos. The register records payments from thirty-four women. All but three of them pay more than Apollos does. It is possible that Apollos, a headman in Aphrodito in this period, uses his position to dodge his tax burden. This could be one of the benefits of the job. However, it is unlikely that he can get large chunks of his land removed from the tax-lists altogether: if he can, why does he appear on the tax lists at all?

If Dioskoros's father pays so little, the family estate may be smaller than it seems, and we may have misunderstood his economic place in life. It is almost unimaginable that the reins of town power would not be in the hands of one of the richest men. Therefore, Dioskoros's family wealth must be hidden in other forms. If he is rich, it is not from land ownership. Even leasing land he owns and passing the tax burden onto the tenant would still show up in the tax register. If family wealth comes from money lending, we would expect some record of it, but loans make up only a small fraction of the records in the Dioskoros archive.[92] We may imagine that Dioskoros's family – like that of the Apions in Oxyrhynchos to the north, but on a much smaller scale – gets rich at least in part through tax collection.[93] Alternatively, it may be that his family earns the bulk of its income through leasing from someone and then subletting to someone else.

This may explain the constant turmoil in local politics. Aphrodito's rental market is a free market. Its leases are typically short-term, leaving room for ongoing turnover. For the major institutional landowners – Aphrodito's churches and monasteries – tenants come and go on a regular basis, with or without their subtenants. This can happen because of changing situations for the tenant, the changing needs of the landowner, or other factors we cannot see. If Dioskoros and his family rely on these arrangements to make their money – and their relatively small landholdings suggest they must – then their own income is inherently volatile. Each year, Apollos, Besarion, Dioskoros, Phoibammon, and others must offer competitive arrangements both to their subtenants and to their landlords.

---

[91] Analyses based on MS Excel spreadsheets of the data in *P.Aphrod.Reg*. See note 39.
[92] See Fournet 2008a, 313–343 for a list of the published texts and their documentary type.
[93] See note 16.

If they do not, they will gradually lose business. In turn, they will gradually lose income, and over time, the political influence that this business and income provides them. Put another way, if you can compete in this town's rental market, you can compete in its politics as well.

We should try to see late Roman peasants not from the point of view of the state and the aristocracy, but from the point of view of the countryside itself.[94] This approach can help make sense of late Roman Egypt. Peasants have agency. Burdened as they may at times be by the demands of the state, they take actions and make decisions separate from and unrelated to those demands. They have lives unrelated to the state.

We hear a great deal about the oppression of the late Roman peasantry, but this oppression is more often alleged than proved. In some cases, the evidence collapses under closer scrutiny. A recent discussion of wage labor and the peasantry claims that Dioskoros "apparently forced such a 'peasant' to accept a wage reduction."[95] However, this misunderstands the situation. The peasant in question, a man named Psais, offers 388 liters of his income from Dioskoros as a guarantee to Dioskoros on behalf of his brother-in-law, a water carrier named Apollos.[96]

This is not a wage reduction, and no one is compelling anyone. Psais presumably makes the guarantee for his wife's brother of his own free will. He faces no oppression greater than obligation to family. But even if Dioskoros does take advantage of the peasants around him, his constant complaints – and the string of thefts he suffers – show that the peasants give as good as they get. If they do not even the playing field, they are at least able to force Dioskoros to play defense.

Ioulianos the pagarch, whom we have already met at various points in our story, makes a more compelling villain than Dioskoros. One scholar has argued that Ioulianos himself ultimately destroys Aphrodito's fiscal independence.[97] Part of this argument makes sense. Time and again Ioulianos encroaches on Aphrodito's territory, seizes some of its property, and tries to incorporate it into his pagarchy.[98] But this argument goes too far. From a single entry in a single Aphrodito account, one scholar argues that Ioulianos owns a large estate that is otherwise completely invisible in the Aphrodito papyri. Comparing that payment to the size of Aphrodito's tax bills, this scholar argues that Aphrodito's tax bills – for land registered both in Aphrodito's own tax accounts and those of nearby Antaiopolis – amount to only two-fifths of the village territory, and that Ioulianos

---

[94] Grey 2011. [95] Banaji 2001, 191. [96] *P.Cair.Masp.* 1.67095 and page 109.
[97] Zuckerman 2004a, 221–222. [98] See page 44.

himself owned the remaining three-fifths. At the end of the day, when Aphrodito's patron Count Ammonios dies, the town's fiscal independence is nothing but a nuisance and Ioulianos is able to gobble it whole.

Not everyone agrees with this theory.[99] It fits the tidy narrative of the powerful aristocrat encroaching on the independence of the peasant. But in fact, the math involved is barely believable. If Aphrodito (in evidence dating to the 530s) pays a combined 712 gold coins in taxes for land registered both in its accounts and the city accounts, and Ioulianos (active in the 550s and 560s) pays 976 gold coins, his property – found nowhere in the Aphrodito papyri – must have dwarfed the roughly 4,000 acres recorded for Aphrodito in the village cadastre.

This is not possible. Aphrodito's region, the Antaiopolite nome, has a total of 34,970 acres. Aphrodito's 4,000 acres makes up over 11 percent of the total. If Ioulianos's proposed large estate is taxed at roughly the same rates as the rest of Aphrodito's land, Ioulianos himself must own over 5,300 acres.[100] If this land is not listed in the cadastre or apparent in the tax register, it is hard to see where it could be hiding. But an Aphrodito that included Ioulianos's hypothetical large estate would be 27 percent of the nome.[101] This makes no sense at an administrative level. It represents a nome with a large tumor sticking out of its side. Assuming the Romans would see this to be as strange as we do, we have one conclusion: there is no large estate belonging to Ioulianos hiding in the evidence. Ioulianos is a nuisance to Aphrodito, a constant threat to its fiscal independence. But he is not a mythical feudal figure whose massive landholdings consume the proud and independent village. This search for a villain comes up short.

It makes far more sense to see the 976 gold coins and change appearing next to his name as an indication of Aphrodito's entire payment after it has been paid by Aphrodito and handed over to Ioulianos. The other entries in the same account, small by comparison, may simply be for late arriving payments, or gold meant for other purposes. This is more than Aphrodito has had to pay in the past, but it makes sense: Aphrodito complains about Ioulianos raising the rates. This text may show exactly what that tax increase looks like, once the money ends up in his hands.

---

[99] Bagnall 2008, 188 is appropriately cautious.
[100] Ioulianos's payment of 976 *solidi* is over 1.37 times Aphrodito's 712 solidi; Aphrodito has 5,906 arouras; 5,906 arouras multiplied by 1.37 is 8,091 arouras.
[101] Aphrodito's 5,906 arouras and Ioulianos's 8,097 arouras are 14,003 arouras, compared to the Antaiopolite's 51,655 arouras. For village and nome figures, see Gascou and MacCoull 1987, 118.

A "generally accepted view" of late antiquity believes that:

> the land was dominated by large estate owners, often imperial bureaucrats (or closely connected with them) who could better shield themselves from the burden of taxation. Those on the bottom rungs of the ladder of wealth probably paid an undue proportion of taxes; under such strain, these farmers fled the land or shed their burdens by giving their holdings to wealthy patrons … From a purely fiscal perspective, this process of elite aggrandizement eroded the tax base upon which the stability of the state depended … Within such a milieu, landowners exerted downward pressure on wages. So long as manpower remained plentiful, income for the majority of rural people remained static or degraded … They were thus starved of capital and overexposed to the risks of daily life, such as food shortage.[102]

This is a tidy picture, and an attractive one in an age of growing concern about income inequality.

However, if this picture is anywhere in Aphrodito, I do not see it. There are no large estates. Count Ammonios is a transitory figure, a newcomer far closer to his tenants in economic clout than one might expect. No farmers flee and no wages shrink. The rich may be better able to avoid taxes. That may explain why Apollos pays so little compared to his peers. But there is no direct evidence and we can never prove it. If the peasantry were starved of capital, Phoibammon's entrepreneurship would not be possible: and yet there it is, for fifty years, sixth-century Aphrodito's longest business career. If my off-the-cuff calculations are correct, ideal conditions would make his career easily in reach for others. Even under worse conditions, Aphrodito's market churn means that as some fall, others soon will rise.

---

[102] Decker 2009, 29.

CHAPTER 6

Town Crafts and Trades

Dioskoros, Phoibammon, and the rest of their family are powerful because of what happens out in the fields below the town. Their agricultural wealth gives them responsibility and power. But when they return to the town to use that power, the streets are full of men and women who make their living through arts and crafts, whose daily lives do not revolve around the farms, the vineyards, and the orchards. Dioskoros and his family appear only on the edges of this world, but their records illustrate it in some detail.

Aphrodito divides itself in half, into its northern and southern parts.[1] No one in the town ever describes himself as from the eastern or western parts. Zooming in closer, past the two main neighborhoods, reveals individual streets with exotic and fragmentary names: Thanekôoutos Street, Solômônos A.ri.tou Street, Isitos Têmountos Street.[2] Some street names are less formal, following the local landscape. One text mentions a street of the Holy Catholic Church. Another text, addressed to Dioskoros's father, mentions a street of the house of old Psimanobet, "your forefather." Without street signs, these names may be completely informal. Maybe everyone calls it Psimanobet Street. Or maybe Dioskoros's enemies roll their eyes and insist on calling it something else.

Zooming in even closer reveals that individual houses have their own names too. A house once called Pselch is now called that of Anouphios the butcher and Ioannes Talbitôn. A house once called the vetch seller Abraamios, son of Hôrouôgchios, is now called that of the heirs of Andreas the shepherd.[3] We have no way of knowing how deep into Aphrodito's history these names reach.[4] In the same neighborhood, a house called that of Psaios, son of Psenthaesios the priest, has no older name. Maybe it is a new house, or its old owners are simply forgotten. It

---

[1] Marthot 2013, 32 with references. [2] Marthot 2013, 33–35.
[3] Marthot 2013, 36, proposing a correction to "the vetch-store of Abraamios."
[4] Marthot 2013, 36.

may sit just on the edge of town: the farm of Promauos the headman is right around the corner.[5] Hints like this show how easy it is to leave town and reach farmland straight away.

One thing leaps out from these names, which is their relatively modest origins: a butcher, a vetch seller, a shepherd. Only the headman is certainly one of the town's elite. These men must own, operate or work in these houses for long enough to leave their mark on the local memory; and all these examples are from one location in a single text. If we zoom back out and remember the satellite view of Kom Ishqaw, the pattern repeats a hundred times over, with a hundred houses on a dozen streets. When the butchers and shepherds walk through the town, they see their own kind everywhere they go, embedded in the very fabric of the landscape for years.

Grouping Aphrodito's workers into broad categories shows that the largest groups are construction workers (8 percent), textile workers (8 percent), food related trades (17 percent), and river trades (19 percent).[6] In each of these categories are smaller subsets, the individual professions. As far as the evidence shows, all the town's specialized workers are members of professional trade guilds. Our understanding of ancient trade associations continues to improve.[7] These ancient associations are not simply mutual aid societies or social groups or burial aid groups; they are economic institutions and give their members economic agency. There is an element of mutual aid, for example in funding and attending funerals. But this mutual aid serves to enhance group trust, precisely to improve the group's economic outcomes.

Guilds serve an economic function not simply for their members, but for the state, using the guilds for tax purposes. In previous generations, when the unpopular *chrysargyron* tax (a tax on traders collected every four years) was still being collected, a guild head or *kephalaiôtês* would be responsible for paying it. One account from our period records payments for troop maintenance by a series of guilds, including the weavers, shipwrights, carpenters, leather workers, and more.[8] The three highest paying guilds in this text all appear in the town's petition to the empress Theodora.

When a guild pays taxes for its members the guild acts as a shield against the state. Indeed, "a protected right to manage their own collection may have been a real privilege that saved association members from coercion." In this sense, guilds have an *autopragia* much like the rights of self-

---

[5] *SB* 18.13320.47–50. [6] van Minnen 2007, 222.
[7] The next several paragraphs follow Venticinque 2016 in detail. [8] *P.Cair.Masp.* 2.67147.

collection Aphrodito itself fought to defend. For this reason, guild "members may have been spared from encounters with the stereotypical rapacious tax collector."[9]

However, it is not clear why some tradesmen pay taxes as individuals when their trade groups pay as well. In some cases, both tradesmen and their guilds own land. Aphrodito's rural place names include: The Dyers' Place, The Oil-Maker's Place, The Mill-Master's Place and The Coppersmith's Field.[10] But only the dyers are grammatically plural: this may be guild land, the other holdings individual. No doubt other guilds own land not so obviously named. This land is an investment for the guild, a predictable source of income, to serve the guild's mutual aid functions.

Guilds serve a social function as well. They help to create and perpetuate social norms. But these norms are internal, sometimes at odds with those of society as a whole. In previous centuries, trade societies were a source of political unrest. This may explain why Aphrodito's shepherds are such a constant problem for Dioskoros: they have a sense of group cohesion that matters more to them than their relationships with outsiders.

Some industries look enormously profitable, or at least enormously productive. The potters are in this group: Psais rents a third of a pottery workshop for 2,400 jars per year in rent for the rest of his life. In addition to the workshop, Psais rents a "third share of the reservoir there and all of the goods and useful things in it, which are the two troughs near Saint Michael and the trough in front of the guest room to the north."[11] The troughs are probably smaller receptacles to draw water from the reservoir, places in which Psais can knead his clay.[12]

This captures a rare visual image of a potter at work, drawing water in sight of a nearby church. He needs to make between six and seven jars per day every day of the year to pay this rent. But since he must take time off, he must produce even more than that for every day he actually works. He must also make more than that, after he has paid his rent, to make any profit.

The workshop owners are a group, the heirs of two sisters named Helene and Mariam. The sisters had their share of the workshop from their father. The rest of the workshop belongs to the monastery of Apa Sourous, their ancestor. This monastery appears in a later chapter: it commands enormous wealth in Aphrodito.[13] Its founding family's surviving members – Helene and Mariam's heirs, and maybe others – are probably still very well-off themselves.

---

[9] Venticinque 2016, 232. [10] Marthot 2013, Volume II, 35, 65–66, 159, and 408.
[11] *P.Cair.Masp.* 1.67110.31–37. [12] van Minnen 1993, 118. [13] See page 113.

This is a tightly-knit family business based on long-term ties. Both the family heirs and the family's monastery have pottery workshop shares, so both sides need empty jars on a large scale. This means that the family and its monastery are probably in the wine business, or the oil business.[14] One of these businesses is probably what brought the family its wealth in the first place, and allowed the rich endowment of its monastery. Moreover, this is a symbiotic relationship: they need the potters as much as the potters need them. Psais agrees to rent his workshop for life. The family and the monastery may have used this arrangement with others in the past and hope for long-term stability. As long as the wine and oil businesses thrive, so will the pottery business.

With the town's other jobs, it is not always easy to tell if a group as a whole is in economically good shape. Aphrodito has over a dozen men explicitly described as carpenters. Two, a father and a son, are carpenter farmers. One is a thief – or at least, Dioskoros thinks so, and records an accusation against him. But most of the other carpenters make unremarkable appearances in tax lists and accounts. Their presence as a collective in the town's fiscal register indicates that they "possessed significant financial capital relative to other groups, [and] owned land in the community."[15] The group as a whole is important enough to sign a petition to the empress Theodora.

Aphrodito's one engineer or *mêchanarios*, Psempnouthios, leases land bordering on an orchard in 565.[16] This raises more questions than it answers. Psempnouthios may make too little as an engineer and need to supplement his income. This is particularly likely if he specializes in irrigation works. His labor might be seasonal, or needed only when something goes wrong. Or he may make more than he needs and use this lease to invest in other income. Functionally, he may be just like the men who call themselves carpenter farmers, but does not yet consider himself a genuine farmer.

Some of these groups leave major traces in the evidence. Take a look at two examples, the oil makers and the goldsmiths. The oil makers are very well documented, but not always because of their day jobs. Oil makers appear in the records lending grain, paying taxes and having land named after them.[17] Once in a while, the evidence shows an oil maker setting up

---

[14] See Hickey 2007, 303 on empty jars. [15] Venticinque 2016, 214.
[16] *P.Cair.Masp.* 1.67109. James Keenan has suggested to me (personal communication) that he is a hydraulic engineer, a specialism relevant to work on the nearby orchard.
[17] *P.Lond.* 5.1699, *P.Aphrod.Reg.*, *SB* 20.14669.

his own business. In 552, an oil maker named Kuriakos leases an olive press from one of Aphrodito's religious institutions.[18] This is economic symbiosis in action, the oil maker avoiding the capital costs of having to buy his own equipment, and the monk in charge of the operation putting equipment to use without the need for specialized in-house labor.

Most information about the oil industry comes from the oil makers' archive. At least thirty ostraca – with still more unpublished – record orders to the oil makers for deliveries to specific groups.[19] Those ostraca may be part of the collection excavated in Aphrodito in 1901.[20] Most likely, they have no direct connection to Dioskoros and his family archive. No one appearing in these texts matches anyone appearing elsewhere in the Aphrodito documents.

These orders for oil are not sales, since no money changes hands. They are requisitions, a tax in kind. While the landowners and tenants in the previous chapter have to convert their crops to cash to pay their taxes, the oil makers' guild ships their product directly to the state apparatus. They make oil payments to slaves, tax collectors, judges, the judges' court reporters, horsemen, soldiers, and others in Antaiopolis, Apollinopolis, Koptos, and possibly even Panopolis. In one offbeat case, they even make payments to some lute players. As with the slaves, the lute players are no doubt part of the retinue of some higher government official.

Even this brief list of payments reveals a good deal of information. If the oil makers are typical of other trades, no one could work in this town without having a sense of their place in the wider world. Their goods are not meant for local consumption alone: the soldiers and other state employees using their product are all over southern Egypt. Furthermore, we remember what it must be like for the people at the receiving end, getting part of their payment or sustenance in kind. To be sure, late antiquity sees a high degree of monetization thanks to the stability of Constantine's gold coinage. Nevertheless, everyday life is full of business done in other ways, with small gaps plugged here and there with the produce of the guilds.

Goldsmiths are a natural source of expertise in a world relying on a gold-based currency. The Aphrodito records make countless references to payments in gold coin, and often specify that payments should be measured according to the "goldsmiths' standard."[21] Because of this, locals with no need of goldwork of any kind would still come to the goldsmiths on a

---

[18] *P.Flor.* 3.285.   [19] Gascou and Worp 1990.   [20] Gascou and Worp 1990, 218.
[21] Gagos and van Minnen 1994, 93.

regular basis. But this relationship is not always happy. Dioskoros himself has ongoing problems with the goldsmiths. In an earlier chapter, we saw how he keeps track of thefts against him.[22] The goldsmiths are front and center in these lists. The goldsmiths Ioannes, Kollouthos, Makarios, Mousaios, and Pacheous all steal from Dioskoros, or at least Dioskoros thinks they do.[23] Two of these goldsmiths also turn around and inform on other thieves.[24]

We do not know why goldsmiths are so frequently accused. But I see no harm in taking a guess or two. Dioskoros's place at the top of Aphrodito society gives him countless opportunities to help his friends and hurt his enemies, most often through over- or under-charging on collections. These goldsmiths may feel themselves cheated, and see a little theft here and there as a tidy way to even the score. Their role as town standard keepers equally gives them countless opportunities to overweigh or underweigh a bag of gold. If someone in the village walks away from a goldsmith unhappy with the count they are given, that person might easily report the goldsmith to Dioskoros for a crime he may not have committed. If these guesses are plausible, they show still more of this village's constant turmoil, the never-ending struggle for information and financial edge.

Other Aphrodito industries are less visible. In fact, some parts of Aphrodito's industrial landscape are unusually blurry. In AD 535, two men named Anouphis promise twelve gold coins to Aphrodito's town police officer if a father and son team, two beekeepers named Hermauos and Mouses, leave town.[25] We can easily imagine why the authorities might worry. Guarantees against flight are usually a sign that someone might try to avoid a tax burden. Whether or not this is the case here, beekeepers are as mobile as shepherds, and their donkeys can do the same sort of damage to crops and property as sheep can. None of the beekeepers ever do business with Dioskoros or his family. Their services may not be needed, or they may be too troublesome to be worth the risk.

In earlier chapters, I argued that Dioskoros and his family are at the head of one of Aphrodito's leading factions, and that a nemesis, an enemy faction, meets them with equal and opposite force. This is probably true of the groups lurking at the edges of our vision and hiding in our blind spots. The groups with no connection to Dioskoros have their supporters, and feel strong enough to challenge other figures with equal strength. The

---

[22] See page 63. [23] *P.Cair.Masp.* 2.67143.
[24] Kollouthos 20 and Mousaios, if Mousais 39 = Mousaios 41.
[25] *P.Cair.Masp.* 3.67296; Ruffini 2008c, 159.

competition in Dioskoros's life is only one of many stories, but the only one we know because of his archive's survival.

Entire pockets of Aphrodito are hidden from view. Aphrodito has a guild of sculptors, but we cannot name a single one of its members.[26] Aphrodito has a *chalkeus* (a type of coppersmith) and a fruiterer, but they appear only in tax lists. We have no record of anyone ever doing business with them.[27] Aphrodito has pockets of social isolation, people whose connections to the rest of the town's social network are tenuous in Dioskoros's records. This group includes a *logophoros* (account keeper), a *taboularios* (accountant), and an *ampelourgos* (vinedresser).[28] These people are marginalized in the records. Dioskoros may be peculiar: he is not in the vine business and does his own accounting. Or we may be looking at one of the quiet corners of Aphrodito's job market, the people with few social connections because they are not particularly needed.

Language itself gives a glimpse into Aphrodito's job market. Dioskoros writes his own dictionary, a Greek to Coptic word list we will examine further in a later chapter.[29] This word list has nearly forty entries for different types of occupation. These words may show which professions are and are not a regular part of Dioskoros's world. Why would Dioskoros write a Coptic definition of a Greek word for a job? Are they jobs he is already completely familiar with? Or are they people he does business with so rarely that he has to look up their names?

Some of his definitions are for essentially administrative functions: crop inspector, measurer, examiner, and weigher. Others are for purely manual labor: grape gatherer, pot carrier, berry picker, leaf picker, pot emptier, potter, water drawer, digger, branch cutter, and ploughman.[30] Here we see Aphrodito's workers in high definition. With the exception of the potters, not a single one of these jobs appears in Aphrodito's other evidence.

We cannot name a single person who does any of these jobs. There may be none, and Dioskoros is word collecting. But there are other possibilities. This word list may simply show which occupations are too trivial to talk about, too small or too fleeting to need the guarantee of the written word. Then the diggers and branch cutters will remain forever unseen and unnamed. Or we know them already, because they hold other jobs at the same time. Tenant farmers do not spend all their time farming, or beekeepers beekeeping. Their digging and branch cutting are side jobs they

---

[26] *P.Cair.Masp.* 2.67147.8.
[27] Ruffini unpublished; Ruffini 2011 index *s.v. chalkeus* and *pômaritês*.   [28] Ruffini unpublished.
[29] Bell and Crum 1925; see page 195.   [30] Bell and Crum 1925, 209–210, and 216.

never need to mention, or small parts of the larger whole that makes up their daily lives. Here, Dioskoros does not know how the Greek language describes the working man: if he ever comes across any of these micro-jobs in a Greek document, he has to look them up.

In some cases, Aphrodito's workers leave only a trace, a teasing hint, raising more questions. Aphrodito has a shipbuilding guild. But we do not know why it has three times as many shipbuilders as it has sailors.[31] One of the shipbuilders takes a payment from the town for the cost of a light wicker boat.[32] This probably means that the guild as a whole works on small-scale projects meant mainly for local use, not for major trips up and down the Nile. Still, they are important enough on the local scene: their guild head appears as a signatory to the town's petition to the empress, even though he cannot read or write.[33]

In AD 538, the hunters of Aphrodito address a letter to Hermauos and Dios, their guild heads.[34] The first part of the letter is a work agreement. The hunters (*agreutai*) work for the "glorious house" of Aphrodito. They tell Hermauos and Dios "that you are our guild heads as long as the most brilliant landowner wants." They agree that they will continue to conduct their affairs according to "the old and ancestral custom" of the guild both in general and in the work they agree to do for the landowner, whose name never appears.

After this work agreement, the letter includes the charter for the guild itself, mapping out the old and ancestral custom the hunters expect to follow. As with so many texts from Aphrodito, damage to the papyrus gets in our way.

> If one of us marries, he will give two jars of wine. If his wife is a daughter of one of us, he will only do one ... Someone having received the price of a ship and longing to [act deceptively?] with those who want to buy the ship [is caught?] selling to the same man another boat without the first man knowing, he will give one gold piece. Someone stealing a piece of (ship?) wood in a leather thong, if it is in the water, he will give one-third of a gold piece ...[35]

Even through all its mangled sentences, story after story comes alive in this short passage. On the one hand, this charter may just be boilerplate, nothing but generic language the hunters sign because this is the way trade guilds have done it for as long as anyone can remember. On the

---

[31] Ruffini 2011 index *s.v. nautês* and *paktônopoios*.   [32] *P.Cair.Masp.* 3.67330.2.19.   [33] Ieremias 21.
[34] *SB* 3.6704.
[35] Adapted from trans. in Hombert 1923, 48, interpolating my speculative interpretations in brackets.

other hand, there may be substance to the conditions, real choices based on the guild's firsthand experience.

The portions of the charter in this quote show three scenarios. First, there is the marriage. We do not know how many hunters are in Aphrodito, and whether an in-house marriage is a likely scenario for one of their own and one of their daughters. The wine is not simply to celebrate the occasion; it builds trust, and shows the community that the groom is a man of his word, true to his signature on the guild's charter. (This is in contrast with the next two scenarios.) The second scenario is a ship sale gone bad, the seller passing off the wrong ship to an unwitting victim. Why these hunters are in the boat business is not clear, but they may need access to the vehicles as a way to transport their own kills. The third scenario is theft – so common in this town – not of sheep or cheese, in this case, but wood. The context, after a ship sale, suggests ship wood or an oar.

In both criminal scenarios, one of the hunters violates the trust of the community. He must pay a fine, and a steep one at that: a gold piece for sales-fraud is what some landowners pay in taxes for a year, or what some ordinary workers might make over the same year. If the hunters think these scenarios are plausible, the fines are set to keep them as rare as possible. Roman guild charters sometimes require that members pay money to their groups when they buy property. Aphrodito's hunters may face a similar requirement here, lost in the damage to the text.[36]

This means that the hunters have a treasurer, someone collecting this money, keeping track of it, paying it back out when the time is right. No evidence indicates whether they farm this work out to someone outside the guild, or have one of their own keep the books. Any signatures at the end of the text are lost, but the first half of the letter mentions the hunters who know how to write, and those who do not. (If some hunters know how to write, it is hard to imagine which occupations in Aphrodito are completely illiterate.)

We are not sure who these hunters work for. The Aphrodito papyri call only two men a most brilliant landowner.[37] Count Ammonios is by far the better known of the two, and a likely candidate. He has close patronage ties to the village throughout our period. The work agreement's vocabulary – particularly references to a "glorious house" – is a reminder of the large estates to the north, in Oxyrhynchos, in this period. But if the landowner is Ammonios, his estate is not even forty-six acres.[38]

---

[36] Venticinque 2016, 234. [37] Ruffini 2011: Ammonios 1 and Theodoros 1 (=Anonymous 19?).
[38] See page 77.

Nonetheless, the power of his patronage appears once again in this work agreement. Both guild heads, Hermauos and Dios, have the honorific title of Flavius, which means that they have some level of imperial service. They may not even be real hunters. But either way, the work agreement makes clear that they are guild heads because Ammonios wants them to be. In this little corner of Aphrodito civil society, there is no democracy, only the influence of the local big man.

Papyri found at Aphrodito introduce us to other aspects of the life of the urban craftsman. Psois is a carpenter and craftsman in Antinoopolis, the capital of southern Egypt. In 568, he and his father-in-law Iosephis sign a contract creating an association between them.[39] They agree to share their work and split the profits. In their own words, they agree

> [to] collaborate with one another in our joint business and that the sale of all merchandise produced that may come to us (from this agreement) shall be made according to joint management and will and approval without any laziness or blame or negligence or dilly-dallying whatsoever.

They promise to live up to the standards of all craftsmen in Antinoopolis. This duty to be diligent is a standard with deep roots in Roman law.[40]

But something more is obviously going on here. This is not simply an agreement between a carpenter and his father-in-law. It is a family matter. Iosephis's wife Tikollouthos – the story's mother-in-law – is "agreeing with him [Iosephis] in regard to his written agreement in accordance with her will in all places." Psois needs her to agree. Without her explicit approval, his future in the family business is unclear. As he puts it himself, he "has the expectation, should it please God, of being taken and being appointed by you [Iosephis] while still alive to (be) your heir and successor after the completion of your life."

A whole family's history comes out from a single work contract. Psois and Iosephis probably worked together long before Psois marries his daughter. Iosephis's decision to arrange the marriage – we may speculate that it happens this way – is probably a conscious decision to invest in the future of his business by bringing in a young and able partner. In a way, their business agreement serves as a substitute for a dowry.[41] While Roman law requires the bride's consent, she is not the central player in this story from the point of view of the contract: we never even learn her name. Furthermore, consider the hunters' charter from Aphrodito: if the

---

[39] *P.Cair.Masp.* 2.67158; subsequent translations adapted from Urbanik 2013, 277–278.
[40] Urbanik 2013, 280.   [41] Urbanik 2013, 280–281.

carpenter craftsmen of Antinoopolis have a similar agreement, Psois does well through this marriage. Marrying the daughter of one of his own guild means he can give smaller gifts to the rest of his guild when it is time to celebrate the marriage.

In December of the same year, two other carpenter craftsmen in Antinoopolis named Daniel and Victor form a similar association.[42] They "agree with common will and non-fraudulent conviction to work together for our trade of fine carpentry through this written agreement without any kind of fraud or fear or force or constraint." We get the sense that Daniel and Victor do not know each other as well as our previous partners.

Their agreement will last only one year from the day it is signed, and they may not trust each other very much. They include a clause agreeing "to receive corresponding wages and to distribute by common consent to ourselves in half-shares, without any theft or defection."[43] Their working relationship may be brand new, or the clause may just be legal boilerplate. Either way, unlike Psois and Iosephis, they have no family ties, so their agreement is temporary and sounds more cautious.[44]

This kind of caution is warranted, and the papyri are full of legal attempts to protect against broken trust. Apollos, Aphrodito's policeman for the better part of two decades in the 520s and 530s, comes into day-to-day contact with a wide range of men and women.[45] He collects guarantees for the good behavior of the town shepherds. The guarantees come from landowners, collective taxpayers, deacons, farmers, and even cumin sellers, and the witnesses include priests and other collective taxpayers. Apollos receives other guarantees of good behavior too, for beekeepers and goldsmiths. He handles an acknowledgment that Anouphios has fallen into arrears on rent owed to a woman named Anna, Dioskoros's wife's aunt. More dramatically, he also handles a petition for a case we have already seen, Victor's complaint that Matheias and Anna have pillaged his house for revenge.[46]

The records hint at the natural connections between men in related occupations. Another man named Victor is a sapper and miner.[47] When he makes payments to the estates of Count Ammonios in the early 540s, he does so in one case through Pakouis the carpenter. The connection may be merely social, or Victor may need Pakouis for his technical woodworking

---

[42] *P.Cair.Masp.* 2.67159; subsequent translations adapted from Urbanik 2013, 283–284.
[43] Urbanik 2013, 284: for *apostasias*, "(secretly) putting anything away." [44] Urbanik 2013, 285.
[45] Apollos 45. [46] See page 35. [47] Biktor 164 *taph(rôruchos)*.

Town Crafts and Trades

skills. We do not know what sort of construction work Victor does: it could be mere ditch digging, or something more complicated such as dams, dikes, or canal works. His payments to Count Ammonios may be for material, parts, and labor that his estate can supply. This is guesswork, but it creates the shadowy outline of one man's career.

Dioskoros's family does business with Konstantinos the door maker later in the same decade.[48] We can bet that the door maker and the carpenter know each other well. Ieremias, the town's only stone cutter, makes a payment in one of the village accounts.[49] We can imagine him working with the town's mill masters on specifications for their mill's grinding stones.[50] At one point, Dioskoros starts a list of people buying legumes from someone named Apollos. He does not get very far: Iosephios the shoemaker is the only entry.[51] We can imagine that the town's shoemaker – if he is indeed the only one – would be known to almost everyone. The same is probably true of the town's two barbers.[52] The same may also be true of Aphrodito's stitchers or clothes menders. The town has four, and anyone who does not get the work done in-house would know them too. Not all the stitchers are stitchers alone. Apollos is a stitcher and a bath man from Psinabla, at some point accused of theft to Dioskoros.[53]

I choose these little stories with an eye to the people who look a little unusual in our record. But the ties that they highlight are no doubt far more typical and far deeper than the evidence shows. Oil working, the textile industry, and small retail trades all appear as family businesses.[54] The same is likely to be true of most of the specialized labor. In a small town the stone cutters, mill masters, carpenters, and door makers not only know each other, but are probably part of a web of connections interlocking their families for generations into the past and the future.

On the one hand, Aphrodito is probably typical of most big villages in Egypt. The evidence from the late antique Fayyum, farther to the north in Egypt, suggests that there is not much difference from one village to the next. It is just not clear "whether those big villages were significantly different in type from the small ones and possessed important public facilities that the hamlets lacked."[55] On the other hand, Aphrodito is a small town that was once legally a city, a regional capital. Aphrodito may even be bigger than its own regional capital.[56]

---

[48] Ko(n)stantinos 10.   [49] *P.Cair.Masp.* 3.67287.
[50] Apollos 15 and Kurikos in the same text; Kollouthos 38 and Palos 17 in the same text.
[51] *P.Cair.Masp.* 2.67141.   [52] On(n)ophrios 4 and Pkouis 1.   [53] Apollos 94; see page 107.
[54] MacCoull 1984, 68–70.   [55] Bagnall 2005, 561.   [56] See page 181.

The Aphrodito papyri give enough evidence from nearby Antinoopolis to tease out the difference between Aphrodito and the great cities of southern Egypt. The working class in the big city is more specialized, while the working class in a small town looks beyond its own specialisms for the income it needs. In some cases, Antinoopolis supports specialization of labor that is marginal or inadequate in a small town.

A few examples show what Antinoopolis has that Aphrodito does not. We will read more about Martha the dried-fish seller in a later chapter.[57] She comes from Antinoopolis, which apparently needs a dried-fish seller. Aphrodito does not. Antinoopolis needs a date seller, Sarapion.[58] Aphrodito does not. No doubt dried fish and dates sell as much in Aphrodito as anywhere else, but in Antinoopolis, the market is large enough that one vendor can provide a specialty in this way. In Aphrodito, everything on offer probably falls to a general grocer.

In Antinoopolis, several different men are carpenter craftsmen, but none in Aphrodito. The small town just has carpenters. Both Aphrodito and Antinoopolis have doctors; they do not seem rare. But in Aphrodito, one doctor, Mouses, is also a farmer, while in Antinoopolis we see evidence of a full hospital administration. Antinoopolis has a pattern weaver and embroiderer, a man named Petros, originally from Lykopolis.[59] Aphrodito does not. Antinoopolis has a doorkeeper.[60] Aphrodito does not.

It does have a good number of weavers. But in the case of a weaver named Victor this job is not his only one; in 548, he rents and sows two-thirds of an acre of land belonging to Dioskoros, who agrees to supply the seed and water for the land.[61] Two-thirds of an acre is precious little land. It is not enough to feed Victor's family, but it may be enough to provide him with helpful income or a little food on the side. For Victor the weaver and Mouses the doctor, their specialisms may not have failed them, but Aphrodito is not a big enough place to give them everything they need through one job alone.

At the edges of the evidence, we can see where even the specialization of the big city starts to fail. Aphrodito has plenty of pork butchers, but no sausage makers. Antinoopolis does have a sausage maker, but in AD 566, the market administrators there worry that he will not stay and do his job through the following year.[62] Antinoopolis is large enough to need a bath attendant, a man named Menas, coincidentally the father of Martha the

---

[57] See page 153; *P.Coll.Youtie* 2.92; and Barns 1976, glossing *tarichopratissa* as "salt-fish seller."
[58] *P.Cair.Masp.* 2.67155.   [59] *P.Cair.Masp.* 2.67163.   [60] *P.Ross.Georg.* 5.32.
[61] *P.Cair.Masp.* 1.67116.   [62] *P.Stras.* 1.46.

dried-fish seller. But that bath attendant falls into poverty, and pledges one of his own daughters for a gold piece.[63] Tending the public baths may not make ends meet in Antinoopolis. Or his need for the gold piece could show that he is involved in other business as well.

Aphrodito's own papyri name no native bath attendants: maybe the town had no baths. The one bathman appearing in its records is Apollos, the bathman from Psinabla we have already met doubling as a stitcher or clothing mender.[64] Psinabla is close enough to Aphrodito that its bathman may come from the neighboring village.[65] If so, Apollos also has a hard time making ends meet. This may be why Apollos appears as an accused thief on one of Dioskoros's lists.

Time and again in these cases, the level of detail is striking. We know that Antinoopolis has a greengrocer, Kollouthos, called a *lachanopôlês*. Aphrodito does not have a *lachanopôlês*, but does have a fruit vendor, Karkau, called a *chedriophoros*. We only know about Kollouthos because he is not originally from Antinoopolis, and has to borrow seven and a half carats from a pork butcher when he is there.[66] This is a trivial sum, but important enough to these two men that they have Dioskoros write up the loan.

In these cases we are dealing with the poorest of the poor or at least the closest to them that our evidence allows. But in all of these cases, the people earn with their labor, either cash or in kind. Below them are those – few, it seems – who have lost control of their own labor, and in some cases, of their own independence. We have just mentioned one such case, in the family of Martha the dried-fish seller.

Kollouthos from Thmounkrekis Nea is another.[67] In 569, he agrees to lease himself to an Antinoopolite lawyer named Phoibammon. He agrees to spend four years as Phoibammon's house servant, and in exchange, Phoibammon will pay him 388 liters of grain, 155 of barley, some oil, some wine, and slightly under one gold piece per year. The labor Kollouthos brings is important enough to require a guarantee: another man from Thmounkrekis promises Phoibammon that Kollouthos will fulfill the contract, and offers surety.

In Egypt, slavery is an urban phenomenon, not very important in the countryside.[68] For agricultural work, slavery cannot compete with hiring

---

[63] *P.Coll.Youtie* 2.92; see page 153.   [64] *P.Cair.Masp.* 2.67143.
[65] Psinabla: in the north of the Panopolite nome; Geens 2014, 114.   [66] *P.Cair.Masp.* 2.67164.
[67] *P.Stras.* 1.40, with Montevecchi 1950, 76–81. Compare the case of Martha and Procla on page 153: "the two documents will at any rate almost certainly have originated from the same office" (Barns 1976, 590).
[68] Keenan 2001, 622 and Urbanik 2010, 221, collecting references to more detailed discussions elsewhere.

free labor. We know of only fourteen slave sales from late antique papyrological data.[69] One of them is a damaged slave sale from Dioskoros's time in Antinoopolis, dating to sometime after 565.[70] The owner, whose name is lost, sells to a financial official named Ioannes

> two female slaves, Eulogia and her daughter Rhodus, born at home and of ordered behaviour and pure conduct whom I have sold to you in good faith and will, without hidden illness or epilepsy or vice or third-party claim, hard-working without inclination to run away.[71]

This is mostly legal boilerplate. It shows only that the buyer and seller want the sale to be legitimate, and the slaves have to be free of defect for that to hold.[72] Down the road, if Eulogia and her daughter prove to be vice-ridden epileptics, the original seller will be liable for damages. The two women – bought in town by a government finance official – are probably not meant for hard labor, but for use as domestic servants.

In 567, a man named Theodoros, an employee in the office of the duke of the Thebaid in Antinoopolis, drafts a will that we will discuss further in a later chapter.[73] The bulk of the will leaves movable and immovable property in three different parts of Egypt to two different monasteries. Representatives of these monasteries, Petros and Phoibammon, will handle the arrangements.

In passing, Theodoros writes, "I want ... to free all my slaves and servants with their property at the time of my death and to give each of them from Petros and Phoibammon my most reverend heirs ... from equal share at six gold coins." This is to some degree an act of faith. The very institutions benefiting from his inheritance will have to make payments out of it to his freed slaves. However, this is true whenever someone frees their slaves at death: the heirs always stand to lose. Nevertheless, ample evidence indicates that this is a common practice. It is one of several clues confirming the impression that slavery is not that important in Egypt in late antiquity. This is, by and large, a land of free people and free labor.

In some cases in this chapter, we argue from silence. But the Aphrodito papyri provide a strong sample size, and in turn a good sense of this town's working world. If the papyri show thousands of people from Aphrodito, and none of them are dried-fish vendors, they are not that thick on the ground. Life in the big city is complicated, life in Aphrodito less so. Its men

---

[69] Harper 2011, 89.   [70] *P.Cair.Masp.* 1.67120.r with Justin II's dating clause in Fr. 1+2.
[71] Adapting the trans. in Urbanik 2010, 223 and incorporating his conclusions regarding *epaphê* at 246–247.
[72] Urbanik 2010, 225–232.   [73] *P.Cair.Masp.* 3.67312; see page 139.

and women have fewer options available to them and can make fewer choices – but they know those choices, personally, as next-door neighbors.

This chapter began with a tour of Aphrodito's street names and house names, and of how the town's working classes see their own kind everywhere they look, written in the very names of the landscape. This is a familiar world, a world they can trust. When we know our neighbors, when we know their names and the places they work, we know where to turn in times of need. Year in and year out, Aphrodito's men and women have to trust their peers. They have to believe that goods and services will arrive as promised. When they cannot be sure, they must turn to others for help.

How do these villagers know where to turn? How do they know whom to trust? Who could vouch for whom? Is there an occupational trust hierarchy? One way to answer these questions is to turn to the town's guarantees, the legal documents in which one person promises another that a third party will do what they say. These agreements reveal how Aphrodito's working classes negotiate life with each other and with their betters.

In April 548, a farmer and hired laborer named Psais vouches for a water carrier named Apollos.[74] Psais is no one particularly important, although his story appears in the previous chapter. He is from out of town, from the village of Arabon, and merely living in Aphrodito, where he marries a local. The water carrier is his brother-in-law, his wife's brother. His promise is simple: he swears to Dioskoros to give part of his salary as surety for his new family member.

In March 553, a cloak weaver named Phib vouches for a "most reverent" church reader named Enoch.[75] Three other men also vouch for Enoch: a sub-deacon named Petros and two men named Ioannes who do not give their occupations. Their promise is also simple: they swear to the pagarch that Enoch will stay in Aphrodito, and if he does not, they will pay the pagarch in compensation – Petros and Phib two gold pieces each, and the two men named Ioannes one gold piece each.

In July 521, an Aphrodito cumin vendor named Mousaios issues a guarantee to the town policeman.[76] His promise is more complex: that a shepherd from the Terkis region named Hermaouos will stay in Aphrodito and that he will fulfill his duties as a field-guard over the course of the coming year. Field-guards have to "work at all public duties, resolutely and unexceptionably, and to keep watch over matters of peace, and to effect the appearance of parties being sought."[77]

---

[74] *P.Cair.Masp.* 1.67095 and page 91.   [75] *P.Cair.Masp.* 1.67094.   [76] *P.Cair.Masp.* 3.67328.
[77] Trans. Keenan 1985a, 256.

Mousaios's promise is only one of twelve made to the town policeman at the start of 521, but he stands out a little from the rest of the crowd. Some of the guarantors do not give their occupations and one is only a shepherd himself. Other guarantors include a deacon, a farmer, a landowner, and a young man named Enoch who will be a village headman thirty years later.[78] A cumin vendor like Mousaios looks much lower in status by comparison: he takes a significant risk, just like everyone else, in this case promising twelve gold pieces if Hermaouos fails to do his job.

Imagine looking for someone to guarantee your own good behavior. Our stereotype of late antiquity expects high-status patrons but that does not happen here. Our villagers turn to almost anyone: a hired laborer, a cloak weaver, a cumin vendor. They turn to the elite, too, but not exclusively. The search for someone to trust is not about status. The only thing all these people have in common is a willingness to put up money.

If someone wants to earn trust and has no money to offer, they need some other kind of collateral. When Dioskoros rents his wagon to Menas in 553, two men – maybe brothers – named Palos and Daueid guarantee that it will be returned unharmed.[79] Their promise comes with no cash on the line. But both men are carpenters. Dioskoros probably imagines that if Menas makes off with the wagon or comes back with it broken, the two carpenters will have to put their own skills to work to make good on their promise.

Once again, the evidence shows how trust works in a village society. Presumably, many dozens, even hundreds of tiny transactions such as this take place on a daily basis and need no paperwork. The men and women involved use their own judgment and good sense. They know that in most cases, their peers will be reliable, and prefer to build their social capital than to cheat their own neighbors. When they do not know the other party quite as well, they need written reassurance. When they get it, they care less about the status of the people involved than their ability to deliver on their promise.

---

[78] Enoch 7.   [79] *P.Cair.Masp.* 3.67303 and page 80.

CHAPTER 7

Looking to Heaven

A century before Dioskoros, and hundreds of miles away in Roman Syria, a shepherd's son named Simeon is driven out of his monastery for the severity of his self-renunciation. Simeon eventually mounts a platform on top of a tall pillar to escape the crowds who have heard about his miracles and come to seek his prayers. Repeated construction of ever-higher pillars cannot keep the crowds away. At the end of his life, after thirty-seven years on top of his pillars, Simeon is famous throughout the Christian world. Even emperors seek his advice.

Saint Simeon the Stylite is not unique. He is part of a movement, a wave of famous monks, ascetics, and holy men in late antiquity. These holy men have earned tremendous attention, for obvious reasons: their lives are colorful, their deeds bizarre. But Simeon is Syrian, and his brand of asceticism is specific to Syria. A recent study of monasticism and poverty in late antiquity notes a profound difference between the religious landscape in Syria and the religious landscape in Egypt, where the holy men also engage in the mundane realities of daily life.[1]

Early Christians wrestle with biblical exhortations to give to the poor and wonder how to reconcile these exhortations with the apparently straightforward words of Saint Paul: "If anyone will not work, let him not eat." The Syrian model, of Simeon the Stylite and those like him, sees the holy poor as angelic, messengers sent as a model to the world.[2] The Egyptian model is more practical, deeply rooted in the peasant life of the Nile valley. In Egypt, the holy poor work for their food. They struggle to achieve a self-reliance that proves they are detached from the value of the gifts they receive.[3] In practice, this creates an intricate web in which Egypt's religious become entangled in the local economy. They both contribute to the wealth of the world through the fruits of their labor and receive from that wealth through the gifts of their peers.

---

[1] Brown 2016. [2] Brown 2016, 110. [3] Brown 2016, 94–95.

Aphrodito's documentary evidence shows what this religious landscape looks like at the business end. The documentary evidence is full of men and women too normal, too typical of their time to earn books of their own. But these men and women are part of a documentary movement, appearing in bequests, rent receipts, and administrative memos. It is an authentic, day-to-day movement, the daily piety of late antiquity. It is the piety of the vast majority of late antiquity's rural Christians, inseparable from the secular fabric of the farms, the vineyards, and the businessmen who run them.

Two hundred years before Dioskoros and his family, in the early 300s, Aphrodito was far from fully Christian. A papyrus from around AD 312 gives the names of nine men from Aphrodito.[4] Four of them are named Besarion, another Sarapion, traditional names based on the old Egyptian gods. Two hundred years later, in the time of Dioskoros, these names survive, but are not nearly as common. The new names we see in sixth-century Aphrodito show how the town has become Christianized. Some of the most frequent names are Christian.[5] In Aphrodito's tax register the three most common names are Victor, Ermauos, and Ioannes. In a larger sample, a more complete register of everyone we know from Aphrodito, the three most common names are Ioannes, Victor, and Apollos.[6] The name Ioannes – for John the Baptist or John the Evangelist – is central to Christianity. The most frequent female names are Maria, Rachel, and Thekla, all names showing the rise of Christianity in Aphrodito.[7]

Names do not tell the full story, but by the sixth century Aphrodito is almost certainly completely Christian. Attempts to apply naming patterns to the records from Egypt suggest that it reaches a tipping point in the process of conversion during the AD 300s: a majority of its population may be Christian by 350, a vast majority by the middle of the fifth century.[8] Even if Aphrodito came late to this conversion curve, by the sixth century the town's last pagans have long since vanished.

By that time, Aphrodito's religious landscape is punctuated with the names of the town's greatest patrons. One of these, an influential office-holder in the region, Count Ammonios, is active in the area from the 520s to the 540s. His estate accounts show a number of charitable contributions over the course of the 540s.[9] These contributions go to a range of recipients, from the personal (two daughters of Loukanos who are nuns and

---

[4] *P.Col.* 8.235. [5] For name frequency, see Ruffini 2006. [6] Ruffini 2011.
[7] Counting Maria and Mariam as variations of the same name.
[8] Depauw and Clarysse 2013, ultimately following Bagnall 1982.
[9] For what follows, see MacCoull 2005.

a priest named Victor) to the institutional (a monastery at nearby Psinabla and the Apa Sourous monastery discussed later). These contributions show an increase early in the decade: one in 541/542, four in 542/543, and thirteen in 543/544, but only one in 544/545 and eight in 545/546.

Ammonios's records of these contributions are tight-lipped. The entries give only the barest amount of information necessary:

To the parish of Apa Agenios	3,878 liters
To the parish of the Holy Apa Patemous	814 liters
To the daughters of Loukanos, nuns	620 liters

Two years later, the same group of recipients receives almost the same amount or more:

To the parish	15,531 liters
To the daughters of Loukanos	776 liters
Apa Patemous	776 liters

Elsewhere in these accounts, entries explain their purpose: for taxes, for example, or for iron or a machine. But these entries and many others like them receive no explanation.

It is unclear what accounts for the dramatic upgrade in contributions in the first three years of these accounts, or why the last two years did not maintain quite the same pace. Ammonios is known in the region for his power as a patron. The gifts he gives may be in response to direct requests from clients. They may be in fearful response to one of the era's greatest signs of divine retribution, the plague sweeping through the Roman world in the 540s. Ammonios and others may be "donating more money and goods to churches and monasteries motivated by fears of their mortality – and their salvation – and so hoping to obtain more and stronger intercession by clergy and monastics."[10]

Unlike Ammonios, the founder of the Apa Sourous monastery is unknown to us. However, we may guess that Sourous was one of the richest men in Aphrodito when he died. The monastery he founded and gave his name to would become the town's largest landowner. Later men –

---

[10] MacCoull 2005, 112.

inspired by his piety – would imitate him on a smaller scale, and Sourous himself may not be the only one in his family to leave a religious institution behind. Several sources mention a church of Apa Romanos, a name known among Sourous's descendants.[11] (Titular churches – named for their founders – are common in late antiquity, and by no means a monopoly of the senatorial elite.[12])

Nevertheless, his foundation is not simply a pious act, it is also an economic one. Scores of men work their whole lives on his monastery's property. Renting that property can earn substantial income.[13] Apa Sourous is one of two monasteries owning several acres of vineyard land in Aphrodito. As one author has pointed out, "Operating a vineyard required substantial investment in both labor and machinery."[14] The monastery probably sells wine on the wider market to supplement or even grow its income.

Apollos, Aphrodito's long-time headman and defender of its *autopragia*, starts his own monastery sometime before his death in the 540s. "Had his glimpse at the pomp and vanities of the capital sickened him of worldly life? or was there enough of disillusionment even at Aphrodite to induce a similar mood?"[15] He may be inspired by the example of Apa Sourous, or moved by a pious desire to recruit for the army of monks who pray for the world's salvation.

His monastery is sometimes called the monastery of the Christ-Bearing Apostles of Pharaous or Pharatopos, or, after him, the monastery of Apa Apollos. The exact location of Pharaous is unknown, but it may be in desert land seven or eight kilometers from the town.[16] The inner workings of the monastery of Apa Sourous are invisible, but the records show more about this monastery of Apa Apollos. Its monks call themselves hermits, suggesting that they lived in separate dwellings without the formal community rules so common in other monasteries.[17]

However, this monastery is not typical. Indeed, some parts of its story are unique. Apollos is not fantastically rich, certainly not on the scale of Ammonios or Sourous, but by starting a monastery he stakes a claim to local patronage much like theirs. In fact, he takes that claim further, by intervening in the internal regulation of the monastery and – through naming Dioskoros to succeed him as the monastery's manager – by prolonging his power over the monastery beyond his own life.[18]

[11] Marthot 2013, Volume II, 303.
[12] Consider the examples from the Latin west in Hillner 2006, with concluding remarks at 68.
[13] Rentals: *P.Cair.Masp.* 2.67133.   [14] MacCoull 2011, 245.   [15] Bell 1944, 26.
[16] Wipszycka 2008, 263.   [17] MacCoull 1988, 29.   [18] Wipszycka 2008, 271.

It is surprising that this does not happen more often. The decision to start this monastery has long-term implications for Apollos's family and Aphrodito's politics. In Aphrodito, various factions constantly compete for power. For Apollos, securing a family member to succeed him in control of his monastery is a move made with this fact in mind. The monastery is a power base for his family, and leaving Dioskoros in charge is a move on the town's chessboard.

Sourous and Apollos do not leave a vision of God in their own words. Dioskoros does. His encomia – poems praising high-ranking office holders – are mystical allegories: they paint a picture of the earthly government and its dignitaries that reveals the truth about the heavens.[19] Sometimes we cannot even tell whether Dioskoros is speaking to a man or God. In one poem, Dioskoros addresses a general he compares to Heracles.[20] But look closer, and the general seems to be Christ himself, the subject of Dioskoros's love. The poet stretches the Greek poetic technique of compound words, creating unparalleled exaggerated compounds with four or more root words.[21] And with these compounds, the lover greets Christ:

> Hail, walking about a gold solidus having the face of an angel!
> Hail, lord! finer than gold silver mother of pearl smaragdus pearl!
> Hail, sovereign! made of topaz agate and onyx ... living brilliantly!
> Hail, lord of the creating of all worthy beast bird star light universe![22]

These verses address the angel on the reverse of a Roman gold coin and the images of Christ on Byzantine icons.

Dioskoros may be writing a parody, a critique of Christian imagery.[23] A sophisticated audience would see this and be invited to enjoy a deeper level of meaning in these verses. In this mystical allegory, Dioskoros's poetry follows the imagery in the Book of Revelation. Dioskoros invites his audience to follow John the Evangelist and move beyond the veneration of images toward a deeper knowledge of the true Christ.[24]

At times, Dioskoros shows his faith in less complex ways. In 570, he writes an agreement for a boat lease between a Flavius Theodoros and

---

[19] Kuehn 1995, 2–6.
[20] *P.Cair.Masp.* 1.67097.v.F = *P.Aphrod.Lit* 4.39–40. This paragraph follows the interpretation of Kuehn 1995, 77–155, asserting the unity of the poem and Christ as its subject. Fournet 1999, 645–650 does not discuss Kuehn's interpretation, taking the poems as distinct and 4.40 as a *chairetismos* for Justin II.
[21] Kuehn 1995, 115. [22] Adapting the translation in Kuehn 1995, 110. [23] Kuehn 1995, 128.
[24] Kuehn 1995, 152–155.

a sailor named Pekusis.[25] In a unique, personal twist, he postpones the usual formula for dating the document by the reign of the emperor, and starts the lease instead with eight lines of religious doodling. "God of grace," he writes, "God leading the way, the God with us in all ways." Then, he continues with the written form of the Christian fish symbol, I X Θ Y Σ, and gives abbreviations for the Greek phrase at the heart of the symbol, "Jesus Christ, God and Son of God, Savior." Only after this quiet display of piety does he begin the legal text of the lease.

Five hundred years of Christian history gave the late antique faithful a wide range of objects for devotion. Anyone's piety may be different from that of the church as a whole. The Holy Trinity, for example, is not a prominent focus of Aphrodito's Christianity. No church or monastery dedicated to the Trinity appears in the records.[26] But Dioskoros himself venerates the Trinity. He emphasizes it in his poetry, and concludes one text to his father's monastery with a call to the Trinity: "guard me through your prayers from above."[27]

Aphrodito's big men have the means to leave a permanent mark on the landscape of their town. But the little men also find ways to express their piety, on a much smaller scale. Giving one's life to God means giving one's things to God as well and these gifts are full of complications. Most of what we know about Aphrodito comes from its Greek papyri. Many of the papyri in Coptic, the final form of Egypt's native tongue, still need to be published. The Greek texts largely show Aphrodito's official life, while the Coptic papyri show more about the private life of Dioskoros's family.[28] The case of the brothers Anoup and Ioulios survives in one of these Coptic papyri, one of the earliest legal documents written in that language.[29]

The text is an arbitration written in AD 569, fragmentary, and hard to understand. Anoup and Ioulios, sons of the same mother by different fathers, decide to become monks, and Dioskoros is involved as the case involves his father's monastery, Apa Apollos. But they must first settle a dispute with the heirs of Apa Papnoute, who was probably the monastery's administrator or head. At the heart of the dispute is nothing more than a tiny cell (a Coptic *ri*), a monk's room once belonging to their father, who had left monastic life and since died. Apparently, their mother,

---

[25] *P.Lond.* 5.1714; see also page 189. [26] MacCoull 1991, 111.
[27] MacCoull 1991, 110–111 with trans. from MacCoull 2009, 3. [28] Vanderheyden 2012, 794.
[29] *P.Cair.Masp.* 2.67176.r + P.Alex.inv. 689 with additional unpublished fragments = *P.Cair.Masp.* 3.67353.r; I am grateful to Anne Boud'hors for providing drafts of a forthcoming edition, translation and discussion of this text, which I follow here in addition to MacCoull 1988, 37–45 and MacCoull 2009, 1–3. See also Richter 2013, 413–415 on the chronology of Aphrodito's Coptic legal texts.

Nemesianê, had ceded the cell to Apa Papnoute, and they had brought a countersuit arguing that the cell was theirs.

Dioskoros does not hide in the shadows in this case. He speaks with his own voice: the disputing parties "asked me together, with a common accord, to examine their case, to study and investigate it, in the manner that the Lord instructs me." He wants the public record of the case to show that he takes his role seriously. Following testimony from the participants, he writes, "I sought proof therefore of these words, as much as a listener in the case as a judge." When it is time for him to give his opinion on the case, he speaks "as the Lord has inspired me."[30]

Everyone ultimately agrees to a convoluted solution, in which Papnoute's heirs receive half ownership of the cell, and the two brothers take the other half share. Dioskoros's intervention is a graceful way to solve the problem, but the entire case shows that family disputes and legal troubles can complicate even the most spiritual of projects. Their case is only one of several like it.

In AD 573, a monk and priest named Psa, but also called Psates, makes a donation to the monastery of Apa Apollos.[31] Psa is not a local: he is originally from the village of Temseu Skordon in the region of Hermopolis, farther to the north. Even his name may mark him as an outsider as there are no other men named Psa from Aphrodito. Nothing explains when or why he originally came to Aphrodito, only that he is now living in the monastery.

He writes through Dioskoros to Enoch, the monastery's administrator, to announce his donation, a building, not yet built, and two gold coins. One of the monastery's previous administrators had given him the disposal rights over another building on monastery land. He intends to convert that building, which originally belonged to Mousaios from the Oxyrhynchite region, into a guesthouse for traveling monks.

Psa's two gold coins may have been a lot of money for a monk from Temseu Skordon. A tax register from that little village from the previous generation, late in the AD 540s, records payments by 283 individuals or heirs from Temseu Skordon made over the course of a single year.[32] Only 12 percent of that group paid more than two gold coins in taxes that year. What someone pays in taxes represents a fraction of his total wealth. If this donation liquidates Psa's wealth, then he comes from the poor end of his

---

[30] Following the unpublished translation by Boud'hors; see note 29.   [31] P.Cair.Masp. 1.67096.
[32] P.Lond.Herm.

village. But his plans to build one building and convert another suggest that he has other means at his disposal that he is not yet getting rid of.

Psa may be more than a mere peasant. It is significant that the monastery's administration gives him disposal rights over one of the monastery's buildings, especially considering that the building had originally been a gift from another monk. Reciprocity is at work here. Perhaps Psa receives disposal rights over that building in exchange for another previous donation, not surviving in our records, or receives those rights precisely on the promise that he would do something with that building that the monastery does not yet have the resources to do itself.

This proposed guesthouse is an interesting story. The site for the project is nothing more than a *kellion*, a little room, but Psa may be planning an extension, or a complete reconstruction. The *kellion* itself had originally belonged to a monk from the region governed by the city of Oxyrhynchos, 125 miles to the north. And Psa himself is also an outsider, a wandering monk of the kind so often viewed with suspicion.[33]

Maybe this is why his plans for a guesthouse for traveling monks run into difficulties. As he says, Enoch did not want to go along with his plan, "and closed the monastery according to the wishes of the founder."[34] In other words, while the Apa Apollos monastery accepts men from Hermopolis and Oxyrhynchos, there is a wariness in regard to strangers. This wariness stems from the founder's own vision for the site, as a monastery for monks dedicated to a settled life, not the wandering kind likely to make use of a guesthouse.

The monk named Enoch, the administrator through whom Psa makes his donation, appears in another document from that same period, a letter from Dioskoros.[35] Here, Dioskoros is complaining: his relationship with Enoch is rocky and he has to convince the administrator to pay more attention to the case of the animals stolen under his supervision. (Again, Dioskoros flustered by animal theft!) The letter gives the impression that the monastery of Apollos "has been losing money," and Dioskoros "is telling the community to pull their socks up and set matters to rights."[36]

It is easy to see why Enoch may not have wanted to pursue the matter. Recall the story from an earlier chapter: the "worthless, impious, and laziest field-guards of our village ... jeered at him daily." We do not know who Dioskoros was writing to, but he begs him to look into the matter, and to

---

[33] Wipszycka 2008, 269–270.
[34] Maspero's note on line 32 prefers a rough rendering: "because the founder (Apa Apollos) had wanted the monastery to be a closed house."
[35] *SB* 20.14626, assuming Enoch 32 = Enoch 33. See also page 72.   [36] MacCoull 1990a, 108.

put a stop to the changes a landowner named Loukanos wants to make to the monastery. Dioskoros thinks the man he writes to is right for the job because of his close connections to Dorotheos, "the most magnificent count."

This magnificent count Dorotheos appears in a number of other texts from the AD 560s and 570s. He receives or appears in half a dozen petitions and panegyrics, twice as an intermediary for or employee of the even more powerful patrician and duke Flavius Athanasios. When the people of the regional capital, Antaiopolis, seek relief from the violence of the soldiers stationed there, an episode seen in an earlier chapter, Dorotheos is one of the officials to whom they appeal.

More directly relevant to this case, the monks of Apa Apollos had already petitioned to him just a few years before.[37] Someone named Iezekiel – "a barber, a slanderer, a bad man" – contests a donation to the monastery of four acres of land by an unnamed widow.[38] He may have been a relative who thinks he has a claim to the land himself, and the monastery asks Dorotheos to intervene to uphold its right to the donation.

This is a sad story. Dioskoros is the *phrontistês kouratôr*, the manager and superintendent, of the monastery his father founded. We do not know whether he wanted the job, but we can guess that it gives him a good chance to follow in his father's footsteps, earning the goodwill of the community and the grace of God. But he has to delegate the day-to-day handling of the monastery's budget to a monk, the *oikonomos* or estate manager.

That estate manager has to negotiate with embittered relatives like Iezekiel, powerful landowners like Loukanos, and prospective donors like Psa. Those negotiations may steer the monastery in a direction Dioskoros does not like, and perhaps in a direction away from what his father had in mind. In moments such as these, Dioskoros can do no more than appeal to more powerful patrons and hope that their influence helps to keep the monastery on track.

Egypt highlights the intense symbiosis between religious institutions and late antique civil society. "Here, enthusiastic patrons made a reality out of John Chrysostom's vision of the widespread dissemination of churches located on large private landholdings."[39] An expert on Egyptian Christianity in this period writes:

---

[37] *P.Cair.Masp.* 1.67003.   [38] *P.Cair.Masp.* 1.67003.23; MacCoull 1988, 31.   [39] Thomas 1987, 59.

> Churches could arise anywhere: at the peripheries of a town or village, or in the desert terrain neighbouring the cultivated zone. Their construction would not necessarily involve any great expense: most of them were small buildings constructed with sun-dried bricks. The liturgical furnishing (vases, crosses, etc.) could be more expensive. Bishops were far from enthusiastic about these activities. It often happened that the families of the founders could not afford the expense of running such churches ... Cult in these churches was frequently irregular, masses being celebrated only on the days of the holy patrons or when ordered by the bishop.[40]

Several of Aphrodito's churches probably fall into this category: including the evidence from the Arab period, we know of twenty-six churches, monasteries, and holy places named for saints in Aphrodito.[41] Some of these places honor well-known figures: the Archangel, the Apostles, and Saint John. Some of them honor much lesser people. A church or monastery of Saint Herakleios recorded in the eighth century may be in honor of one of a group of twenty-three Alexandrian martyrs, or another lesser known saint.[42]

For all that we know about Aphrodito, and all the institutions we know by name, there are some unexpected blind spots. "We cannot even find out from the sources whether Aphrodito had a patron saint." We cannot tell which saint Aphroditans turn to "at moments of crisis."[43] Nor do we have any sense of the physical geography of Aphrodito's faith. The 1901 excavations in Kom Ishqaw apparently found an elite part of town, now under the Islamic cemetery. Those excavations were in the south part of town, near the modern town's main church.[44] (See Figure 7.1 and Figure 7.2.) That main church may be the modern descendant of long-lost structures going back on that site to the main church of late antiquity.

Aphrodito may have had a cult to Saint Menas, but the evidence is slim.[45] A priest of the Saint Apa Mena church appears in the town's archives, as does a poem in honor of the saint. Dioskoros may have written this poem himself, but it does not seem to be in his style. The poem honors Menas, who died a martyr in AD 296, as a "champion of Christ" who "accomplished a fearful struggle and won victory for God." Menas, whose cult spread far throughout the Nile Valley, has become "like the angels: you dwell with and join in the liturgy with the Cherubim and Seraphim."

---

[40] Wipszycka 2007, 333–334.
[41] Marthot 2013, Volume II with Papaconstantinou 2001, 296–298 and references *s.n.*
[42] Papaconstantinou 2001, 92. [43] MacCoull 1988, 152. [44] Quibell 1902, 86.
[45] *P.Aphrod.Lit.* 4.48 introduction, 659, adapting trans. from MacCoull 1986b, 52.

Figure 7.1 "Church Door," Kom Ishqaw (Egypt), Photo © 1995–2015 Clement Kuehn

Figure 7.2 "Crosses," Kom Ishqaw (Egypt), Photo © 1995–2015 Clement Kuehn

He is a patron for living sinners: the poem closes with a call to Menas to "speak with God [and] ask him to have mercy on us."

This role is not reserved for long dead martyrs. The saints of tomorrow are the monks of today. Aphrodito shows this to be true better than anywhere else in late antiquity.[46] The papyri from the sixth and the eighth centuries give a great "before and after" picture of this process in action. In the sixth century, Aphrodito has just over a dozen shrines. Only one of them is to a local monastic saint. Most of the rest are in honor of saints and martyrs from elsewhere in the Roman world.

However, this same period records a monastic superior named Abba Enoch and an institution called "The Place of Apa Psoios." In the eighth century, these names reappear as "The Place of Saint Enoch" and Saint Psoios.[47] A priest of the church of Saint Apa Promaos the Martyr of the village of Aphrodito signs the town's petition to the empress Theodora in 547. Saint Promaos is not mentioned anywhere else, and his popularity may be very local.[48]

---

[46] Papaconstantinou 2007, 356–357.
[47] For Enoch, the time elapsed may be even shorter: see *P.Cair.Masp.* 2.67242 (547) and 67234 (VI).
[48] Papaconstantinou 2001, 181.

Later evidence gives more examples. An eighth-century reference to an unknown Saint Psempnouthios and a monastery of Abba Psempnouthios may be evidence of a purely local saint.[49] Similarly, eighth-century references to an Abba Papnouthios, a Saint Papnouthios, and the heirs of Saint Papnouthios all suggest a local figure.[50] These little details are a constant reminder: local society forms its own shape. Aphrodito's religious landscape is a collection of figures both foreign and familiar, figures of the town's own choosing.

In the medieval world, the Christian church is a tremendous economic power, owning vast stretches of land. With this in mind, people look to late antiquity expecting to find a similar situation. But Aphrodito's landscape is hardly dominated by church holdings.[51] The Aphrodito cadastre and register show that Aphrodito's churches own very little of the local land, less than 4 percent of the land registered in the village accounts.[52]

Religious institutions do own over a third of the land registered in the city accounts, a separate category of Aphrodito's land. But most of these institutions are far away, churches in the big cities of Antaiopolis or Apollinopolis, or the famous White Monastery of Shenoute, the great monastic leader and founding figure of Coptic literature who lived in the fourth and fifth centuries. By far the largest landowner in this category is the monastery of Apa Sourous. As we have seen, this is a local institution founded with the wealth of a local family. Since land in the city accounts adds up to only a little over a quarter of Aphrodito's land, this hardly represents a picture of church dominance of local farmland.

Instead, the records show a complex tapestry of connections between various churches and farms.[53] A farmer named Phoibammon works land owned by three different religious institutions. A farmer named Palos works land owned by the oratory of the Archangel Michael and the monastery of Smin. Pnis, who also works the Archangel Michael land, has three sons who work land belonging to the Apa Sourous monastery and the Apa Zenobios monastery. These two monasteries are a repeating pair: several men and women handle land belonging to both.

These examples are only those known. Aphrodito's men and women almost inevitably do business with a church or monastery, if not more than one, or know someone who does. Which institution you work with

---

[49] Papaconstantinou 2001, 219.   [50] Papaconstantinou 2001, 166.
[51] Compare the impression given by Gascou and MacCoull 1987, 118; Gagos and van Minnen 1994, 17, and Alston 2002, 304 (discussing the cadastre); and Zuckerman 2004a, 226 (discussing the register) with the contrasting image in Bagnall 2008, 184.
[52] Bagnall 2008, 184.   [53] MacCoull 2011, 246 with references for the following summary.

depends on your own social connections, your own needs and your own line of work.⁵⁴ The church of Apollinopolis owns garden land near Aphrodito that it may use to bring excess product to market in the town. The monastery of Apa Zenobios grows reeds it may use to make mats, baskets, or rope. The conclusion is the same in Aphrodito as in so many places in late antique Egypt: a Christian church firmly embedded in the economic life of the world at large.

Religious life in Aphrodito has an annual rhythm to it, as it does throughout the rest of the Christian world. Feast days for the saints come and go throughout the year.⁵⁵ One of Dioskoros's long accounts includes payments on the 23rd of Pachon for the feast day and alms (*agapê*) of Mary, the feast day of Saint Kollouthos, and the feast day of Saint Phoibammon. The next entry, for the 16th of Pauni, includes payments for the feast day of Saint Onnophrios, and the entry after that, for the 15th of Epeiph, includes payments for the feast day of Saint Makarios and the feast day of Saint Apa Enoch.

These payments are second nature to Dioskoros. They come casually. He records them only when they occur to him, and then, with no dividing line between the sacred and the profane.⁵⁶ These examples are selective excerpts, omitting some entries and payment amounts.

Pharmouthi 1:

> To the parish of Ama Mary.
> To Rachel's daughters.
> To Psoukios the shepherd.

Pachon 23:

> For the day of Saint Onnophrios.
> On the same, for Pelias for the little birds that she rears.
> On the same, for Apa Mena the monk.
> On the same, to my sister Rachel.

As with entries from the accounts of Count Ammonios, these entries tell us little.

We can only speculate why Dioskoros makes some of these payments. The entries themselves have no notes. He may turn to Mary or Kollouthos

---

⁵⁴ MacCoull 2011, 244–245 with references.
⁵⁵ Keenan 1984, 62, note 43. Note how some of the dates of payments recorded by Dioskoros compare to the feast days recorded in later Coptic synaxaries (Papaconstantinou 2001, 407–414): Kollouthos comes two days later in the synaxaries, Onnophrios on the same day.
⁵⁶ *P.Cair.Masp.* 2.67141.5.r with Pelias 1, Rachel 13 and Psoukios 2. See also page 79.

or Phoibammon as an act of personal piety. He may see himself as a patron of the churches or people in charge of those holy days. It may even be nothing more than force of habit, continuing payments his father made for decades before him. He does not, it seems, make any offerings to the town's Holy Catholic Church, where his cousin may have been a priest several decades before.

One striking feature is the absence of church hierarchy. Egypt's larger church hierarchy plays hardly any role in Aphrodito. All the religious action – from Count Ammonios down to the small donors to the local monastery – comes from private individuals. This fits a pattern present in other parts of the story: large administrative structures – the provincial and imperial governments – are less central to the story than it might seem at first glance, and give way to the importance of interpersonal relationships. Similarly, the church hierarchy is less important than the nature of specific arrangements with specific people.

Bishops appear only once in a long while, and never in a spiritual role. To the people of Aphrodito, bishops are no different from anyone else above them. When they behave well, we turn to them for help. When they behave poorly, we turn to someone else. When some in town write to the empress Theodora to defend their fiscal rights, they also include an appeal to the piety of the local bishop.[57] Bishops are, in short, powerbrokers and patrons like any other.

In 539 or 554, Bishop Ioannes – probably the bishop of nearby Antaiopolis, the regional capital – acts on behalf of the church to alienate some church property. A man from Aphrodito named Apollos takes over two separate plots of church land in the villages of Thmounameris and Pteme. These are cessions, not sales: Ioannes charges nothing for the land, and Apollos only agrees to pay the taxes on them. Nothing explains why Ioannes is getting rid of church land. Fiscal or economic motives are possible,[58] but the bishop may equally be trading favors, perhaps giving away underproductive land for a song in expectation of future donations to the church in Apollos's name.

A Bishop Kephalon – again, probably the bishop of Antaiopolis – appears in a rent receipt from the first half of the sixth century. His son and heir is an intermediary for a payment made to Dioskoros's father Apollos for rent on land in nearby Phthla.[59] Kephalon appears again in

---

[57] *P.Cair.Masp.* 3.67283.13, if correctly restored.
[58] *P.Michael.* 41 with page 80: "The transfer ... suggests that taxation was a crushing burden."
[59] *P.Cair.Masp.* 3.67326.

a letter from a public official named Ioannes to the bishop himself.[60] Accused of criminal violence, Ioannes repents to the bishop, but adds that his boss Victor is actually the man responsible. Here, Kephalon appears as an intercessor, a man to ask for forgiveness.

It is not clear why this is in writing or why Dioskoros has a copy of it.[61] If this letter of repentance comes from public papers – either the city archives in Antaiopolis or the town archives in Aphrodito – then it may have been stored in proceedings against Ioannes or his boss, Victor. In that case, Bishop Kephalon is not simply a forgiver of sins, but a powerful figure in the middle of a potential political dispute. His sacramental role also gives him secular influence, to speak for Ioannes if he chooses, in defense of his crimes.

Finally, the Aphrodito papyri give three references to Theodoros, Bishop of the Pentapolis, a region far to the north, along the Mediterranean shore. His relationship with Dioskoros is pure conflict. Two complaints from Dioskoros survive: poetic petitions he writes around the year 551.[62] In one poem, addressed to a high official in Constantinople, Dioskoros complains of the "violent acts" of Theodoros, who in person "stole for himself the harvest of my threshing floors." He has "harvested all of our fields of honey-oozing grape clusters, the ewes, the oxen ... all of our goods he has handed over to Arsas."

Maybe the bishop is wine dealing at Dioskoros's expense.[63] But what this means is unclear. In the second poem, addressed to another high imperial official, Dioskoros again complains of Theodoros's violence. This time, he adds that Theodoros has robbed him of four pounds of gold.[64] Nothing in the poem gives any clue as to what is going on: this much gold – 288 gold pieces – is a serious sum. It would be a significant chunk of Aphrodito's entire cash tax bill for this period, when Dioskoros himself is a village headman.[65]

The bishop also appears in a receipt he writes to the monastery of Pouinkoreus in the Hermopolite nome.[66] It acknowledges that the bishop has received a shipment of 1,500 *knidia* of wine, delivered to him in Alexandria, for which he paid in advance. This is, to put it mildly, far from Aphrodito. It is not clear why Dioskoros has a copy of this receipt for

---

[60] *P.Cair.Masp.* 3.67295.
[61] *P.Cair.Masp.* 3 page 48: Maspero credits the copyist's interest in the letter's pretentious style.
[62] *P.Aphrod.Lit.* 4.1 and 5 with MacCoull 1988, 66–68, adapting both translations.
[63] MacCoull 1988, 68.   [64] Not four solidi, as in Theodoros 9.
[65] Banaji 2001, App. 1 Table 7: compare the figures for 525 and c. 567 CE. Dioskoros 3: headman in 552.
[66] *P.Cair.Masp.* 2.67168.

a wine sale that does not involve him. Possibly he is part of the transaction in some way, as a middleman.[67]

Dioskoros must have some business arrangement with the bishop. He may manage vineyards for a distant monastery and act as their agent, selling their wine to the bishop. Or he may have his own vineyards, and the monastery is using his product to fulfill its own agreement with the bishop. Theodoros, Dioskoros, and the monastery may all disagree over who owes what to whom. Maybe Dioskoros's tax collecting responsibilities somehow get tangled up in his work for the bishop, who takes Dioskoros's share of Aphrodito's tax collection to make good on some other debt.

However, this is just guesswork. The main point is that religion is irrelevant here. Theodoros's religious role matters only because it limits Dioskoros's options. The only people Dioskoros can turn to in a struggle with an Egyptian bishop are high-ranking imperial officials in distant Constantinople. This conflict is just one among many, the bishop no different from any of the other competing parties in this book.

I mean none of this to trivialize the role of the church in late antiquity, quite the contrary. Christian faith is part of the air in Aphrodito. Its scribes follow Christian conventions reflexively: notaries use three crosses to note section breaks in documents, and invocations of the Holy Trinity appear in letters, rent agreements, and even rent receipts.[68] But this pervasiveness of the faith in all aspects of life means that Christianity appears not at the top of a stylite's pillar, but in day-to-day brass tacks, the practical and the secular.

This is how the world of Aphrodito intersects with the world of Shenoute and of Simeon, with the world of the late antique holy man – through business. The men and women of late antiquity reach up to heaven through patronage, and patronage takes money. In one poem, Dioskoros praises a local notable, "You have settled limitless gold upon the monasteries of Shenoute and Saborios."[69] But this praise can just as quickly turn the other way. In another context, in the 560s, Aphrodito residents complain about aggression by the pagarch Menas, including his attempts to divert Aphrodito's resources to Shenoute's White Monastery.[70] Consider the pagarch's aggression from another point of view, and we can imagine some other poet in some other town praising Menas for showering gold on the White Monastery.

---

[67] Or some other business of Theodoros: Fournet 1999, 493.   [68] MacCoull 1991.
[69] P.Cair.Masp. 3.67338, trans. in MacCoull 1988, 128.   [70] P.Cair.Masp. 1.67002.20.

Kollouthos and Markos, the sons of Christophoros, give another hint of Aphrodito's ties to the White Monastery. We will read more about their complex land exchange with Thaumastê and Anastasia in a later chapter. In that exchange, we hear about a specific plot of land in Aphrodito which Paul, Thaumastê's father, had donated to the White Monastery.[71] The monastery can then profit from renting that land, and Paul would receive spiritual benefit from that gift. At some point, however, the White Monastery decides to sell the plot to Kollouthos and Markos – it may need the money or decide that it takes too much effort to manage the land – who in turn cede it to Thaumastê and her daughter Anastasia, thus returning the land to the family of its original owner.

In these two cases – Paul's donation and the pagarch Menas's depredations – the White Monastery is not a center of Coptic literary culture or the source of divine rules for the monks at less famous monasteries. It is more worldly than that and more practical. It is both resource-rich and resource-hungry. It buys and sells like a good entrepreneur.[72] It changes life in Aphrodito not simply through its spirituality, through the good it does for its souls, but also through its market transactions, through the ripples that its gifts and sales send through Aphrodito's land market.

We began this chapter with a brief look outside Egypt, at Simeon the Stylite and the world of the holy man. Remember that late antiquity's holy men are mirrors for their society, giving a glimpse of the "average" Roman "from a surprising angle."[73] Holy men take for themselves a role society as a whole once held, the role of a community's professional guardian. They are leaders, anchors of certainty in a changing world. But we see little of this in Aphrodito. It produces no miracle workers, seems to have no patron saint, makes no monk a lawgiver or intercessor with the powers above. This apparent difference between Simeon's world and Dioskoros's world may just be an illusion. Aphrodito may look the way it does because we know it through documents, not literary texts. In the documentary record, Aphrodito's holy men may simply blend in with their peers.

Throughout this book, the Aphrodito documents show two exceptional worlds, of chaos and control, rising above the mundane landscape of the everyday. These people generate documents to keep things from going wrong, and they generate documents when things do go wrong. Below the examples we see in this chapter, for less important people playing with

---

[71] See page 157, following MacCoull 2009, 14 and correcting Kollouthos 66 et al.
[72] The comment in MacCoull 2009, 12 about this text's Aphrodito families applies just as much to the White Monastery.
[73] Brown 1971, 81.

smaller stakes, we might find thousands of quiet moments of personal piety, saint-day offerings too small to record, or Christian fish scratched on a church wall instead of a papyrus. And running parallel to these examples, there is room for Simeon the Stylite's world as well.

Imagine a missing *Life of Apa Apollos*, the patron saint of Aphrodito, written by later generations of Dioskoros's family and friends. This lost saint's life might tell the story not only of his monastery, but of his actions in defense of his own hometown against the aggression of impious outsiders. The *Life* of Shenoute shows the great monk raiding pagan homes and miraculously teleporting to the court of the emperor Theodosius. Similarly, the lost *Life* of Apollos might show Dioskoros's father rebuking the local Blemmyes as they backslide toward their ancestral paganism, and miraculously teleporting to the court of the emperor Justinian as he defends the rights of his hometown.

This is just a thought experiment, a fantasy. But it shows that we are at the mercy of our evidence, divided in strict binary between the documentary and the literary.[74] One group of texts shows an exotic world of saints and miracles, the other group only the mundane. We have Aphrodito's documents, not its monastic libraries, and so we see no holy men in Aphrodito, or anywhere in the immediate area.

At some point in the sixth century, Antinoopolis has a stylite, a holy man living on a pillar, Father Ioannes the Stylite.[75] But even here, we are not praying but doing business. Father Ioannes appears only in a letter written to him guaranteeing that Iôsephis the donkey driver will make daily shipments of water to his monastery for the next six months. Father Ioannes is not famous: we know nothing else about him. He may be the classic late antique holy man. But he lives in the real world, and when he buys water, he needs a written guarantee that someone will deliver it.

Some of Aphrodito's sixth-century monks become its eighth-century saints, including one who starts his own monastery. Apollos, who helps to run the town in the sixth century, and starts his own monastery before he dies, is not one of them. Despite our thought experiment, sainthood is not in his future. The difficulties Dioskoros has managing his father's monastery may explain why. The consequences of a weak, sloppy or corrupt monastery administration are clear. These institutions rely on agricultural gifts and income from them. That income evaporates if the monks do not handle tenant relations with care. A poorly run monastery will not survive,

---

[74] Although Dioskoros himself straddles this divide: see Fournet 2004; Fournet 2013b.
[75] *P. Turner* 54.

and its founder's sainthood will fall victim to secular mismanagement of his estate. Such a fate might await Apollos when Dioskoros finally dies.

This is just a guess, but it is also a reminder of how closely intertwined the sacred and profane are in this world. A sixth-century document describes Count Ioannes undertaking "an inspection of the administration of the monasteries of Aphrodito" because the "monks of one of these monasteries had brought charges of fiscal misadministration against their *proestos*" or monastic superior.[76] Ioannes "seems to have regarded his inspection duties as an irksome and time-consuming diversion from more important duties."[77] The distraction of a single inspector or the attention of an able administrator can ruin an institution or build it into the foundations for a future saint.

Furthermore, the only real contact Dioskoros has with any higher member of the church hierarchy is the bishop Theodoros. Theodoros is not caught up in the theological controversies and ecclesiastical schisms of the day: he is moving wine, caught up instead in accusations of theft and violence. Theodoros may not be typical, but nothing in Aphrodito makes him particularly exceptional either. If we view late antiquity from this angle, there are no holy men here. With no way to access the daily lives of the average Christian, we can only imagine what else is missing. In these archives, there is only business.

---

[76] Thomas 1987, 65.   [77] Thomas 1987, 65.

CHAPTER 8

From Cradle to Grave

When Dioskoros writes his Greek to Coptic glossary, he adds an entry for "abortion" or "miscarriage."[1] The death of unborn babies, newborns, and children is common in this world. However, the lives of Aphrodito's children are invisible to our eyes. The town's inhabitants act in their own right only as adults, and children appear in our records only in passing, as bystanders in family disputes. What their lives may be like is a gap in the history, in Aphrodito as in most places in the ancient world. Remember the small finds from Aphrodito in Chapter 1.[2] The 1901 excavations at Kom Ishqaw uncovered a doll made of rough red earthenware; a horse's head made of pottery; and wooden writing tablets, including one with wax still in it.[3] These dolls and tablets may be the best glimpse we will ever get of Aphrodito's children.

The levels of child mortality in Roman Egypt probably vary little from one period to another. Census records from other places in Roman Egypt, from earlier periods of Roman rule, provide raw data for reference. Life expectancy is low for both men and women, in the low to mid-twenties, and infant mortality is high.[4] Dioskoros is one of three siblings that we know of. Others may have died in childhood. Likewise, Dioskoros has four children that we know of, and may have lost still more. These lost brothers and sisters, these lost children, are ghosts hidden throughout the town. The people of Aphrodito grow up hearing about the ones before them, knowing the ones after them, seeing them in ways we never can.

Aphrodito's marriages are much clearer. The Michaïlides collection held twenty-one papyri from Aphrodito, bought on the open market around the end of the Second World War. The large majority of these papyri relate to the life and career of Phoibammon, the son of Triadelphos whom we have met in earlier chapters. The lone exceptions are three papyri allegedly

---

[1] Bell and Crum 1925, 214.   [2] See Figure 1.3.   [3] Quibell 1902, 88.
[4] Males: "*at least* 25.0 years" (Bagnall and Frier 1994, 100). Females: 22.5 years (ibid., 87).

"found together, in a different spot from the rest of the collection, in a box made of 'mud', each roll resting in a separate groove in the box."[5]

When collectors buy papyri that do not come from controlled archaeological excavations, we have no way to know whether we should believe these stories. The box, if it existed, was "described as being rectangular, and provided with a lid of the same material, which was possibly sun-dried mud-brick, or a sun-dried clay." It may have been the ancient equivalent of a scribe's desk drawer. The modern editors suggested that the three texts were the notary's copies.[6]

One of the papyri has two documents on a single roll, the two together forming a marriage settlement between Rachel and Besarion on December 30, 566. The main characters in both pieces are Jacob and Irene, the parents of Besarion, the prospective groom. In the first text, Jacob and Irene acknowledge that they owe Rachel, their future daughter-in-law, "the customary marriage-gift," in this case thirty gold pieces. As a guarantee for that sum, they offer Rachel just under seven acres of land for her to choose from their holdings in Aphrodito. In the second text, Jacob and Irene then lease the seven acres from Rachel for the cost of the taxes on the land.

This may seem like a strange arrangement. The whole thing is fictional: no gold changes hands, and no land.[7] The point of this marriage gift is to guarantee that Rachel will have claim to the gold – or the land – if her husband divorces her or dies. In effect, Jacob and Irene are offering Rachel marriage insurance. This sort of arrangement has deep roots in indigenous Egyptian practice, appearing in Egyptian-language marriage contracts centuries before the start of Roman rule.[8]

Why would Rachel think such insurance necessary? Is she taking a risk in marrying Besarion? Are Jacob and Irene willing to risk having to pay a hefty sum as a way to buy a good marriage for their son? Is she marrying down while they are marrying up? Jacob is no small man himself: he signs the village's petition to the empress Theodora in the 540s, and has served as a village tax contributor. Even the best of marriages may need a guarantee.

The modern world imagines weddings as large celebrations with friends and family, parties full of friction and fun. The paperwork and formalities are always present, but not necessarily prominent in public. But the ancient world's paperwork is all that survives. It is also the evidence for the real friction, the moments of tension and awkwardness. The groom's parents both need help to get the paperwork done. The groom's mother is illiterate,

---

[5] *P.Michael.* page 71. [6] *P.Michael.* page 80. [7] *P.Michael.* page 85. [8] Pestman 1961, 40–41.

and a priest named Dioskoros signs for her. But as the editors note, "the priest seems almost as illiterate as the lady for whom he wrote."[9]

The groom's father gets interrupted as he signs the lease. He starts one word in his acknowledgment too close to the end of the line and stops, unsure how to fix the mistake. The rest of the word is in different handwriting. "One might guess that Jacob was slow in finishing" his signature, and that "Dioskoros impatiently snatched pen and papyrus and finished it for him."[10] If the groom's father is nervous at the signing, we can understand why. The standard form of marriage contract in this period is a hefty declaration of debt to the bride. One contract, most likely from Antinoopolis, the capital of southern Egypt, in the 560s or 570s, includes an acknowledgment of a debt of six gold pieces. The groom or one of his relatives signs the text with the promise that he is "ready to hand these over to Your Grace [the bride] whenever you want, free from all malice and procrastination, at my own hazard and liability, and at the cost of my family and personal possessions."[11]

This is generic language, and reappears almost word for word in another marriage contract from the same period, between Horouogchis and Scholastikia.[12] Their agreement begins with a clause acknowledging that the groom owes the bride just under six gold pieces as a counter-dowry, but it is far more interesting for the conditions it places on both parties. To my mind, the burden of the agreement lies more heavily on the husband than the wife. He promises her

> I won't despise you or throw you out of my marital home except on account of unchastity and shameful transactions and bodily disorder made known by three trusted free men either from the country or the city … I, your spouse, further promise not to invite anyone unsuitable to the house, nor to dine with a friend or relative when you're at home unless you are willing.

The list of conditions goes on at length, and the groom claims that he is not making his promises from fear or through deceit or under duress.

In fact, these conditions tell us hardly anything about Horouogchis and Scholastikia as husband and wife, but they do reveal a fair amount about typical expectations for married life. Accusations of infidelity might come easily, but demanding three witnesses sets a high standard of proof.[13] The note about witnesses from the country and the city is an interesting touch.

---

[9] *P.Michael.* 42.A.40.n.   [10] *P.Michael.* 42.B.24.n.
[11] *SB* 22.15633 with translation from Kuehn 1993, 107.
[12] See Scholastikia 1, *P.Lond.* 5.1711 and its draft version, *P.Cair.Masp.* 3.67310.
[13] A standard of proof with old roots: compare *P.Eleph.* 1 (311/310 BC).

Even in the status-conscious late Roman world, all that matters to witness infidelity is to be free. Husbands misbehave, bring home obnoxious friends, and take over the home with unwanted guests. But here too, the wife has protection, an expectation that she has some say, some level of control over that home.

Elsewhere, we meet a bride named Theodora, also called Sega, and her husband, apparently named Kollouthos.[14] One part of the text includes a declaration of debt to the bride, but whether it is from the groom himself or one of his relatives, we cannot tell. Hardly anything shows who these people are. The groom may be a *singularis*, a messenger or assistant in a provincial office. One of the bride's family, a man named Pithiodoros, may be a fruiterer.[15] This is not society's elite, and yet the documentation of their marriage amounts to over one hundred lines of text.

In another marriage contract, we meet Viktorine and Aphous.[16] This document survives today in fragments written "in very bad Greek, full of spelling errors and grammatical mistakes."[17] Dioskoros works with this couple during his time in Antinoopolis, the provincial capital. They are from the Lykopolite nome and own property both there and in the Antaiopolite nome. The property survey gives a rare peak into the closet of a late antique Egyptian woman.[18] Viktorine's property includes roughly three ounces of gold jewelry and an assorted list of other clothes and jewelry: linen fabrics, handkerchiefs, cushions, cloaks, jewelry boxes, perfume containers, and much more.

Their agreements to each other are much like the others. Aphous agrees that he will "neither commit any outrage against her, nor to her body, nor to her face, and not expel her … and not bring in another wife or (?) a concubine."[19] Viktorine agrees "to cherish the marriage and to love her husband in everything and to stay in the house … and not to do anything without her husband's knowledge."[20] Some of the language in these marriage contracts is generic, and does not show the human side of the marriages. A petition from Antinoopolis in the late 560s or early 570s gives more detail about the marriage at the heart of its story. "My father," the petitioner writes:

---

[14] See Theodora 1 and Kuehn 1993 for *SB* 22.15633's potential relationship to *P.Flor.* 3.294 and *P.Lond.* 5.1710.
[15] *P.Lond.* 5.1710.15, absent from Ruffini 2011.   [16] Who appear again, page 138.
[17] APIS Catalog Record for *P.Cair.Masp.* 1.67006.v.
[18] *P.Cair.Masp.* 1.67006.v.80–91, with Italian trans. in Russo 1998, 150–151.
[19] Trans. altered from Urbanik 2011, 144.   [20] Trans. in Urbanik 2011, 136, note 25.

abandoned me, then a little child, and preferred the life of a monk to the life of an Antaiopolite defensor. He sent me away from Antaiopolis with few things to my uncle on my mother's side. Later on, when I grew up, my uncle became my father-in-law, for he married me to his daughter, and gave me, as is customary, some property according to a dowry contract, for he was a kind man.[21]

Bitterness at the petitioner's father – unable or unwilling to provide for his son – gives way to gratitude to his mother's brother, a man named Kollouthos. This marriage between two first cousins is a bit of good luck for the husband, who will now have financial resources he once lacked. It is also a smart move by Kollouthos, who can leave his daughter in the safe hands of a grateful relative.

Some of these marriage contracts are basically debt agreements.[22] After the consummation of marriage, the groom agrees to give a gift to his bride; this gift becomes, legally, the groom's debt to the bride, and it may be a payment for the bride's virginity.[23] The gift or debt agreement comes after the wedding itself in order to wait for proof on the wedding night. Indeed, Horouogchis tells Scholastikia that her gift comes now that he has "found your holy and steadfast virginity."

Depending on the status of the newlyweds, such gifts and a dowry may be a legal requirement. Recent imperial legislation banned marriage by agreement alone for high-ranking officials, adding that "there shall always be a dowry and bridal gifts and everything that becomes the noble persons."[24] This helps eliminate uncertainty about a marriage's exact legal standing: if a dowry and bridal gifts have been given and documented, everything is in order.

These gifts to the bride are not just the couple's business. Marriage comes with in-laws and the potential for conflict between them. One of the longest texts found at Aphrodito is a complex dispute from Antinoopolis for which Dioskoros himself may have been the arbitrator. On one side of the case are Anastasia, her husband Phoibammon, her sister Maria, and her husband, also named Phoibammon. On the other side of the case is Anastasia's brother, Psates. The case is a tangled mess. Dispute over the wedding gift is mixed up with a dispute over inheritance and a further dispute over money spent maintaining disabled relatives and decaying homes.

---

[21] *P.Lond.* 5.1676.1–11, slightly altering the "paraphrase" in Kovelman 1991, 144–145.
[22] A *donatio propter nuptias*: see Papathomas 2004, 139–140 for a brief discussion of the genre.
[23] Rowlandson 1998, 210 with Kuehn 1993, 108, note 19 for references.
[24] *Nov.* 74.1.4; trans. in Urbanik 2011, 132.

The beginning of the text is damaged, but soon gets to the heart of the matter. Phoibammon the tow worker complains about his brother-in-law, Psates the bootmaker:

> Although he had promised me when I married his sister that immediately after the solemnization of the marriage he would hand over all her share of household utensils inherited from her parents and also my share, in right of my wife, of the house-property to live in – which indeed ... was the very reason why I was anxious to marry his sister ... as I had no house; but up to the present he has given us nothing of all this, though we have grown weary first of demands and then of reproaches.[25]

Phoibammon's honesty is striking. He does not wax sentimental for his wife, but has his eyes firmly on the prizes marriage brings with it.

Phoibammon's testimony is only part of the story. The bulk of the document focuses on statements by the disputants. Psates sees himself as a helpful victim: complaining about his family, "And this, this is the return I get for my *philadelphia*: they are suing me!"[26] Psates works making *tzagkaria*, "Persian shoes, perhaps an upscale specialty that would have sold well in the fashionable society of the ducal seat."[27] Dioskoros tells his story in almost poetic language. His father died, Dioskoros writes, "having laid down the final liturgy, his life."[28] When Dioskoros helps to resolve the dispute, proposing a division of the inheritance into equal shares, he calls the resolution itself a "quenching," as if the dispute is a fire raging through the family and its society.[29]

Not all stories end so well. In September 573, a doctor in Aphrodito named Isakos divorces his wife Tegrompia.[30] The marriage's surviving *perilusis* or cancellation begins with a brief summary of the events:

> Whereas I, Isakos, took you in partnership as wife with good hopes for the marriage and for having children, wanting my marriage to come to peaceful fruition, now, a grievous demon bearing ill-will towards our life together, we have been driven away from one another.

Isakos and Tegrompia release each other from all further obligations, and acknowledge that they are each free to remarry or, should they choose, to join a monastery. No court proceedings will be necessary to finalize their divorce.

On the one hand, their case is rare in the records: we do not have as many divorce records for cases in Aphrodito itself as we have divorce

---

[25] *P.Lond.* 5.1708 introduction. [26] Trans. in MacCoull 1988, 34. [27] MacCoull 1988, 32.
[28] Trans. in MacCoull 1988, 32–33. [29] MacCoull 1988, 34.
[30] *P.Cair.Masp.* 1.67121; see Tetrompia 1 in Ruffini 2011.

records found at Aphrodito but originally from Antinoopolis. On the other hand, the heart of the matter is all too common: a grievous demon is the standard reason for a failed marriage.[31] Menas divorces Maria in 568, also citing a grievous demon bringing ill will between the two.[32] When Mathias, a crewman in a state galley, divorces his wife Kura in 569, he blames an evil demon for their separation.[33] When Theodoros divorces his wife Amaresia, also in 569, he blames an "evil grievous demon."[34]

Sarapion, a date seller whose father had been a doctor, divorces his wife Mariam at some point in the same period.[35] Although both Sarapion and Mariam are originally from other regions, they, like all the previous examples, now live in Antinoopolis. However, unlike the previous examples, they do not quite blame a demon for their divorce. Sarapion says that they have been split asunder by "a full-grown grievous ill-will between the two of us from I don't know where."

Thinking about these demons, the modern mind might instantly recognize the language of a no-fault divorce.[36] The demons shift the blame from the husband and wife. This helps ease one's conscience: despite formal church condemnation of divorce, the spouses are not in fact to blame.[37] Indeed, invocation of a demon may be legally necessary: in 566, imperial legislation explicitly bans consensual divorce.[38] The text of the divorce between Mathias and Kura stresses that the two are in complete agreement:

> We agree and each party agrees that it has received back its personal property in full ... and we are not charging one another and we shall never make any charge in any court whatsoever, or outside of court, because we have been ... paid in full and have been reconciled with one another.[39]

Each of them is free to start their life anew: "it shall be possible for each one of us to enter into marriage with someone else if he (or she) should wish, without hindrance or impediment or reproach."[40]

At the same time, these demons are truly part of a pervasive popular superstition. The evil eye plays an ongoing part in Greek magic. Surviving Greek amulets and exorcisms attack the demon *Baskosunê* (Envy) and blame this demon for separating husband and wife. In one Byzantine text, Jesus himself blames separation between husband and wife on the work of the devil.[41] Thus these demons are two sides of the same coin, a

---

[31] For the format of divorce settlements, see Urbanik 2014, 158–159.
[32] *P.Cair.Masp.* 2.67153 and 67253, with trans. in Urbanik 2014, 167–169.   [33] *P.Lond.* 5.1712.
[34] *P.Lond.* 5.1713.   [35] *P.Cair.Masp.* 2.67155.   [36] Keenan 2007, 239.   [37] Urbanik 2005, 215.
[38] *Nov.* 134.   [39] Trans. in Rowlandson 1998, 212.   [40] Trans. in Rowlandson 1998, 212.
[41] Dickie 1993, 13.

"widespread conception" in late antiquity that serves at the same time as a convenient way to avoid legal blame.⁴²

Once the demons drive these marriages apart, one of the most important problems is the future of the children. Mathias and Kura, whose full agreement on their divorce we have already discussed, finish with the following note:

> And it has been additionally decided between us that, if the fetus of the above-written Kura should survive and be born, on condition that Mathias, oarsman, give for the expense of the said childbirth six gold [carats] without judgment or trial, his father should receive the little child.⁴³

In short, Mathias agrees to buy full custody of his unborn child. Modern readers might find the transactional nature of this text strange, but it is a convenient and businesslike way to avoid disputes farther down the road.

Marriages driven apart by demons end more happily than those without them. The case of an Aphrodito woman named Eirene offers a good example of how much more could go wrong.⁴⁴ In September 553, Eirene files a police petition against a coppersmith named Makarios. In the petition, she claims that Makarios "illegally dared to harm me and broke his oath to me, the petitioner Eirene, that 'I take you as wife,' but now mocks me." Eirene asks that the police arrest Makarios and hold him until her case comes to court. At the end of the petition, she adds Makarios's mother, Tkouiskouis, to the complaint as well.

This petition says little, but we may guess what has happened. One modern author pins the blame on the mother-in-law, whose name means "the tiny tiny one." Maybe she interferes in the marriage and pushes her son to leave Eirene.⁴⁵ Eirene's grounds for legal complaint against Makarios are unclear. She says only that he dares to outrage her or harm her. The Greek verb *hubrizein* (to treat despitefully, outrage, insult, maltreat) is the same verb Aphous uses when he agrees to marry Viktorine and do her no harm.⁴⁶ Legally, Eirene is accusing Makarios of *iniuria*, a violation suggesting sexual assault under Roman law.⁴⁷ Deeply buried here may be a hint that Makarios consummated the marriage with an act of rape.⁴⁸ Recent legislation outlines financial penalties – one-quarter of the man's estate – against men who lure women into false marriages, sleep

---

⁴² See references to earlier arguments in Bagnall 1987, 55, note 46.
⁴³ Trans. in Rowlandson 1998, 212.
⁴⁴ *P.Cair.Masp.* 1.67092 with Urbanik 2011, modifying his translation on page 141.
⁴⁵ Urbanik 2011, 142–143. ⁴⁶ See page 134. ⁴⁷ Urbanik 2011, 145.
⁴⁸ Sexual misconduct, consummation: Urbanik 2011, 147.

with them and then expel them. Eirene may hope for exactly this sort of settlement against the man she thought would be her husband.[49]

In a strange juxtaposition, the back of one of the divorce contracts in Dioskoros's archive has the text of a father's will to his daughter.[50] Both father and daughter go unnamed. "An old man from sixth-century Antinoopolis left his daughter his property as a *donatio mortis causa* in return for her continuous care in his sickness and old age."[51] Some people have wondered why any parent would want this kind of contract with a child. They may think that their children will not honor their moral obligations, or want a formal agreement when more informal arrangements have already failed.[52]

Death is as much a legal transaction as marriage and divorce. But wills are rare in late antiquity. Not even two dozen survive from the start of the fourth to the start of the eighth century.[53] Three of them are from the Aphrodito archives.[54] We have already seen the story of the monk named Psa, and his donation to the monastery of Apa Apollos. Several others, mostly from Antinoopolis, have also left their plan for what should happen when they are gone.

Pauchab, who dies in late 525, leaves a will which only partly survives.[55] Because we only have the end of the text, many of the important details are lost. He leaves to a monastery some property designed to provide it with revenue in wine and grain. That property will, apparently, remain in the hands of his daughters or their heirs, but the monastery can ask for it back "if it comes to pass that the heirs, my daughters, in heedlessness do not pay [the monastery] in a reasonable spirit."

In an earlier chapter, we met Theodoros, an employee in the duke's office in Antinoopolis who draws up his will in 567.[56] He has no legal heirs, but his grandmother is still alive, and Theodoros remembers her in his will:

> I want and deem it worthy that my noblest maternal grandmother shall have by the title of succession a plot of land with all that justly belongs to it and in all its extent, and I want it to suffice for her, that she shall not sue for anything else either of the two monasteries or Petros and Phoibammon on account of the *Falkidion*.[57]

---

[49] Urbanik 2011, 149. [50] *P.Cair.Masp.* 2.67154.v.
[51] Huebner 2013, 138 citing *P.Cair.Masp.* 2.67154.v.   [52] Huebner 2013, 138.   [53] Bagnall 1986, 2.
[54] A fourth (*P.Lond.* 5.1894) survives in a small fragment containing only subscriptions. A fifth (*P.Michael.* 53) survives in a much larger fragment, not yielding continuous sense.
[55] *P.Cair.Masp.* 3.67324. Date: Ruffini 2011 *s.n.*
[56] See page 108 and extensive discussion of this will in Keenan 2001, 618–625.
[57] Trans. altered, with some omissions, from Urbanik 2008, 127.

In this extract, his will sounds a bit defensive.

Under Roman law – specifically, the *lex falcidia* mentioned here – legal heirs are entitled to the "Falcidian portion," a quarter of an estate. But that law does not apply here, because the grandmother is an ancestor of Theodoros. She is not one of the people automatically entitled to a share of the estate.[58] Theodoros may expect a grandmother to be grumpy on hearing that so much of her grandson's goods are going to the monasteries. Alternatively, Dioskoros may be doing nothing more than flexing his legal muscles and showing off his learning.

Other wills naturally show other priorities. In November 570, Phoibammon, the head doctor in Antinoopolis, drafts a will leaving the administration of the hospital to his brother Ioannes; the education of his children to Besa or his successor at the Apa Ieremias monastery; an annual sum in kind for Athanasios, his pupil, until his majority; and an instruction for Besa to get fifty of the sixty gold coins owed to Phoibammon by Petros for his annual fee to use in payment of a debt to Christophoros.[59]

Much of the will focuses on practical issues. One clause includes provision for a dependent named Athanasios, who may be the doctor's love-child.[60] Phoibammon leaves the Apa Ieremias monastery a new boat, along with a bill of sale: the monastery will be able to show that its ownership of the boat is clear. He also leaves the monastery two-thirds of an acre of vineyard land – his father's old property – along with its irrigation machinery, "for the salvation of my soul and a holy offering on behalf of the departed."[61]

A spiritual thread runs through the text. Early in his will, Phoibammon writes that "The end of all things and of the human race is death, and it is totally impossible to escape."[62] We wonder whether we are hearing his words, or those of Dioskoros. Either way, Phoibammon cares about his fate. He instructs his sons to wrap his body for the funeral, and asks the head of the monastery

> to receive my remains into the holy monastery at a memorial, for a commemoration of my all-too-short life, and to reckon my name in the catalogue of all the saints who are at rest, when you make a recital of them by name.[63]

In classic form, a man dies and an immortal patron is born.

---

[58] Urbanik 2008, 134–135.
[59] *P.Cair.Masp.* 2.67151; this section follows MacCoull 1988, 50–54. Cf. also Amelotti 1972, 62–63.
[60] MacCoull 1988, 54. [61] MacCoull 1988, 51.
[62] MacCoull 1988, 50. See also Fournet 2013b, 143. [63] MacCoull 1988, 52.

All three wills leave goods to monasteries. It becomes almost a standard practice to include a monastic bequest in preparation for death.[64] Phoibammon shows – more openly than many people in this book – that everything in life and death is a transaction, even the road to sainthood. We find a quid pro quo in death as much as we do in marriage and divorce. This may be a symptom of the evidence: truly selfless works need no paper trail.

Sometimes inheritance appears only much later, long after a will has already taken effect. Widows are often given extended use of their husbands' estates "on the condition that they [take] responsibility for the administration of the property for the benefit of their common children."[65] When we meet the widow Tekrompia in 570, she claims to have done just that: "I worked with diligence day and night."[66] But this does not sway her daughter Anna, who wants her share of the paternal inheritance and expects to charge her mother rent for living in her dead father's home.

Earlier, we met a petitioner from the regional capital, Antaiopolis, whose father abandoned him, only to have his mother's brother take him in and marry him to his first cousin.[67] The story seems to begin happily but ultimately, Kollouthos, the uncle turned father-in-law, falls badly ill. At this stage of the story, the petitioner and his new wife are no longer living with him: "together with his servants he was in need of daily bread, for he had no person to supervise his meager property." This is the real reason this story survives:

> The malice and intrigues of tax-collectors increased his discomfort and fever, and he longed for death ... everywhere he saw oppression both for his suffering body and for his soul suffering from hunger and thirst.[68]

Buckling under pressure from the taxman, he transfers part of his property to a third party named Peter, who agrees to handle the tax burden.

Later, with Kollouthos dead, Peter goes back on his agreement and tries to pass the tax burden for the property onto our petitioner's dowry.[69] This is a classic case of economic uncertainty coming at life's major turning points: the father's disappearance followed by the father-in-law's death.

---

[64] Maspero in a note to *P.Cair.Masp.* 3.67324.4.
[65] Huebner 2013, 98. See Yiftach-Firanko 2006 for the evolving role of spouses in wills in earlier periods.
[66] *P.Cair.Masp.* 2.67156 with trans. in Kovelman 1991, 145.   [67] See page 134.
[68] *P.Lond.* 5.1676, slightly altering the "paraphrase" in Kovelman 1991, 145.
[69] *P.Lond.* 5.1676 introduction.

The anonymous petitioner lands on his feet the first time, and we may guess that he will do so again. Something about the picture of his father-in-law near starvation "together with his servants" does not quite ring true. We may guess that this family has at least some resources to use in times of trouble. However, the petition itself is part of this process, the never-ending search for someone one step above you to give you leverage against the others around you.

As this case shows, wills and inheritance can have a dark side. They sometimes include conscious decisions to leave people out. In 569, a man from Antinoopolis whose name is lost announces his decision to disown his children:

> Having my mind and understanding unaffected, with true and unerring judgment ... this I transmit to my parricidal children, though children in name only, that is, to Dionysia and John and Paulina and Andrew the outcast ones ... thinking to find you helpful in all things, a comfort to my old age, submissive and obedient, and on the contrary you in your prime have set yourselves against me like rancorous things ... I fell grievously ill through you ... it is no longer lawful for you in future to call me father, inasmuch as I reject and abhor you from now to the utter end of all succeeding time as outcasts and bastards and lower than slaves ... for ravens to devour the flesh and peck out the eyes, in this manner I debar you from receiving or giving anything on my behalf, whether I be alive or dead.[70]

A few years later, someone prepares a draft for another disinheritance but with the names of the children left out. In that draft, the father announces

> I have decided by writing in this very moment for a lawful renunciation and disownment of you, daughter, useless and unworthy of being called by name ... I expel you ... I have already disowned you in every legal way today for all the course of the sun, from now on, for centuries of centuries ... you shall be as if you were a stranger, separated forever from my blood and family and from my whole estate ... you shall not be counted among all of my children ... all my assets ... shall belong to my [other] children ... who have obeyed, being submissive to my will in everything, and having followed my orders ... they respect eternally the same paternal stock with natural goodness and good-heartiness.[71]

These two angry fathers sound similar. Both insist that the disinheritance will last for all time. Only subtle differences sneak in: the ravens devouring flesh and pecking eyes, for example. While these are legal deeds, neither

---

[70] *P.Cair.Masp.* 3.67353.v.A. Trans. *Sel.Pap.* 1.87.
[71] *P.Cair.Masp.* 1.67097.v.D. Trans. slightly altered from Urbanik 2008, 123–124. Date: Urbanik 2008, 122, note 6. Draft, not rhetorical exercise: Urbanik 2008, 124 with references in note 7.

father claims that his children have done any legal wrong. (The first man claims that he fell ill because of his children, but this sounds more like a generalization than an actual accusation.) Both men instead complain that their children are disobedient and disrespectful. Gross insults and disrespect are circumstances under which disowning is legally permitted.[72]

Whatever the children have actually done, they shame their parents and this shame is public. Disowning them is only a legal action in response. Shame demands a public action as well. And so the first father calls upon several city officials "to give the customary publicity to the decisions" he has made to disown his children.[73] It is not enough that they be disowned: everyone has to know. This is a reminder of the dispute begun by Psaios and Talous discussed in an earlier chapter.[74] As their legal claims against Ioannes the priest stall, they use "loud complaints" against him in his own church. The law matters, but one's honor and dignity matter just as much, if not more.

Despite all we know about the preparations these people take for death, we never know how it finally comes, to any of them. On the way to their deaths, these men and women most likely have experiences very different from ours. Anyone reading this book has already been poked and prodded by a nameless array of doctors, nurses, and other health professionals. Another endless array still lies ahead as the end draws near. Late antique health care is very different.

Aphrodito has at least two hospitals, including one at Dioskoros's family monastery.[75] It also has a treatment center (a *therapeutêrion*) and – in the eighth century, at least – a Doctor's Place.[76] But the treatment center may be religious, not medical, and the doctor's place a plot of land known by its owner. By my count, the town has only seven doctors through the span of the sixth century.[77] Crudely put, this is roughly one doctor for every 1,000 people we know from Aphrodito. Assuming that some people never saw a doctor, and assuming that others did so only in extreme emergencies, this ratio may mean a pretty light caseload.

The evidence says very little about these seven doctors, but two stand out. The Aphrodito land records from the 520s register land that had once

---

[72] *Nov.* 115.3.1–14; Urbanik 2008, 126. [73] Urbanik 2008, 121. [74] See page 56.
[75] MacCoull 1988, 6, citing *P.Cair.Masp.* 1.67096.29 for Apa Apollos.
[76] Marthot 2013, Volume II, 86 and 92.
[77] Biktor 173, Isak(i)(os) 60, Makarios 52, Mouses 6, Papnouthis 8, Theodoros 24, and Jai 2.

been held by the heirs of a doctor named Papnoute.[78] The same records register three different plots of land in the hands of Mouses, who is described as a doctor and farmer.[79] These two men may be different points on a spectrum. A small-town doctor may need or want other forms of income. One might own land to get it, and another might need to work that land himself. How a doctor farmer could balance these two jobs, the land records give no clue.

Dioskoros's documents give more detail about health care in the big city. Where Aphrodito only has doctors, Antinoopolis has head doctors. The head doctor Phoibammon succeeds his father in the position, and, at least according to his will, is to be succeeded by his brother in the position when he dies. But the doctors also have students, so the trade is not kept exclusively in the family.

Phoibammon's hospital, which his father had founded, "provided patients with medical care, food, and housing."[80] Hospitals just like this must have been relatively common in cities throughout Egypt.[81] Generally speaking, the late antique hospital emerged in the fourth century when monastic health care became part of a larger, institutionalized Christian charity.[82] But the hospitals in Antinoopolis are not simply independent institutions for the common good: Phoibammon's hospital was his property, part of his patrimonial estate, to be passed on to his heirs.[83]

Another head doctor, Sophronios, appears in the heat of the action. A report by the headman Arsenios is badly damaged and the context missing. A patient "was strong enough at that moment to beg Sophronios the head doctor to take hold of him and give him medical treatment to stop the bleeding, since he was altogether laid out by a stroke in his head and his whole body had been worn down."[84] But ultimately, the report admits, God is the one who helps save the sick from disease.

Where we imagine doctors, we easily imagine nurses. When Theodoros drafts his will, he includes an inheritance for his nurse Tadelphe and her daughter Leontia.[85] The dispute between the bootmaker Psates and his family mentions a nurse as well.[86] A letter from Dioskoros mentions a "great nurse."[87] But the word in these cases, *trophos*, is etymologically related to wet nursing and feeding.[88] These are not nurses in our sense of the word. They are caregivers and workers of another kind, for those at the beginning of life, not its end.

---

[78] *SB* 20.14669 and 14670. [79] *SB* 20.14669. [80] Miller 1997, 48. [81] Miller 1997, 94.
[82] Crislip 2005, 138–142. [83] Miller 1997, 107. [84] *P.Cair.Masp.* 1.67077.9–12.
[85] *P.Cair.Masp.* 3.67312.105. [86] *P.Lond.* 5.1708.257. [87] *SB* 20.14626.25.
[88] Tawfik 1997, particularly references at 943, note 58.

We do not know what it is like to fall ill in Aphrodito. Very little evidence survives. People may be reluctant to record specific illnesses in the papyri. One letter writer mentions in passing that "the pustular disease has not settled upon me."[89] A petitioner from Antaiopolis describes his father-in-law as "half-dead and completely helpless" because of "fever from gout in his feet."[90] This sort of detail is rare, probably because most sickness takes place out of sight, receiving nothing more than traditional home remedies. One papyrus shows such a home remedy for a common malady:

> For a migraine, take a little myrrh and thorn and saffron residuum (*krokomagma*) and gum, rubbing them (on your head) with a smearing of vinegar. Fumigate your head with bitumen and bird horn. Another recipe: plaster *euphorbia* with egg white on the side of your forehead.[91]

The euphorbia is a common genus of flowering plant. The first modern editor of this recipe noted that euphorbia sap is a violent caustic and the egg white is intended to act as a sweetener.[92] Sweetened or not, euphorbic sap on the forehead is dangerously close to the eyes, where it can cause permanent damage, including blindness.[93]

This risky potential side effect might give the impression that we are dealing with quack medicine. But these migraine recipes are in the mainstream of classical medicine. Euphorbia gets its name from Euphorbos, physician to the famous African king Juba, son-in-law of Anthony and Cleopatra. Euphorbos had noted the laxative powers of these plants in his writing.[94] Medical uses for saffron appear in no less an ancient authority than Galen.[95]

As striking as the recipe itself is its place in the text. It is written in a different hand in the middle of a long set of estate accounts, after nearly fifty lines and before over one hundred more lines of tedious, precisely dated payment entries to shepherds, butchers, monks, and many others. We can almost imagine Dioskoros, our accountant, taking a break on the eighth day of Tybi, rubbing his eyes and sending for the local doctor to ask for help writing a prescription for his headache before he picks up later with other entries for the same day.[96]

---

[89] MacCoull 1993, 28: for "pustular disease," the Coptic *pihe*.
[90] P.Lond. 5.1676.16 (*pephlegmenê podalgeia*); see page 141.
[91] P.Cair.Masp. 2.67141.II.r.20-29; cf. Maspero's trans. in the introduction; notes ad.loc; Fournet 1994, 320, note 22.
[92] P.Cair.Masp. 2 page 60.   [93] Eke et al. 2000.   [94] Totelin 2012, 137.
[95] Galen *de alim.* II.89B.   [96] Eighth day of Tybi: P.Cair.Masp. 2.67141.II.r.17.

Other hints of illness or disability hide in the papyri. At least three men from Aphrodito are named Cholos.⁹⁷ The word means "lame" in Greek, or halting, limping. Cholos may not be a name, but a nickname. In every single case, it appears in a private account, where the author needs no legal formality. It may be easier for his memory to make note of payments from "Enoch, son of the cripple" or from "the crippled potter" than to remember their real names. In another case, an account records payment from Ioannes, son of Kertos. Kertos may be a misspelling for the Greek *kurtos*, and the payment from Ioannes the hunchback's son.⁹⁸

Blindness is equally common. Apollos "the blind" appears in one of Dioskoros's theft records next to an entry recording "the rendering of the pledge."⁹⁹ Apollos may be promising to return whatever has to do with the son of Talous in the account's previous line. In his next appearance in the records, Dioskoros calls Apollos "his uncle," apparently referring to the informant Ieremias, son of Pathelpe the shepherd. It seems that the blind Apollos is indeed a shepherd promising the return of stolen property.¹⁰⁰

Apollos is not the town's only blind man. Dioskoros makes a small payment to the unnamed wife of Victor, another blind shepherd, on three separate occasions in the Egyptian months of Hathur, Choiak, and Tubi.¹⁰¹ On the 30th of the same Choiak, Dioskoros makes another small payment through the unnamed wife of a blind man named Soul.¹⁰²

Why? Is Dioskoros giving charity to the blind? And why does he do it through their wives? When the men are disabled, are they unable to come to him? Is it considered more appropriate or less embarrassing for their wives to seek charity than for the men themselves to do so? Dioskoros uses *polublepôn*, a grimly ironic euphemism, to describe all these men. Literally, these men "see many things" rather than nothing at all. He could call them *tuphlos*, a common enough classical word for blindness he lists in his own customized Greek dictionary and knows how to use in context.¹⁰³ Instead, he chooses another word he had put in his dictionary, one that is much more obscure.¹⁰⁴

---

⁹⁷ Ruffini 2011 *s.n.*   ⁹⁸ Ruffini 2011, Kertos 1.   ⁹⁹ Apollos 95; *P.Cair.Masp.* 2.67143.
¹⁰⁰ If Pathelpe 1 = Pathelpe 2 = the brother of Apollos 95, then Apollos 95's extended family includes both Ieremias 14 and Apollos 107 and his son Ieremias 24.
¹⁰¹ Biktor 174, assuming that *P.Cair.Masp.* 2.67141.2.r continues 1.v, that a reference to Choiak is lost somewhere in this continuation, and that the entries in 1.v.31, 2.r.6 and 2.r.19 are all to the same Biktor.
¹⁰² *P.Cair.Masp.* 2.67141.2.r.12.
¹⁰³ The word appears in *P.Cair.Masp.* 1.67020.11, which Dioskoros himself possibly wrote.
¹⁰⁴ Bell and Crum 1925, 193 with note at 211.

Maybe he is showing off, to himself. Or perhaps his word choice reveals a more general attitude toward the disabled, of unease, of discomfort, or – toward the blind specifically – of almost religious reverence. Alternatively, his word choice in these quiet and out of the way moments may show how hard it can be to look at the world through bilingual eyes. Dioskoros lists seven Greek adjectives for blindness in his dictionary, but can only find two ways to translate them into Egyptian.[105] In some languages, our bodies and their failings are less complicated than they are in others.

To my mind, this chapter more than most others in this book shows the gaps in our evidence. The fragility of life hides from us. We know little about the disabled and the sick and see them only when they need help from others. We know even less about the children, so many of whom never leave childhood. We do not know what sorrow feels like to any of those who live on after they die. We know only what needs to be put on paper.

More precisely, much of the evidence for marriage, divorce and death comes from legal texts. It is not always clear what this evidence means. In some situations it seems that imperial law has little reach in the distant provinces, and that civil courts in Egypt no longer work.[106] This "may in part be a result of Coptic disaffection with the Chalcedonian central government."[107] But it is easy to be skeptical of this view, since there is ample evidence of imperial legislation in Egypt.[108] This chapter is full of contemporary law, in some cases used very effectively.

This reveals another problem. Roman marriage is created by the "will of the parties and dissolved by the simple lack of it." Under these rules, divorce is "formless" and does not really need any documentation.[109] Marriage and divorce records are rare, which means those that we do have do not represent typical experiences. Most marriages will not end with women as unhappy as Eirene, bringing Makarios to court. This may mean that marriages begin and end much more easily, practically, when needed and without fuss.

We do not find evidence for love anywhere in Aphrodito's marriages. Besarion's marriage settlement calls him the "most beloved" or "most longed-for," but his parents are speaking, not his bride.[110] The one exception I can find is in Horouogchis's marriage contract with Scholastikia. Here, the groom tells Scholastikia that she "will altogether be home-

---

[105] Bell and Crum 1925, 192–193.   [106] For the historiography, see Keenan 2014.
[107] Bagnall 1987, 57.   [108] Beaucamp 2007, particularly 283–285.   [109] Urbanik 2014, 155.
[110] P.Michael. 42.B.7.

minded and accordingly will be husband-loving towards me, worthy in the things I set before you and prudent in your inclinations."[111]

But this is not love. It is a contractual condition, and one vague enough that it cannot be enforced. The eighteen gold pieces she would have to pay if she were not husband-loving are presumably the husband's bargaining chip if the marriage turns out badly and he wants a divorce. Here too, late antiquity is a world of people jostling for position, always trying to find a way to protect themselves.

---

[111] *P.Lond.* 5.1711.40–42 with *P.Cair.Masp.* 3.67310.r.18–19.

CHAPTER 9

Aphrodito's Women

Ama Rachel is a rare woman. Her name appears again and again in tax registers handling a range of landed estates. She appears in the 520s managing land belonging to the monastery of Apa Sourous, the monastery of Apa Zenobios, and the monastery of Smin, as well as land belonging to the heirs of men named Romanos and Hermeias.[1] It is not clear whether she manages this land in a personal or professional capacity, but her status as an Ama (literally "mother") is a clue. She may be the head of a women's monastery, managing land left to her monastery in private bequests or delegated by men's monasteries for the support of her women.

A "duplicate record of Maria's wine for the assessment of the 11th indiction," also labeled an "account of gifts of wine from Maria," says nothing about Maria herself, but hints at her business.[2] Each line in the account gives the cash value of a gift of wine, followed at the end by a calculation converting those gifts into a total amount of wine. By the end of the account, Maria has given away six and a third gold pieces' worth of wine, or 532 jugs. She may be in the wine business, or an estate owner giving away surplus. She does very well, if this is what she gives away in a single year.

Three of the first five gifts go to Aphrodito's cumin sellers, three of the four known in our records. Another gift goes to Apollos the baker. Two other gifts go to Pkouis the barber and his brother Isak. Maria's account gives no reason for her gifts. Maybe the barber and the baker work for her and receive payment in kind for their services. Perhaps the cumin goes into a sort of spiced wine, and Maria thanks the cumin sellers with a taste of their own product. We never see Maria's male relatives, and no one else is involved in the business but her.

Land managers such as Ama Rachel and businesswomen such as Maria are exceptional in Aphrodito's records. More common in the papyri are the

[1] Rachel 4. [2] *P.Cair.Masp.* 2.67146.

eugenestatai, the "most well-born" women. Most of these women appear only briefly, in tax or loan records. Aphrodito's fiscal register records three women named Mariam, Sophia, and Thaesia paying for the heirs of a man named Eulogios in AD 525/526.[3] They are probably sisters, Eulogios their father. Mariam, the "well-born" daughter of Eulogios, appears in the records ten years earlier, repaying a loan of five gold coins. She had borrowed the money from another woman, Tariste, but repays her son instead, as Tariste has died since the time of the loan.[4]

The well-born women Sibulla and Herais are their generation's representatives of the family's fortune in the 520s and 530s.[5] They are sisters, daughters of a former village tax contributor named Mousaios. Land they own is leased out to a father and son team, Victor and Psachos.[6] In both cases, someone else seems to be leasing the land for them. It is possible they are still minors, and Aphrodito's public treasury manages their property for them.[7]

Sophia, another of Aphrodito's well-born women, is a woman long absent from our story, Dioskoros's wife and the mother of his sons. As her status suggests, she comes from an important family in her own right.[8] Her paternal great-grandfather's name, Philantinoos, suggests some ancestral connection to Antinoopolis, the capital of southern Egypt. No one else from Aphrodito has that name.

Sophia's papers – found with her husband's – show the central role she plays in merging the business affairs of her father's family and her husband's.[9] Throughout the 550s, she makes tax payments on behalf of both Dioskoros and her grandfather, Kornelios. But her business connections are not just family: she also makes payments for the family of Pbekios, whom we do not know.[10] In the 580s, when her husband Dioskoros is dead, Sophia runs the family affairs on her own. She leases family land three separate times, to a tenant farmer, a monastery, and two shepherds.[11] These lease agreements all call Sophia a *suntelestria*, a tax contributor, marking her as one of the village's fiscal heavyweights. As far as we know, she is the first in her father's family to hold the position, which both her husband and father-in-law held thirty to fifty years before.

---

[3] Ruffini 2011, Stemma 6, with entries *s.n.*   [4] *P.Cair.Masp.* 3.67306.
[5] Sibulla 2 and Herais 1, as is Ioannes 67; see Ruffini 2011, Stemma 7, with discussion, page 201.
[6] Biktor 74 and Psachos 2.   [7] See the introduction to *P.Lond.* 5.1695.
[8] Fournet 2008a, 17–30 and Ruffini 2008b, 226–228.   [9] Sophia 13.
[10] As did Dioskoros: note the entry for Pbekios 2, speculating on a possible family relationship.
[11] Sophia 13, taking her name to be restored in *P.Cair.Masp.* 3.67325.r.IV.

It is not obvious whether the village headman Dioskoros or his well-born wife Sophia get the better of this marriage. Her father and grandfather obviously command considerable resources. Their connections to the powerful Count Ammonios strengthen Dioskoros's similar family ties. But the two families encounter something of a cultural gap between them. Apollos had obviously wanted the best education available for his son. He may have had a similar background himself. It seems unlikely that Sophia's father Ioannes had any such advantage. He can write well enough, but would fail spelling. When he and Apollos write the same seven-word sentence, Apollos is perfect, but Ioannes misspells nearly half the words.[12] As we will see, Sophia's own children probably receive a much better education than her father.

These are Aphrodito's well-born women. A comparable number of the well-born women named in the town's papyri are in fact from somewhere else, in most cases from the big city. A well-born woman named Maria agrees to guarantee a loan of six gold pieces as part of a wedding contract between two others from Antinoopolis.[13] While her husband has to sign the agreement for her, she acts on her own initiative, putting forward her own money.

Maria may be the sister of another interesting woman, Asteria. We meet Asteria in a support agreement signed by her five sons.[14] They agree to provide her annual income from land she has inherited from her dead husband. The agreement makes clear that she is to receive this payment even if she is no longer mentally competent, while a separate payment for room rent is assigned to Asteria's sister Maria.[15]

In a previous chapter, we met Rachel, a woman engaged to marry Besarion in AD 566.[16] Her marriage settlement entitles her to thirty gold pieces if the marriage to Besarion fails. This is real money, proportionate to her status, since the marriage settlement addresses her as well-born. The marriage contract for a woman from Antinoopolis named Scholastikia calls her well-born as well.[17] Another woman from Antinoopolis – her name may be Theodora – is also called well-born in her marriage contract.[18] That contract acknowledges a debt to her of six gold pieces.

---

[12] Compare Apollos in *P.Cair.Masp.* 3.67300 to Ioannes in *P.Lond.* 5.1687, misspelling three of the six extant words, not four, correcting Ruffini 2008b, 227.
[13] Maria 31; *P.Lond.* 5.1711.77.   [14] *P.Cair.Masp.* 3.67314; MacCoull 1988, 35–36.
[15] *P.Cair.Masp.* 3.67314.2.10–12.   [16] *P.Michael.* 42; see page 132.   [17] *P.Lond.* 5.1711.37.
[18] *SB* 22.15633: for *eugeneiai*, Kuehn 1993, "Your Grace." See also Ruffini 2011, Theodora 1.

Other well-born women do not come into focus as clearly as these previous examples. Athanasia, a Lykopolite woman staying in Antinoopolis, enlists Dioskoros to help her in an inheritance dispute with her uncle, Theodoros.[19] Eudoxia, another woman Dioskoros knows from his time in Antinoopolis, is the co-owner of a vineyard.[20] Heraïs is a beneficiary in a will drafted by her grandson, who has property in three different parts of Egypt.[21] A well-born woman named Thekla appears in a legal settlement the terms of which are lost.[22] We know little about these women. We can only assume, from the context, that they are financially well-off, or at the very least, that they come from well-off families.

The evidence does not say what makes one well-born. There is no formal process granting a right to use the adjective. Note how many of these well-born women appear in marriage contracts, wills, and settlements. On the one hand, calling the bride-to-be well-born may be a generic polite formality in wedding contracts and in other formal settings. On the other hand, the marriage contracts show that these women are able to command significant sums of money on their wedding days. They are presumably prominent and the right to use the adjective may be something everyone knows.

In most cases we know nothing about their parents except bare names. Nothing indicates that these women have fathers who are or were high-ranking officeholders. On the contrary, their fathers, when known, tend to be no more than local officials: village headmen and tax contributors.[23] The documents themselves have no reason to draw much attention to this fact, and everyone involved may know it or take it for granted.

If these women are part of a well-born nobility of sorts, whatever offices conferred on that nobility in the past are unmentioned in the records, and presumably are no longer really important. What matters to these women and to the people dealing with them now are the sums of money at stake in their marriages, their wills, and their inheritances: their status is not really political, but economic.

In some cases, rich and influential women appear in the records with no explanation. We know very little, for example, about Maria of Antinoopolis.[24] She is the daughter of a lawyer named Kuriakos and granddaughter of an *illoustrios* named Theodosios. Whether her wealth comes from them or somewhere else, she can afford to lend just under

---

[19] Athanasia 4.   [20] Eudoxia 1.   [21] Heraïs 7.   [22] Thekla 13.
[23] Eirene 1 is the daughter of a *suntelestês*; Mariam 2 is the daughter of a *prôtokômêtês*; Rachel 17 is herself a *suntelestês* (sic, ed.); Sophia 13 is the daughter of a *ktêtôr* and a *suntelestria*.
[24] Maria 37; *P.Cair.Masp.* 3.67309.

fifteen gold pieces at interest to Ioannes, a local government official described as a "calculator."[25]

When Aphrodito and its neighboring village of Phthla find themselves pitted in a legal struggle over taxation and land rights, a man named Kuros is one of the central characters. As the *boêthos* or assistant for Phthla, he is crucial to the tax collecting apparatus of his little village. But in one text, his unnamed wife makes an unexpected appearance.[26] She, not her husband, is approaching government authorities in Antinoopolis and she, not her husband, is to receive receipts for Phthla's payment for the thirteenth indiction. Maybe she acts for her village because her husband is absent and the family must act for him. Or perhaps she has some power in her own right that we cannot yet understand. This is just a brief glimpse, nothing more.

Several of these examples are from Antinoopolis or from Aphrodito's neighbors. However, Aphrodito has a female elite of its own as well. The town's fiscal records highlight this elite's small size: "At Aphrodito, 34 women (or 14.7 percent of the individual taxpayers) pay 10.9 percent of the total taxes and 11.6 percent of the taxes paid by individuals." In Aphrodito land registered in the region's urban accounts, "7 women (or 13.7 percent of the individual taxpayers) own 11.9 percent of the land."[27]

These women – a few dozen at most – probably form a clear and visible group in Aphrodito. In a town of a few thousand, all of these women are probably known by sight, by name, by reputation. They might expect deference in the streets, in the markets, in the churches. But they are exceptional, and make up only about 10 percent of the women in the surviving evidence. Most women in Aphrodito are powerless and impoverished by comparison.

Procla and her sister Martha in Antinoopolis show the difficulties facing women in servile manual labor.[28] We hear their story in 569, but their hardship began with their father, Menas. In Martha's words, "My father having fallen into the utmost poverty," he then "made a pledge of my orphan sister, junior to myself, called Procla, to the most illustrious lord Nonnus for one solidus of gold in keeping with the deed of pledge made by him at the time to the most illustrious gentleman." In short, Menas has a debt he cannot pay, and offers his daughter's labor in exchange.[29]

---

[25] Ioannes 230 (*psêphistês*). Vanderheyden 2012, 798: "professeur de calcul."
[26] Vanderheyden 2012, 797; see page 167.   [27] Bagnall 2008, 185.
[28] P.Coll.Youtie 2.92 = P.Cair.Masp. 1.67023 + P.Fitzhugh; trans. slightly altered from Barns 1976, 593–594.
[29] For Menas, see page 106.

The arrangement is difficult for Procla, "who was being overworked" by Nonnus. After their father Menas dies, Martha writes that she "managed to earn half of the aforesaid one solidus by [her] manual labor and [has] paid it to the said gentleman Nonnus with the intent of redeeming [her] sister." But her own manual labor only goes so far, and she cannot raise the rest of the sum.

She turns to a third party, a man named Helladios who works as a secretary on the staff of the local duke. She writes, "I have entreated you to advance the remainder as a loan for the redemption of this same orphan sister." Helladios, "motivated" as he has been "by Godly charity," agrees. This effectively cancels the debt to Nonnus. But now, Martha owes Helladios, and has to offer Procla to him instead, "on condition of her residing in your household, performing all servile offices and requirements of yours ... until the satisfaction of the debt."

This may seem to be structural oppression of the poor. It may seem to be commodification of labor driven by the demand for gold coin. This ignores everything we do not know about the story, and ignores how the players themselves see things. We do not know how Menas got into debt in the first place. Nor do we know anything about Nonnus and Helladios. If we believe Martha, her own hard work shows her love – or at least her sense of responsibility – for her younger sister, who is only fifteen years old. But it also shows her control over the situation. Her family is essentially shopping for a patron. Her father, Menas, chose poorly, and Nonnus works Procla too hard. Martha is considering her options, asking herself whom in Antinoopolis she knows, and then approaches an employee of the duke's own staff. In the marketplace of patronage, Nonnus is the loser and Helladios the winner. Even the poorest find flexibility and power through their face-to-face connections.

In some cases, pledged labor can seem close to slavery. This gray area is probably at the heart of Aphrodito's so-called Cinderella story, the marriage of Martha, daughter of Rebekka. The story survives in two different texts, which combine to give the testimony of an anonymous man who hopes to be Martha's husband.[30] The testimony starts with a curious but legally accurate claim, that "neither time nor error can diminish freedom." The anonymous speaker introduces Jacob and his wife Sophia, "who came from the Antaiopolite and spent no little time with my father and furnished him care." The speaker's father is dead now, but the speaker insists

---

[30] *SB* 18.13274; translations condense those in MacCoull 1992a, 381–382.

that he had "never found any indication of any kind whatever, either from my father or anyone else, that Jacob and Sophia were slaves."

At this point, the speaker gives a complicated summary of Jacob's family history.[31] Jacob and Sophia had three daughters named Leah, Rachel, and Rebecca. Jacob's first daughter Leah had two children, a son named Mark and a daughter named Sophia. Sophia in turn had three sons and other children whose names we never learn. Jacob's second daughter Rachel became a nun. Jacob's third daughter Rebecca had two daughters, Eulogia and Martha. Eulogia became a nun as well.

Her sister Martha is the focus of the story. The anonymous speaker knows all four generations of this family because Jacob and Sophia served or cared for his father. But after his father dies, their granddaughter Martha is still living in his house. The arrangement is confusing, at least to Martha. The speaker notes that he has "heard from her even at the present time that she has been asked concerning some of the capital paid to her, answering 'I am not free.'"

The speaker – whoever he is – sees things differently. He writes that he has written the surviving text "by which I understand and know that Martha is not in any way a slave nor born of a slave." Further, he says, "I enjoin that she is already in a position to perform the actions of free people and to do what befits free people." Obviously, there would be no need for such a statement if the speaker did not anticipate objections:

> If, as might happen, anyone should dare to say that she is a slave, let her by the present written agreement be free for the future, not harassed by anyone, not even by my most learned and beloved heir, who by my command and wish has agreed to this written agreement.

This is basically an emancipation proclamation, setting Martha free from slavery.[32] But the speaker's heir is the real heart of the problem.

This strange insistence on Martha's free status is really a love story.[33] The speaker wants to clear the good name of the woman he plans to marry. At the same time, he claims that Martha already has property of her own and hopes that "heaven protect and give long life to my most learned son and heir Victor." Both points are meant as reassurance for his son: the speaker will take a new wife, but this will not threaten his son's inheritance.

The very need for this text shows how marginal Martha is. She is not alone. Her cousin Sophia – the only other woman still alive who did not

---

[31] Ruffini 2011, Stemma 5.
[32] MacCoull 1992a, 383 for references to Taubenschlag's work on these texts.
[33] MacCoull 1992a, 387.

become a nun – has problems of her own. The anonymous speaker makes a passing reference, never fully explained, to "those who drag her (Sophia) into slavery together with her children," and hopes that they "shall see what they find before the fearsome judgement-seat of the All-Powerful."

Jacob and Sophia's decision to serve the speaker's father obviously damages the family's reputation. The author of the text seems to have a fairly sophisticated grasp of current legal vocabulary. He describes Sophia's stay in his father's home with a term similar to that describing a free person entering a contractual provision to remain and provide work.[34] The very care – *therapeia* – Jacob and Sophia provide is similar to a word – *therapaina* – for a handmaiden or female slave. They exist in a gray area, it seems, between enslaved and free, in which the distinction is less a matter of law than a matter for the beholder.

We are struck throughout the speaker's description of this family by the almost total absence of men. We see three generations of descendants without explicit reference to marriages. With the exception of Jacob himself, not a single father appears by name.[35] We may have cause and effect here: the absence of men as husbands and fathers compounds Sophia and Martha's already vague legal status.

Remember Eirene's complaint in the previous chapter, concerning a man who promised to marry but now mocks her.[36] Leah, Rebecca, and Sophia may themselves have met such men, who make them similar promises, or take advantage of their ambiguous legal status, or are themselves in similar states, in no position to marry or provide material support. This Cinderella story shows the plight of marginal women in late antiquity.[37] These women need privileged men to assert their freedom for them when their own voices are not enough to stop the whispers against them.

Martha's Cinderella story inadvertently provides an interesting statistic. Ten descendants of Jacob and Sophia appear by name: six of them are women. Of those six, two become nuns, one out of three in the first generation and one out of three in the next. These figures may be high: this is a poor marginalized family, and this could be what drives these women into religious orders. Even so, we learn something from the story.

Women with religious vocations are not rare in Aphrodito. In some sectors of society they are going to be statistically common. Think back to

---

[34] MacCoull 1992a, 384–385: *paramenousa* and *paramonê*. [35] MacCoull 1992a, 386.
[36] See page 138.
[37] Compare the high percentage of fatherless women in the Kysis *nekrotaphoi* archive; see Bagnall et al. 2015, 176. Women without men in their lives may be hiding in plain sight in much of our evidence.

Ama Rachel in the 520s, when she manages monastic land and probably runs a female monastery of her own. She probably comes to this position through her own high status. Most likely she oversees women much less like her, and much more like Rachel and Eulogia, nuns whose own relatives are barely free. Knowing so little about these women is yet another reminder of how much is lost, even in the midst of so much information about this community.

Some widows do better than others. We have already met Maria, the widow who stars in the famous Aphrodito murder mystery, and Sophia, when she accuses Senouthes of murdering her second husband.[38] These are extreme cases. Aphrodito has other widows, but they are invisible. In most cases, Aphrodito's women probably do not appear in the town's record because they have nothing worth litigating, nothing worth buying or renting, and nothing that needs a papyrus to record.

The Aphrodito papyri call only one woman in town a widow, and that is Sophia, Dioskoros's own wife.[39] As so often with these records, other examples ended up in the Aphrodito archives by connection with Dioskoros. A widow named Maria, not from Aphrodito but from the Theodosiopolite village of Sabbis, complains that the leading men of her village want to impose some public agricultural service on her, but she insists that she is exempt.[40]

In a separate case from the early 630s, another woman, Thaumastê, has outlived two husbands and a son named Paul.[41] Her first husband Constantine had left her a share of a place called Byllê Field, just west of the town. This field includes an old well, a watchman's hut, a tower, a house, a livestock pen, palm and fruit trees, and adjoining land. Shenoute's famous White Monastery held land in the same place, which Thaumastê has bought. She and her daughter Anastasia now cede both pieces of land to two brothers named Kollouthos and Markos.

Kollouthos and Markos then cede to Thaumastê another piece of property in the same area west of the town. This land had once belonged to Thaumastê's father, Paul. He had donated the land to the White Monastery, who had in turn sold it to the locals, Kollouthos and Markos. In short, Thaumastê gives up some of her marital inheritance as a way of reclaiming some of her ancestral property. And there are tax consequences as well: "We are ready, we, Thaumastê and Anastasia her

---

[38] See page 149. [39] If Sophia 13 is to be restored in *P.Cair.Masp.* 3.67325.r.IV; see page 150.
[40] *P.Cair.Masp.* 1.67006.r, which Drescher 1944, 93, note 2 cites along with *P.Oxy.* 6.899.
[41] The following paragraphs summarize MacCoull 2009, 11–17. Translations are hers.

daughter to act as contributors with regard to the contributorship of the sown-land that we gave."

These are women acting alone, under their own power and without male supervision, but this brief moment is deceiving. In her second marriage, Thaumastê has no legal power. Her husband Jacob renovates and sells her property as he sees fit.[42] The one document from this marriage is damaged on the right margin, so it is not clear what is going on. Jacob sells property that he describes in considerable detail. Some of that property – possibly where he sets up a water source and a wine press – belonged to Constantine, Thaumastê's first husband, and must have come to Jacob through her. But the sale is in his name, with no hint of Thaumastê being involved.

Kollouthos and Markos, who swap plots with Thaumastê, also do business with another widow, a woman named Taham.[43] In 640 she sells them land that she has inherited from her dead husband, another Markos, land he had bought from someone else. As with Thaumastê, Taham is careful to note who has the tax liability: "as far as the old tax is concerned, I have paid it in full legally." But, she tells Kollouthos and Markos, "you complete the contribution of the half-portion . . . (complete with) tax in money and transport tax."

A third widow, a woman named Tsyra, sells something to Kollouthos. She sells "that which belongs to my son David, namely the fifth portion of my husband's wagon, with its iron wheels and all its wood interior and its reclining bench."[44] We do not know what it means to sell a fifth of a wagon, or why Tsyra is acting in her son's name. David may be under age. But the common factor in all these stories is Kollouthos himself. Three times he buys or trades for property from widows. This is a reminder of how little we really know about these women. Perhaps they are empowered, making these transactions without a husband's intervention. Or maybe they are exploited by Kollouthos, an entrepreneur in his own right, who acquires land and property from widows without other ways to support themselves. Too much is missing from the picture.

Aphrodito papyri record over 5,000 men and women from that town, but the vast majority of the total are men. By my count – and it is a very rough count – fewer than one person in ten in the Aphrodito papyri is

---

[42] MacCoull 2009, 19–20.
[43] MacCoull 2009, 21–23. Kollouthos 66 and Markos 4, now badly out of date, with the publication in MacCoull 2009 of *P.Vat.Copti Doresse* 1, 2 and 5. (Preparation for Ruffini 2011 overlooked an earlier publication of the first of these texts.)
[44] Slightly altering the trans. in MacCoull 2009, 27.

a woman. In other words, a man from Aphrodito is more than ten times more likely to find his way into writing than a woman. Thousands of Aphrodito's women are missing from our records. Many of the women we know best from the Aphrodito papyri are from the big city, their stories surviving only because Dioskoros takes his papers with him when he goes back home. His career in Antinoopolis, the capital of southern Egypt, is full of legal work on marriage and divorce, which concerns him much less when he is back home looking after the family business.

Some clues help us to find the town women lost in the documentary record's gender gap. Aphrodito hides its women in different ways. Women are less likely to appear in the written record, and when they do appear in it, they are more likely to be anonymous. In formal legal texts, everyone must have a name, but in private documents, in accounts kept for managing one's own business, precision matters less. In Aphrodito's private accounts, traces of its women become faint.

The accounts for Dioskoros's family estates show him referring to women in a number of ways.[45] He mentions "the sister Pelias" or simply "Pelias" six times. He mentions "the sister Rachel" or "my sister Rachel" five times and "the mother Rebekka" three times. He knows these women well, and they need no better label. He names other women more precisely, such as "Maria from Telbonth," who appears twice, or "Maria, Palol's wife" and "Kura, Iosephios's wife," who each appear once.

However, among these women are others with no names. He mentions "Victor's wife" four times, "Ptapar's wife" once, "Apa Abraam's wife" once, "blind Soul's wife" once, and "Ieremias's daughter" once. In short, almost as many women are anonymous in Dioskoros's accounts as those he records by name. Either he does not know their names, or he finds it easier to think of them as extensions of their husbands or fathers. Nor is Dioskoros simply using the names of owners who might matter for tax registration purposes. If this were the case, some anonymous sons or brothers would appear in his accounts as well, but this simply never happens. Dioskoros's anonymous women make an interesting contrast to the widows we have just met. If Ptapar and blind Soul die, Dioskoros may have to learn their widows' names: alone, without husbands, there will be no other way to identify them.

We have spoken of Aphrodito's women, but not about what it means to be a woman in Aphrodito. A specialist in gender in late antique Egypt wrote that:

---

[45] P.Cair.Masp. 2.67141.

> The extensive archive of sixth-century poet and lawyer Dioskoros of Aphrodite, for example, seems to be an ideal area for the investigation of gender. These papers allow us to investigate gender in private and public documents, as well as in the effusions of the only poet of antiquity from whom we have autograph manuscripts. Dioskoros' documentary activities took place in a largely male world, but one in which women appear in a number of economic and social guises, while his poetry draws on earlier classical imagery for its understandings of gender roles and relations.[46]

This call to investigate gender in Aphrodito raises interesting questions. So far this chapter has shown women almost exclusively in an economic context. But several other parts of the Aphrodito papyri also show how that town imagines its women.

The first issue we should examine is that of women's names. Comparisons show what we can learn here. Medieval Nubian women – not too far from late antique Egypt in time and space – had a more narrow range of naming options available to them than their male counterparts.[47] Their names were disproportionately variations of Mary, Elisabeth, and Anna. In short, their parents were choosing religious role models for their daughters, but had a smaller list of options than they did for their sons.

Aphrodito shows the same phenomenon at work in Byzantine Egypt. Treating Maria and Mariam as versions of the same name, the Aphrodito papyri record fifty-eight women with the name of the Virgin Mary, the most common female name, compared to 250 men named Ioannes, the most common male name. This occurs in a town where the surviving evidence records more than ten men for every woman. If we knew as many of Aphrodito's women by name as we know men, nearly 600 would be named Maria or something similar. By comparison, Aphrodito's men receive the most popular male name less than half as often.

In other words, when parents in this town imagine their daughters, they are more than twice as likely to imagine them as hundreds of other families have, as a version of the Virgin Mary. Aphrodito's families choose names for their children with one eye on gender roles. Men have more options available to them in life, and so they have more names available to them as well. Women have fewer options, fewer appropriate gender roles, and only one woman who can stand as the perfect role model.

After female names, the second place we should look is Aphrodito's literature. Dioskoros has left five *epithalamia* – poems in praise of a bride and bridegroom – and one possible fragment from a sixth.[48] These poems

---

[46] Wilfong 2007, 319.   [47] Ruffini 2012, 238–239.   [48] *P.Aphrod.Lit.* 4.32–37.

date from the late 560s or early 570s, his period away from Aphrodito. In this group, only one poem is addressed to the bride, a woman named Patrikia, the rest to the groom. Indeed, Patrikia is the only woman addressed in any of Dioskoros's poems. We will save that one poem to the bride Patrikia for later. Dioskoros's other *epithalamia* provide an interesting glimpse into how he imagines the provincial elite think about their women.

He consistently uses mythological imagery, expecting his listeners to catch the references. The poem in honor of the marriage of Kallinikos compares his bride Theophile to Ariadne and Helen of Troy.[49] The comparison to Helen is awkward, at best: in this scenario, Kallinikos is Menelaus and Theophile a Helen "who will not leave you."[50] The poem in honor of the marriage of Mathaios also compares his bride to Ariadne, Leda, Europa, and Daphne, and praises her "nobility of descent," saying that she is "ripe as a honeycomb" or, in the words of another translator, "firm as a young grape."[51] The poem in honor of the marriage of Isakios compares the bride to Aglaia, the goddess of beauty.[52]

The comparisons to Ariadne and Aglaia are flattering enough, but the other analogies seem strange today. Zeus seduces Leda only by disguising himself as a swan. Zeus kidnaps Europa while disguised as a bull, rapes her, and abandons her. Apollo pursues Daphne, who avoids a similar fate by transforming into a laurel. These comparisons say nothing about how the average villager views women: the classical allusions would be meaningless to most people in Aphrodito. However, they suggest that the provincial elite – to whom Dioskoros addresses these poems – see women as works of nature to be chased, seduced and – if necessary – forced into love. Dioskoros must know his audience, or he would be foolish to write so many poems with such consistent themes.

The exception among these marriage poems is written for "the most glorious Patrikia," marrying an otherwise unknown man named Paulos. We know Patrikia from elsewhere, a contract for tax collection in the nearby village of Phthla. This contract is undated, but probably drawn up in the early 550s.[53] An obscure pun in Dioskoros's poem for her suggests

---

[49] *P.Aphrod.Lit.* 4.32.A.4 and 17 (the "Tyndaride"). [50] MacCoull 1988, 89.

[51] Compare MacCoull 1988, 108 with Fournet 1999, 435. The divergent translations highlight the curiosity of the term *omphakoentos*, from *omphax* ("unripe grape") which metaphorically means "young girl not yet ripe for marriage," hardly an appropriate description to our eyes.

[52] *P.Aphrod.Lit.* 4.34 with Fournet 1999, 630.

[53] *P.Lond.* 5.1660, which Bell dated to c. 553 because of the appearance in it of Ioulianos 2 and Menas 13, who also appear together in the precisely dated *P.Lond.* 5.1661, from that year. Ioulianos is known from texts dating from 547 to 553, and one from 559/560.

that Patrikia is originally from Aphrodito.⁵⁴ She is probably a large landholder in the Antaiopolite nome, and an important person in her own right.⁵⁵ In that tax-collecting contract, she is one of the local pagarchs, the officials ultimately responsible for regional tax collection. She may have held the office only by succession after her father's death, but this assumes too much about the role of women to be certain.⁵⁶ In any case, the office gives her real power and prestige.

Dioskoros's poem begins by praising Patrikia's virtues, claiming they are so great that her mother must have been loved by Phaethon, son of the sun god Apollo. (We may guess that Patrikia's real father was indeed no longer alive, or at any rate, not around to hear this poem!) Her beauty is striking, comparable to that of Aphrodite herself. Her ancestors bring distinction to the marriage, and she is *noarôteran* than the Graces themselves. But this word can mean many things: more beautiful, wiser, or younger. All three suggestions appear in modern translations.⁵⁷ The confusion, based on Dioskoros's use of an unknown word, is frustrating: praising a woman for her beauty or her brains makes quite a difference.

He could not really claim her to be younger than the Graces, with a straight face. Patrikia marries in 566 or 567, most likely ten to fifteen years after she appears in charge of regional tax collection. She either holds the office of pagarch at an extremely young age – early childhood – or marries Paulos later in life than we might reasonably expect. (In earlier periods of Roman Egypt, three-fifths of women were married by the age of twenty.⁵⁸) This may be her second marriage. Or perhaps her status as "most glorious" and the accompanying prestige empower her, letting her marry when and whom she chooses.

However, this is purely speculation. We can be more certain about Patrikia's position in relation to Dioskoros. When she appears as pagarch in the tax-collection contract from the early 550s, she delegates her position to Menas and serves in office at the same time as Ioulianos. This is ominous company: Ioulianos had tried many times to place Aphrodito under his own authority as tax collector, and had, after Dioskoros's father had died, seized some of his cousins' property. Menas had been worse, reportedly guilty of any number of transgressions against Dioskoros, his friends, and family.

---

[54] Rowlandson 1998, 154, note 2.   [55] Fournet 1999, 634.   [56] *P.Lond.* 5.1660 introduction.
[57] *P.Aphrod.Lit.* 4.35.15 note, with "more skilful" appearing in Rowlandson 1998, 154.
[58] Bagnall and Frier 1994, 113.

Dioskoros is not interested in Patrikia's marriage, or in her unknown husband Paulos. Her marriage is merely an opportunity: she interests him because she is powerful, because she keeps company with people who threaten him. Her virtues, her beauty, her wisdom are all gates through which Dioskoros can enter in search of leverage, of patronage, of protection. When Dioskoros looks up at the social classes above him, what he sees is similar to what he sees when he looks up at the heavens: many powerful and holy men ready to intercede for him, but only one powerful woman in a position to do so, whether it is Mary in heaven or the most glorious Patrikia here on earth.

CHAPTER 10

Big Men and Strangers

At some point in the sixth century, a provincial record keeper (*kommentarêsios*) most likely working for the duke of the Thebaid gives Aphrodito's headmen – three men named Enoch, Papnouthis, and Phoibammon – a guarantee of travel protection: "Holding a document from me, find yourselves unharmed and without loss from all people and all business that may befall you."[1] This safe passage also covers Aphrodito's shepherds and shepherd guild heads. Taking the sheep to market may leave them exposed, threatened by thieves and bandits. Or some of them may have warrants out for their arrest, and someone in the duke's office needs them on more important business. In short, they need the protection of a powerful patron.

This reminds us that Aphrodito is a "fluid society," a potentially "threatening" place "with both the powerful and the weak capable of using violence."[2] The people of Aphrodito have strong economic ties to more than one person. In this "kaleidoscope of economic relationships, even if reinforced by violence or menace, stable dominance was almost impossible."[3] This society works through political openness: "peasants could use the patronage system in the same way that village leaders could, using influential outsiders" such as Ammonios "to balance out the power of the local elite."[4]

That local elite also needs and benefits from higher powers and protection. Ammonios protects Dioskoros from certain required payments, and mediates transitions of power among Aphrodito headmen.[5] When Ammonios exits the scene in the late 540s, his son Theodosios is not as supportive of Aphrodito's cause.[6] Two decades follow in which Aphrodito struggles to retain its autonomy and constantly finds itself in tax

---

[1] *P.Cair.Masp.* 1.67090.3–4.   [2] Wickham 2005, 415.   [3] Wickham 2005, 416.
[4] Wickham 2005, 416.   [5] See page 47, and Ammonios 1(b), an uncertain identification.
[6] Theodosios 16, following the identification in Zuckerman 2004b, 77.

difficulties. Without a local patron, Dioskoros and his town look to the dukes in Antinoopolis and imperial officials in Constantinople for their support.

In 567, Aphrodito sends a petition to Athanasios, the duke of the Thebaid. Athanasios is well known, a man of many names and titles. One papyrus calls him Flavius Marianos Michaelios Gabrielios Sergios Bachos Narses Konon Anastasios Domninos Theodoros Kallinikos, the most glorious, the commander, the former consul, and most noble-statured patrician. He receives several petitions and poems from Dioskoros over the years, some on behalf of Aphrodito and himself, some on behalf of other people in other towns, and some with no goal but praising the duke's magnificence.[7]

The last of these starts with a striking image, comparing Athanasios to Jesus.[8] Dioskoros praises the "justice and just dealing" of Athanasios, whom "we have long expected as the dead in Hades once awaited the coming of the Christ, the everlasting God." The petition is long and covers many complaints, but the first major issue is a land seizure. Menas, the pagarch of Antaiopolis, the regional capital, bestows

> on the Assistant of the village of Phthla and on its shepherds free of rent and taxes, to appropriate to themselves, [Dioskoros's] acres, which they enjoy without rent and taxes, leaving to him, to his utter destruction, the tax quota on them, assigned to his charge.

Put more simply, the local tax collector has taken his land and given it to someone else, but still expects him to foot the bill.

In another petition to a later duke, the complaint is once again about taxes.[9] The petitioners from Aphrodito write:

> Our land is sandy and dry ... Owing to the unfruitfulness of our lands, which are of poor quality, we were formerly assessed, along with all the landowners of the most unhappy pagarchy of Antaiopolis, at only two carats per aroura [roughly two-thirds of an acre] of arable land and eight carats for vineyards.

They remind the new duke of the generosity of his predecessor:

> When the all-honored patrician Athanasios learned of our great straits and poverty, how that in the winter we live on vegetables instead of bread food and nothing is left over to us and our children from our holdings for our

---

[7] See Palme 2014 for the most recent discussion of Dioskoros's petitions to Athanasios against Menas.
[8] *P.Cair.Masp.* 1.67002 with trans. by Bell 1944, 33; compare MacCoull 1988, 26–27.
[9] *P.Lond.* 5.1674 with trans. adapted from commentary to ed. princ. and Bell 1944, 23.

maintenance (for the village is composed of small holders) he had compassion on us.

Some of this is plausible and some of it is not. The tax rates are probably correct: it would be too brazen to lie about something so easily verified. But it seems unlikely that the village lands are really so bad. The late Roman Empire taxed land at rates based on its perceived quality.[10] Aphrodito would not be assessed at the same rate as the rest of the region if its land is so bad, unless the entire Antaiopolite nome has nothing but sandy and dry land.

Ultimately, the facts do not matter: this is not a land survey, but an emotional appeal. The real complaint concerns the later tax hikes by the pagarchs Ioulianos and Menas, which we saw in an earlier chapter.[11] "Our lives, which were honorably and freely spent, were dragged under the yoke of the pagarchy." However, bigger men come to the rescue: the emperor "has graciously granted your supreme humanity as a gift to the all-miserable Thebaid to rule over it."

The petition to Athanasios in 567 highlights a subtle feature of the late antique world. Aphrodito can be dangerous, but outsiders can be more so. At home, you know who your friends are and where to find them. Away from home, almost anyone can be an enemy. The pattern repeats itself several times: contact between villagers and the outside world leads to violence at the hands of local big men – invariably as part of an attempt to collect taxes or fees of some kind – and the only solution is to turn to even bigger men for help.

We see this first when travelers from Aphrodito visit Thynis for the annual cattle market.[12] The pagarch Menas orders them to be arrested and their animals confiscated. They spend the next ten months moving from jail to jail, in Thynis, Antinoopolis, and Antaiopolis. They are insulted, tortured, and charged several hundred gold pieces. When they are finally freed, they have to buy back their own animals at auction. If Dioskoros is telling the story honestly, this is part of a much larger attempt by Menas to collect over 800 gold coins from the village tax on arable land.[13]

A half dozen of the Aphrodito papyri deal with tense relations between Aphrodito and the shepherds of nearby Phthla.[14] We have just seen one of these papyri, a petition in which Dioskoros complains that the pagarch

---

[10] For late Roman taxation, see page 43 with note 3.   [11] See page 83.
[12] *P.Cair.Masp.* 1.67002.II; see Bell 1944, 34, Keenan 2008, 174–177 and Keenan 2007, 238.
[13] Keenan 2008, 176, following Zuckerman 2004a, 213–214.
[14] Vanderheyden 2012, 795: "un sous-dossier."

Menas has given some of his land to the shepherds of Phthla essentially free of charge. Earlier in this book, we saw another one of these papyri, in which Menas arrests Dioskoros's son and pillages his brother-in-law's house.[15]

Other records fill in the story. In a poem he writes after the petition, in the summer of 567, Dioskoros begs the duke to, "protect me from the violence of Menas, a carnivore, cruel, a great plunderer."[16] In the spring of 568, he writes another poem, over ninety lines long, to the next duke. He starts with some flattery: "Oh descendant of a truly divine race, without contest from a race of gold!"[17] The flattery goes on rather long for modern tastes, more than half the poem, before Dioskoros gets down to business. The "harmful tax collectors" are "defiling married women." He – Dioskoros probably means Menas – "threw them to the ground, pummeling them with kicks ... abusing wives." Dioskoros has made claims of sexual violence before, and then as now, they are too vague to be completely credible.[18]

But they are a prequel to the real pain: "He has taken five carats under the pretext of tax collection. He has added a new and enormous tax to the books. Not receiving the gold, he appropriated wheat from people who do not have anything to eat." The whole story is unclear, but the main complaint may come down to nothing more than Menas doing his job. We do not know how people learn of new taxes, or how they can verify tax-collector claims. Here, when Dioskoros faces a new tax, he simply refuses to believe it.

Most of these texts tell the story from Aphrodito's point of view. Only one text tells part of the story from a more neutral, third-party point of view.[19] Ioannes, an assistant at the public accounts office in Antinoopolis, writes to the shepherds of Phthla in 566.[20] The text is fragmentary, but Ioannes is clearly complaining: the shepherds of Phthla have not paid the full tax assessment that they are supposed to, and they have damaged the fields. Here, we see striking confirmation from an outside observer that Dioskoros's complaints against shepherds are legitimate.

The tensions between Aphrodito and Phthla are the natural push and pull between any town and one of its economic satellites. But the violence

---

[15] See pages 34 and 47.
[16] *P.Aphrod.Lit.* 4.3 with trans.; see note on dating in Fournet 1999, 472. For *ômophagos*, Dijkstra 2004 prefers "cannibal."
[17] *P.Aphrod.Lit.* 4.11, following the editor's translation.   [18] See page 37.
[19] Vanderheyden 2012, 795. Note also the fragmentary mention in *P.Flor.* 3.296 of tax transfers to Phthla.
[20] Ruffini 2011's Anonymous 124 shown to be Ioannes 230 by Vanderheyden 2012, 796–797.

also has a broader context in the ancient world. Other sources show that resource competition between neighbors is perfectly natural. Palladius, a fourth- and fifth-century Christian author from Galatia in Asia Minor, wrote a work called the Lausiac History, recording a series of biographical anecdotes about the monks of Egypt and Palestine. One story involves the life of Piamoun, a pious virgin with the gift of prophecy. Her prophetic gift revealed itself during an episode of village-on-village violence:

> It happened once in Egypt during the overflow (of the Nile) that one village attacked another. For they fight over the distribution of the water, so that murders and woundings ensue. Well, a stronger village attacked her village, and men came in a crowd with spears and clubs to destroy her village.[21]

An angel appeared to her, revealing the attack, which her prayers were able to prevent. However, divine intervention is not really the point of this story. The main challenge for Piamoun's village and those nearby is resource distribution: how to ensure that their lands have enough water, and thus how to ensure that they grow enough crops to feed their people and pay their taxes. This is always worth violence if you are close enough to the brink.

Documentary evidence for tension between villages survives as well. Farther north in Egypt, in the Fayum, the leading villagers of Karanis swore an oath in AD 439 that nobody in the village would steal water from one of the neighboring villages.[22] This is going far afield, but for a good reason: Aphrodito's local problems are not unique. Conflict over resources can boil over into theft and violence anywhere in the ancient world. When this happens, the natural response is for the villages involved to look for a protecting patron, whether it is one like the patrician Athanasios or the pious virgin Piamoun.

Indeed, the vision of violence Dioskoros paints extends outside his immediate hometown and its region to other parts of Egypt. In 567, while working in Antinoopolis, he writes a petition for the town councillors of Omboi in southern Egypt.[23] This petition also goes to Athanasios, this time called Triadios Marianos Michaelios Gabrielios Theodoros Constantinos Iulianos Athanasios. The text describes itself as a "petition and supplication from the most pitiable councillors of Omboi."[24]

---

[21] Palladius *Lausiac History* 31.1, from trans. in Clarke 1918.   [22] *P.Haun.* 3.58 = *SB* 14.11357.
[23] *P.Cair.Masp.* 1.67004.
[24] Trans. here and in subsequent paragraphs adapted from Dijkstra 2008, 353–354; see also Dijkstra 2004.

In their words, they "were the victims of greed out of proportions and had no chance to explain [their] case." The petition as it survives never names the man about whom they complain.[25] Whoever he is, they claim he "set aside the taught Christian worship ... consecrating shrines with demons and wooden statues." Worse, he had "renewed the temples for the barbarians, the Blemmyes," who had – or so they claim – converted to Christianity, but begin to backslide under the influence of this unnamed man. The consequences are devastating:

> They plundered us completely and he destroyed our houses, so that they became uninhabitable ... While we were absent and present here in this city, Antinoopolis, on account of official (tax) business ... He collected [taxes], appropriating them for himself with the band of outlaws accompanying him. They also fearlessly spent the taxes on themselves ... Moreover, after he had even sent the choicest gifts to barbarian tribes and worshipped together with these people, the wretched man ... fearlessly violated his own grand-daughter (?). And on top of that he melted the imperial standards into gold to make a bracelet for a favorite barbarian slave girl ... We therefore entreat your extraordinary honor ... that he be totally eliminated ... in order that we find means to live peacefully ... [and to pay (?)] our part (of the taxes) to the fisc and to assist according to custom in the collection of this (part) ... that we find means to pass our time in peace.

Scholars have made more of this in the past than they should. This is not really evidence for a nomadic Blemmyan invasion of Egypt in the 560s. Nor is it evidence about Blemmyan religious convictions. It only shows that some unnamed official recruited barbarians to help collect taxes from Omboi, a job the people of Omboi thought should be left to themselves alone.[26]

Dioskoros puts rhetoric to good effect. His reference to the evil-doer sleeping with his granddaughter is probably nothing but gossip,[27] and claims that the Blemmyes had converted to Christianity are unlikely. In this passage, Dioskoros alludes to the Second Letter of Peter, with its warnings about false prophets who lead people from truth into lawlessness. This allusion to Peter makes his claims about the Blemmyes seem more like a rhetorical crutch than an historical fact.[28]

Dioskoros sometimes talks about barbarians generally and Blemmyes specifically in a purely metaphorical sense.[29] In one of the poem-petitions against the village of Phthla, Dioskoros begs the governor to "reject the race

---

[25] Not, as believed by some previous scholars, Kollouthos 53; see Dijkstra 2008, 4, note 15.
[26] Dijkstra 2008, 5.   [27] Dijkstra 2008, 6.   [28] Dijkstra 2008, 6, citing 2 Peter 2.21.
[29] Dijkstra 2008, 8.

of Blemmyes, that is to say, these *boêthoi*."[30] The word *boêthos* – *boêthoi* in the plural – means nothing more than "assistant," the title of a petty government official.

This is clever: Dioskoros complains about a man named Victor, himself a government assistant. In another complaint against the village of Phthla, Dioskoros claims that Menas has given his family land at Phthla to the assistants (*boêthoi*) and shepherds there. We have entered the mind of a man obsessed with the county clerk. He resorts to name-calling – the clerks are barbarians, Blemmyes – but in truth, the real barbarians are nothing like what we imagine.

We have met the Blemmyes, a nomadic tribal people in the eastern deserts, in an earlier chapter.[31] I do not mean to suggest that there are never any Blemmyes anywhere on the horizon or that no tension ever erupts between nomads and the settled people of the Nile valley.[32] There are hints of a Blemmyan presence in the area around Aphrodito. The Aphrodito cadastre, which we discussed in previous chapters, is drafted in the 520s, four decades before Dioskoros's petition for the councillors of Omboi.[33] And that cadastre refers to a small orchard in the "place of the Blemmyes" in the catalog of Aphrodito's agricultural land.

Apollonides the *skriniarios*, a secretary in some public office, registers land there in the hands of one of Aphrodito's farmers. The name of the place is never explained. Maybe Blemmyes had settled there, or nearby. The casual nature of the reference makes it seem almost normal: the Blemmyes have been part of the landscape for so long that they barely merit explanation.

For centuries, the Roman Empire recruits soldiers from the barbarian tribes near its borders. The Visigoths and Ostrogoths who bring so much chaos to the European part of the empire are two of the most famous examples. The emperors and generals responsible for these arrangements could make a virtue out of necessity, but civilians coming face-to-face with the new recruits could easily wrinkle their noses in disgust. Dioskoros's complaints against the Blemmyes are the same thing, a civilized native's frustration at seeing local officials relying on immigrant labor instead of traditional arrangements with the locals.

---

[30] *P.Aphrod.Lit.* 4.11.82 with commentary ad loc. and in Dijkstra 2008, 8. [31] See page 38.
[32] But surely not where MacCoull 1992b, 108–109 finds them, in obscure references to buried money and the "ten thousand men [who] have gone south." MacCoull's speculation seems safer when it leans toward the plague or malnutrition due to famine. The Blemmyes appear nowhere in this text, and cannot reasonably be blamed for the situation it describes.
[33] *SB* 20.14669.

As with so much else, we have to follow the money. Aphrodito tries so hard to preserve its tax independence because this allows its elites to collect less and pocket more than they could if the empire's regional officials were in charge of the collection. The same is true for the councillors of Omboi. When imperial officials recruit local barbarian tribes to help collect taxes, this means that Omboi's elite sees less of the revenue stream. Complaints about Blemmyes are, in this case, complaints about one group's rent-seeking to the detriment of another group's rent-seeking.

When Theodoros, an official in the office of the local duke, writes his will in the late 560s or early 570s, he includes a substantial donation to Shenoute's White Monastery "for rescuing captives and other pious distributions."[34] On the one hand, we can assume that Theodoros has the Blemmyes in mind when he imagines ransoming captives, even though he does not mention them.[35] On the other hand, this is probably nothing more than legalistic boilerplate: a good lawyer or notary in this period would know that "rescuing captives" is a special action under the laws of the emperor Justinian. It is one of the special circumstances under which alienation of church property is legally permissible.[36] Theodoros's will does not show the violence of the times so much as it shows two parties agreeing about the legal limits of an inheritance.

Throughout this book, I have argued that life in Aphrodito is competitive and sometimes erupts into violence. But the Blemmyes are not really part of this picture. A thorough look at all the evidence about the Blemmyes shows that their status "as an ethnic group remains enigmatic. Neither historical nor archaeological research so far provides clear evidence for their existence other than as a construct by contemporary or modern outsiders."[37] Put another way, the Blemmyes seem so violent and dangerous only because Dioskoros is so good at his job, because Dioskoros is so convincing when he complains about his enemies.

Looking at these complaints from the other side, from the point of view of Dioskoros's enemies, they might even be slander. Slander appears several times in the Aphrodito papyri. The Greek verb *dusphêmeô* (to "use ill words") has a number of related forms referring to words of ill omen, slander, blasphemy, and shame. These words are rare in the papyri from Roman Egypt. Terms relating to *dusphêmeô* appear only six times in all

---

[34] *P.Cair.Masp.* 3.67312.69–70.
[35] Maspero's note at *P.Cair.Masp.* 3.67312.69; MacCoull 1987, 97; Keenan 2001, 623–624.
[36] Just. *Nov.* 7.8; *Nov.* 65.1 (permitting alienation if no income derives from the initial inheritance); *Nov.* 115.3.13; *Nov.* 120.9.
[37] Barnard 2005, 38.

published papyri. Five of those times are in papyri from Aphrodito.[38] We have seen the first several times before, in a tax-collection contract involving the most glorious Patrikia. The person agreeing to collect a middleman's share of the taxes in Phthla under the pagarchs Ioulianos and Patrikia also agrees to protect this middleman from slander.[39]

The other cases follow a similar pattern. A letter most likely addressed to Dioskoros or his father Apollos notes that the most magnificent count has sent out an order with the knowledge of the local advocate, instructing the release of an imprisoned woman. The letter, complaining that the order has not been carried out, breaks off in the middle of a complaint about slander.[40] A petition by Dioskoros against the pagarch Menas complains about "many slanderous words," but again, right before a break in the papyrus.[41] An arbitration from an earlier chapter includes Phoibammon's note that he and his wife shame his brother-in-law in an attempt to win his wife's inheritance.[42]

In all these cases, slander and power go hand in hand. Tax collectors care about their reputations because of their power. Likewise, counts and pagarchs care about their reputations because of their power. An attack on reputation is an attack on power. Someone with a crumbling reputation is less able to do his job. This is true even at the lowest level, in the inheritance dispute between a tow worker and a bootmaker: these men attack each other's reputations to reduce their power. Here again, we see the personal nature of late antique society. There is no abstract legal power or authority somehow separate from each individual. There is first and foremost the person and his reputation. When someone agrees to protect someone else from slander, as the tax collector does in Phthla, they work on a rhetorical spectrum. Slander is an act of envy, an attack against someone who has what you want.

Envy also appears repeatedly in the Aphrodito papyri, and the big men are the cure. In one petition, Dioskoros complains to the duke of the pagarch's envy.[43] In a poem praising a high-ranking official named Romanos, Dioskoros tells him that "It is not for the envious to recite your worth" and that his life will be "free from grief, unblighted by envy."[44]

---

[38] A DDBDP search for "dusfhm" on October 1, 2014 produces *CPR* 30.3; *P.Cair.Masp.* 2.67202; *P.Lond.* 5.1660, 1677, 1708; and *P.Ross.Georg.* 3.16. This disproportionality may be a symptom of the evidence: the Dioskoros archive cares more about slander precisely because it zooms in so much more closely than other collections of papyri from Greco-Roman Egypt.

[39] *P.Lond.* 5.1660.25. [40] *P.Cair.Masp.* 2.67202. [41] *P.Lond.* 5.1677.16.

[42] See 136, and *P.Lond.* 5.1708.53. [43] *P.Lond.* 5.1674.17; see MacCoull 1988, 48.

[44] *P.Aphrod.Lit.* 4.4 with trans. in MacCoull 1988, 69–70 and discussion of the identity of Romanos in Fournet 1999, 476–477.

In a poem praising the emperor Justin, Dioskoros hopes that "creeping envy ever be banished from your reign."[45] In a poem praising the marriage of a high official named Isakios, Dioskoros hopes that Isakios will "live forever ... free from envy," and commands, "Go away, evil eye; this marriage is graced by God."[46]

The big men in these poems and petitions – the dukes and the emperors – are pristine, blameless. They neither envy others nor suffer their envy, and this sets them apart from the little people. Dioskoros envies the men who take his money and slanders them as barbarians. These men in turn envy Aphrodito and Omboi for their independence and slander those who stand up to protect it. Dioskoros appears to contradict himself: pagarchs are envious because of their great power, while emperors are equally free of envy because of their great power. But this reinforces what everyone in late antiquity already knows: some people are simply better than others. These stories have good guys and bad guys, enemies who bring violence and heroes who can stop them. But the heroes – the patrons – are strange heroes, passive, waiting in the wings. They do not act on their own initiative, but in response to requests. When Dioskoros praises Athanasios as a redeemer comparable to Jesus, he is not simply asking for a favor, but also extending an invitation, giving his potential patron a chance to prove his worth.

At first glance, the tax collector, the soldier, and the abusive functionary are all extensions of Byzantine state power. This is certainly how people saw it in the first half of the twentieth century, when these papyri were discovered. But there is no such thing as the state, at least as a monolithic block. Much more immediately, there are individuals, particularly in a world where the state's civil service is not physically present at the local level. The state is the hidden infrastructure, the skeleton giving specific shape to some of the world's patronage networks. The patronage networks themselves are the muscle moving the bone, the real source of action and reaction in this world. When the men of Omboi confront their oppressor, when Dioskoros confronts Menas or the assistants at Phthla, they do not face a monolithic state, but a single man. They know full well that every man has a place in a hierarchy. Above every man in the hierarchy is another man more Christlike. Every man has a superior.

To find the better men, there is no better place than the imperial city itself, Constantinople, the capital of the Roman Empire. Apollos – father

---

[45] *P.Aphrod.Lit.* 4.17 with trans. in MacCoull 1988, 74.
[46] *P.Aphrod.Lit.* 4.34 with trans. in MacCoull 1988, 112.

of the poet Dioskoros – is one of Aphrodito's headmen on and off from the 510s to the 540s. At the peak of his career, Apollos goes to Constantinople in late 540.[47] He travels with his nephew, a priest named Victor. We do not really know why the two men go to the capital. Since Dioskoros would do so later, to defend his village's tax rights and his own property rights, it seems likely that Apollos and Victor go for the same reasons. We can imagine them sending petitions to imperial officials, cultivating connections, going to the city's great church and palace to win the favor of strangers. The result is a colorful picture of the two men as "country bumpkins gawking around in the Byzantine capital," going to mass at the Hagia Sophia and soaking up the sights.[48]

But in the end, no evidence for the trip survives except for a single loan the two men make while there.[49] They borrow twenty gold pieces from an imperial banker named Anastasios. They may have run out of money during the winter in the capital, and expect to be able to repay the debt at a branch office when they get back to Egypt at the start of the spring sailing season. There is some small risk for the lender here, and Apollos and Victor put up all their property as collateral against the loan. We assume they make good on their debt: the loan agreement itself may survive as nothing more than a souvenir to remind them of their trip.

This is the first and only time in his life in which Apollos holds the rank of Flavius.[50] He appears as a regular Aurelius Apollos earlier in 540 and never appears as a Flavius again at any point in the remaining six years of his life. Flaviate status normally comes from holding specific imperial offices. But sometimes, it is less precise: people seem to receive promotion to the rank of Flavius or earn the honor of the Flaviate without a corresponding imperial office. We might imagine a formal system, someone in an office somewhere giving out the empire's official permission for a person to become an honorific Flavius.[51]

The case of Apollos makes this seem rather unclear. He may receive the title at court, even from the emperor himself.[52] If he receives the honor in Constantinople, or somewhere else along the way, it would be the perfect credential to bring home to small-town Aphrodito. He would instantly be a better man. But he never seems to use the title again. Instead, we only see it in Constantinople, at the very moment he needs to present himself before some of the best men of all.

---

[47] Ruffini 2008a, 153–154. [48] Keenan 1992, 177. [49] Keenan 1992.
[50] Ruffini 2008a, 153, note 33 and Apollos 2 (although the date given for *P.Flor.* 3.342 should read 524).
[51] On the "mechanics" of the system, see Keenan 1974, 297–301. [52] Keenan 1974, 299.

Big Men and Strangers 175

If Apollos wants to claim to be a Flavius, it seems unlikely that anyone could really stop him. A new title might be just what he needs to present himself to higher officials, to make himself heard in the capital. His nephew Victor drafts the loan agreement himself. (Apollos is literate, but not up for a job like this.[53]) It is Victor himself who calls his uncle a Flavius, who promotes him in the eyes of imperial officials. This is partly guesswork, and it may be unfair to Apollos and Victor, but it makes sense. If these two men are in Constantinople to seek justice and ask for favors, if they are there to find and cultivate patrons, they need to look as attractive as possible. They are engaged in a balancing act: they must be both needy and worthy. They must be humble men needing help, but at the same time important enough as clients to reflect the glory of the patrons.

Dioskoros soon follows in his father's footsteps, twice making the trip to Constantinople. The first trip, in 548, is known from only two texts. These complaints claim that a higher official has received Aphrodito's taxes, but put the funds to personal use, not crediting the town's account in the public treasury.[54] Dioskoros's trip a few years later, in 551, comes alive through many more sources. Several detailed stories show Dioskoros playing the hapless provincial in search of a powerful patron at the imperial court.

This begins practically the moment Dioskoros arrives at the docks. Once in Constantinople, he makes a great deal out of the hardships of the voyage. In one petition to an official in the capital, his claims of suffering at the hands of the sea on the way to Constantinople sound like a provincial landlubber complaining of sea-sickness: "I have suffered enough pain on the impetuous waves of the sea because of the violence of Theodoros of Pentapolis," one of the men he comes to the capital to complain about.[55]

A letter survives, most likely from this trip in 551, as a calling card written for Dioskoros by an unknown official in the capital.[56]

> The admirable Dioscorus who delivers this letter of mine to your renowned eminence is a native of the Thebaid. Being wronged, as he says, by certain persons there he came to this royal city with a report of the damage thereby caused ... Rightly conceiving that his only sure help lies in the support of your justice he seeks to obtain this from you ... I beg you to see that some more than usual attention be bestowed upon the admirable Dioscorus, so

---

[53] Keenan 1992, 178, note 17.   [54] Theodosios 16: *P.Cair.Masp.* 1.67029 and *SB* 6.9102.
[55] *P.Aphrod.Lit.* 4.5.19–20.   [56] *SB* 4.7438 with trans. in *Sel.Pap.* 2.431.

that I may appear to have been of service to him and you again may receive a much increased reward from the Lord God.

This letter is surprisingly vague. It does not say what "wrong" faces Dioskoros, or why the letter survives, stashed in Dioskoros's own archive. Dioskoros may have never delivered it. More likely, its recipient handed it back to Dioskoros after reading it and giving his answer.[57]

More importantly, note the author's most basic assumptions. He does not expect the letter's recipient, whoever he is, to do his job, to follow the law to employ the power of the state. He expects the recipient to think of favors given and received, to think of the author's service as a patron to Dioskoros, his own service as a patron to the author, and God's service in turn as a patron to him.

An imperial decree survives giving Dioskoros the weapon he needs to return home with.[58] As we have already seen, this decree restates the situation back home in Aphrodito, most likely in Dioskoros's own words.[59] Apollos of Aphrodito "used to collect the contributions for the whole place." Facing injustice from the governors, Apollos and others sought protection from the imperial court, the so-called divine house. In their absence, someone named Theodosius "collected the taxes of the village, but paid nothing whatever into the public account." As a result, local officials had to collect taxes from Aphrodito a second time in a single year.

This is all backstory. An earlier imperial decree in Aphrodito's favor had no effect: "the intrigues of that person were of more avail than our orders." Apollos had to go to Constantinople a second time. Now, the emperor decrees that Dioskoros deserves recourse, that "his village shall not be deprived year after year of what is due to them, so that they shall not on this account be shortly reduced to exhaustion over the payment of the public taxes."

The decree repeats Dioskoros's complaint against the pagarch Ioulianos, that he "wished to place their village under his own pagarchy ... he attacked them and was guilty of seizing their property." Furthermore, Dioskoros scores a more personal victory as well: the decree notes that "some of the proprietors in that village have robbed the petitioner and his brothers of certain property," and orders an official investigation.

After the decree states Dioskoros's claim, it includes specific instructions to the recipient. The person carrying out the decree should

---

[57] Martin 1929, 102. [58] *P.Cair.Masp.* 1.67024 with trans. in *Sel.Pap.* 2.218. [59] See page 21.

examine this case with as much strictness as the law rules ... if you find that in truth the inhabitants of the said village [Aphrodito] have never been subject to a pagarchy for taxation, you shall stop the aforesaid Ioulianos from meddling with them and cause him to make good to the petitioners the harm which he has inflicted on them according to the provisions of the laws on that subject.

The call for investigation is a standard response by higher officials to these kinds of petitions. However, the claim that earlier imperial decrees made no impact on the situation is striking.

The late Roman state is regularly seen as a crushing weight around the neck of its people, and Justinian himself as an all-consuming autocrat. But here, the state does not even have basic records about the tax status of its own provincial villages or confidence that its own decrees are followed. The records that do exist are local, effectively out of sight of the central state and in the hands of local players. As at so many other times in Aphrodito's history, the future depends less on the law than on face-to-face interactions, and big men turning up to help little ones.

Even armed with the imperial decree, Dioskoros still needs further assurance. In fact, the law requires that he have someone file his case for him in the courts back home. Consequently, Dioskoros approaches two high-ranking officials named Palladios and Epigonos, and asks them to come back to Egypt with him. Palladios is a count of the sacred consistory, one of the highest ranks in the imperial court, and Epigonos is also a count.

Dioskoros is asking a big favor. Palladios and Epigonos have been living in Constantinople in recent years, but are originally natives of Cappadocia, in modern Turkey. They are not Egyptians, and have no clear connection to Egypt. Still, they could be powerful allies. We do not know Palladios and Epigonos from anywhere else. As a count of the sacred consistory, Palladios would move in the highest circles of the imperial government.[60]

Palladios agrees to help, but Epigonos's decision is unknown. The surviving agreement records the request to both men, but only Palladios signs. Having the imperial decree – the agreement calls it the "divine order" – in hand, Palladios agrees to "come to the Thebaid [in southern Egypt] and take the said divine order ... and lay it before the local courts." Palladios further agrees to

---

[60] *PLRE* 3.445 and 3.960–961. Zuckerman 2004b, 87 considers the title honorary.

devote all goodwill ... and watchfulness and furtherance to our suit ... and produce before the court all the persons mentioned in the said order under safe security ... and prosecute the suit till the end of the case.[61]

In exchange, Dioskoros and the other men from Aphrodito who come with him agree to pay all of Palladios's expenses, and award him a portion of any reward that comes from their suit.

So far this trip looks like official business, with representatives of one level of local government complaining about a higher level of local government to the highest powers of central government. But family matters are at stake too. Unfortunately, Dioskoros is not the only one in his family with his grandfather's name, and this gets confusing.[62] Apollos had been looking after his nephew, another Dioskoros. When Apollos died, local officials took advantage of this other Dioskoros's weakness to seize some of his property.[63] This same Dioskoros has – to make matters worse – lost his paternal inheritance to his step-mother, and seeks an imperial rescript enforcing traditional inheritance law in his favor.[64] These are, in the grand scheme of things, basically trivial issues. But Dioskoros's prospects for a local solution are so slim that friends at the imperial court seem a safer bet.

While in Constantinople, the first Dioskoros, our story's main character, also helps other Egyptians with their own petitions.[65] One papyrus, which must have survived the return trip to Egypt, includes two separate rough draft attempts at a petition on behalf of someone from the region of Hermopolis, also in southern Egypt. The petition itself is a complaint to the emperor that the petitioner's paternal uncle has sold an inheritance that the petitioner has coming from his father.

We do not know whether Dioskoros knew this person before arriving in Constantinople, or was introduced to him while there. We do know that he has other Egyptian contacts already in the city. His rough-draft copy of the petitioner's complaint is interrupted by notes to find Ioulios and Theodoretos the ex-duke in Constantinople. Whoever suggested to Dioskoros that he find these people even gave their addresses, and brief notes on which neighborhoods in Constantinople they call home.

During the same trip, Dioskoros writes what becomes the best known of his poems, an *enkômion* addressed to an official named Romanos.[66] This

---

[61] *P.Cair.Masp.* 1.67032 with trans. in *Sel.Pal.* 2.363.
[62] Following Zuckerman 2004b contra van Minnen 2003; Ruffini 2011 remains agnostic and keeps Dioskoros 31 and Dioskoros 35 separate.
[63] *P.Cair.Masp.* 1.67026. [64] *P.Cair.Masp.* 1.67028.
[65] *P.Cair.Masp.* 3.67352 with Fournet 2010a. [66] *P.Aphrod.Lit.* 4.4.

may be Romanos the Melodist, a famous Christian hymn writer then living in Constantinople, but not everyone is convinced of this.[67] The poem is in two parts, one in iambic trimeter, the other hexameter. The first letters of the lines spell short phrases: Lord Romanos, Romanos the Amazing. The poem starts with pure praise:

> Blessed in every respect, blessed with a pedigree and intelligence, you deserve the best: here you are, Sir ... You are Menander, wise man of old, in your intelligence! Isocrates speaking with manly power ... you are honored by all because of your fortune and pedigree ... Your intelligence has surpassed that of the wisest men.[68]

But every poem has a purpose, and Dioskoros soon turns to his: "Stretch out to me your hand that heaps up good fortune, saving my dear children and their excellent mother, because in my land tenure I am suffering the unexpected troubles of violence."[69] Once again, we realize why Dioskoros and his team travel so far. Romanos must be someone with access to the halls of power in Constantinople. So at least Dioskoros thinks him to be.

We do not know the outcome of these cases. It is easy to assume that Dioskoros loses his cases and Aphrodito loses its independence.[70] This assumption rests on the fact that Dioskoros eventually leaves Aphrodito and finds work in the provincial capital, a phase of his life we will describe in the next chapter. But really, this proves nothing. His archive's silence on the outcome of the trip to the capital supports suspicion of victory as much as suspicion of defeat.

In his petitions, Dioskoros "very successfully mingles the sober and prosaic account of the facts and state of affairs with occasional evocation of emotional sentiments by a subtle play on words."[71] His petitions to Athanasios complaining against Menas are the best examples. Indeed, Dioskoros has been so successful in his petitions that "papyrologists, philologists and historians generally tended to believe" all of his accusations.[72] Throughout these petitions, Dioskoros uses a set of emotional strategies. He plays on the duke's "parental affection and compassion for children," uses words designed to evoke "sympathy or antipathy in characterizing persons," uses metaphors "insinuating common pictures of anxiety and dread," and creates "progressive disdain" for Menas himself.[73]

---

[67] Kuehn 1990, 103–107, rejected by van Minnen 1992, 97–98 and Fournet 1999, 475–477.
[68] van Minnen 1992, 90.   [69] MacCoull 1988, 70.
[70] As has Zuckerman: see page 91 with note 97.   [71] Palme 2014, 5.   [72] Palme 2014, 18.
[73] Palme 2014, 10.

Although the long and slow trip from southern Egypt to the imperial capital must take a certain amount of courage, Dioskoros and his family are not unusual in making it. The instinct in the provinces to travel as far as the imperial capital to plead a case is so common that the imperial government legislates against it, publishing a law in this period urging the capital's numerous rural petitioners to return to their provinces.[74] Others from Egypt with connections to Dioskoros are part of that crowd. It is possible that his father Apollos is not the first from his town to make the trip to the imperial capital, but is merely one in a long line of traveling petitioners in Aphrodito's history dating back generations, even centuries, to the start of Roman rule over Egypt.

As we have seen, two mountains of evidence emerge from the otherwise flat Nile valley landscape: evidence for contracts and evidence for conflict. When everything goes well, and no legal requirements loom, nothing gets written down. As a result, we have no texts in which Dioskoros describes all of the good things high-ranking patrons have done for him in the past. There is only grievance against past wrongs and hope for future help, side by side. This chapter shows an abundance of both.

However, we do not bother our betters with pleas for help we know will never come. Implicit in comparing Athanasios to Jesus – and implicit in the long trips to Constantinople – is a brimming optimism. The future help will meet and defeat the past wrongs, and become the evidence missing from our records, the hidden favors from high-ranking patrons. Just because we cannot see these victories does not mean they are not there. Dioskoros's own behavior makes no sense without them.

---

[74] *Nov.* 80.2.

CHAPTER 11

Life in the Big City

Villagers from a small town in southern Egypt making it all the way to the imperial capital are probably on the longest trip they or anyone they know will ever make. But Aphrodito and its residents are also part of a vibrant local network of travel and trade. Imagine Egypt from their vantage point, looking out. The nearby villages – Phthla and Thmonachthe in particular – are in walking distance and hardly count as a serious trip.

However, go down to the Nile and get in a boat, and a range of options unfold. Egypt's other big towns and smaller cities are on the distant horizon, coming into view once a year or on only a few occasions in a lifetime. The biggest cities dominate the view. They may need dozens of visits, or take years of your life.

This sort of travel can be dangerous. We have already seen the danger some Aphrodito residents face when they are arrested traveling to the livestock fair at Thynis, a village in southern Egypt's Hermopolite region.[1] Since livestock fairs and markets frequently coincide with religious festivals, the annual livestock market at Thynis probably overlaps with the Festival of Thynis.[2] The festival, which may be or coincide with Easter, is a well-known annual event in the area of Hermopolis, and requires an "obligatory contribution" of wine for its supplies.[3]

Several major cities are closer to home. Surprisingly, we hear little of Aphrodito's closest city, the nome or regional capital of Antaiopolis. It is not even clear whether Antaiopolis is larger than Aphrodito, itself a former city.[4] Aphrodito has close ties to Antaiopolis. Aphrodito's cadastre records a place called "of those from Antaio." The cadastre itself is basically the city's view of Aphrodito, the central state's apparatus recording its fixed vision of what Aphrodito's land and landowners look like.

---

[1] Not the early pharaonic capital of Thinis. See page 166. [2] Keenan 2008, 177.
[3] Mandilaras 1991, 115–116. [4] Keenan 2007, 232, note 30.

The Aphrodito papyri mention Antaiopolis once in a while, with the occasional reference to an Antaiopolite church or to soldiers stationed there. But this is a thin record of ties between a town and its capital. The Antaiopolite churches own land here and there in the fields of Aphrodito, but little indicates that Aphrodito's residents do much business with the men and women of their nome capital. The relationship – full of recurring political tension – is almost completely fiscal, nothing more.[5]

Aphrodito, in the Antaiopolite region, is between the Antinoopolite region to the north and the Panopolite region to the south. Aphrodito has significant ties to this region and its capital, Panopolis.[6] In the AD 520s, the family of Tryphiodoros of Panopolis is one of the largest non-institutional landowners in Aphrodito. Later, in the seventh century AD, Theodoros, a wine dealer from Panopolis, owns a paternal share of a house in Aphrodito.[7]

Several churches and monasteries from the Panopolite region own land in Aphrodito as well. Sohag is about twenty-five miles away from Aphrodito. There, we find the Red and White Monasteries, two of the most famous monastic institutions of Coptic Christianity. By Dioskoros's day, both are over a century old, the White Monastery best known as the home of Shenoute, one of the fathers of Coptic literature. The Panopolite monastery of Smin, the monastery of Apa Zenobios, and the guesthouse of Apa Dios all own small plots of land appearing in the Aphrodito cadastre. For these religious houses, a small tie to Aphrodito is just part of a much wider collection of landholdings throughout the region.[8]

The capital of southern Egypt, Antinoopolis, is not quite seventy-five miles in a straight line to the northwest of Aphrodito, and only a little farther following the slow curve of the Nile. Its Roman foundations, on top of an older Pharaonic site, date to the early AD 130s and a visit to Egypt by the emperor Hadrian.[9] Following the death on this trip of his favorite, Antinoos, Hadrian founded a city in his honor in central Egypt. Hadrian's decision may have been motivated by a desire to strengthen classical Greek institutions in one of Rome's least Hellenized provinces. From the beginning, Antinoopolis followed a classical urban layout, forming a grid organized around two central intersecting streets.[10] (See Figure 11.1.) The streets ended with gates and were lined with columns along their route past major public buildings: a theater, baths, and temples. A racecourse lay outside the city to the east.

---

[5] Exceptions such as *P.Flor.* 3.281 notwithstanding.   [6] Geens 2014, 254–255.
[7] Theodoros 27: *SB* 18.13320.   [8] Geens 2014, 255.   [9] Bell 1940, 133–134.   [10] Bell 1940, 135.

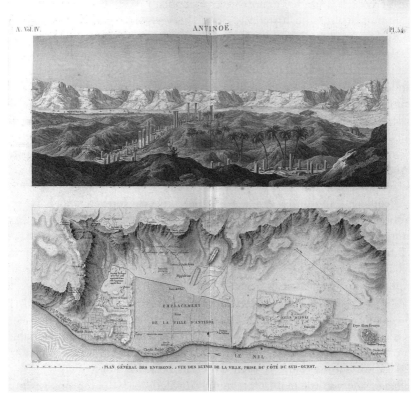

Figure 11.1 Antinoopolis: an illustration of the ruins, published in 1809 in the *Description de l'Égypte*

Italian excavations of ancient Antinoopolis continue to discover more about the city in late antiquity. The excavations include a fifth-century church with a burial chamber inside. The deceased were "mainly young women" but included "two men and one very small child." This church may have been dedicated to an important saint.[11] Excavations at a quarry in the mountains nearby found a camp, which likely "served as a police-post for the supervision and control of the workers in the quarry among whom many would have been criminals."[12] The quarries themselves, when abandoned, became home to monks seeking escape from worldly life.

[11] Grossmann 2010, 169.   [12] Grossmann 2010, 173.

A city of this size has a more diverse population. Here, we see minority communities for the first time, or at the very least, find hints of their existence. In 569, a Jewish craftsman named Peret – the papyrus calls him *Hebraios*, "the Hebrew" – leases a workshop on the ground floor of a house on the southern edge of the public market in Antinoopolis.[13] Peret is a dyer, and the workshop is presumably for his trade. We know nothing else about him. Is he alone in Antinoopolis? Does he have a family? Is he part of a larger Jewish community in town? Is this workshop his sole source of income or part of a larger operation? His is the only Jewish name in the Aphrodito papyri. This is worth remembering: for all the subtle variation in their stories, everyone we have met so far is essentially the same, a Christian in a universe of Christians.

People in Aphrodito can stay in that universe forever, and have no notion of anything different until they go to the big city. Nor do we find any documentary evidence of the doctrinal rifts slowly dividing Christendom. If there is a difference between Monophysite and Chalcedonian Christians, we do not see it in the evidence from Aphrodito or its nearest big city.

Not everyone in this big city is from there originally. Villagers live there on a more or less permanent basis. Nikantinoos, the man whose debt settlement we discussed in a previous chapter, is from Aphrodito, but in his own words, "resides here in the fair city of the Antinoites." In 566, Dioskoros moves there. A man who had been his hometown's highest official is now a little man, a face in the crowd, doing work for hire: we find him writing petitions to local officials on behalf of third parties, doing scribal work and acting as a mediator in legal disputes.[14]

We do not really know why he moves. It may be that in Antinoopolis, Dioskoros is working for the office of the duke.[15] This is an almost modern picture of Dioskoros moving to the big city as a job seeker taking a step up. In this picture, he is a sort of "country cousin" in relation to the sophisticated elite of Antinoopolis.[16] Considering the complaints he lodges against the local pagarchs in this period, he may have fled Aphrodito because it is no longer safe for him, the confiscation of at least part of his property having left him in dire straits.[17]

Whether this is true or not, there are many other reasons to go to Antinoopolis. Entertainment and education are near the top of the list.

---

[13] *P.Ross.Georg.* 3.38.   [14] MacCoull 1988, 24–47; Ruffini 2011, Dioskoros 3(ba)-(bp) et al.
[15] MacCoull 1988, 24 and 31.   [16] Bell 1940, 146.
[17] Bell 1944, 34 and *P.Lond.* 5.1674 introduction, 56, following Maspero.

In one case, Dioskoros combines his interest in both, copying a Greek poem in honor of the great athletic contests of ancient Greece.[18] "There were four contests in Greece," he writes, "two sacred to mortals and two to immortals: to Zeus, Apollo, Palaemon, and Archemorus, and their prizes are wild-olive, apples, celery, and pine-branches." The lines describe the Olympic, Pythian, Isthmian, and Nemean games. These games and their prizes are dead by this time, relegated to ancient history by virtue of their close association with ancestral – that is, pagan – Greek religion. To the average man in the street in the sixth century, these games are likely to be no more than names. If not for his own interest in poetry and classical literature, even Dioskoros might not know what they are.

The real athletic entertainment in this period comes through the circus races. The four dominant circus factions in the late Roman Empire are the Blues, Greens, Whites, and Reds, with the Blues and the Greens being the most important of the four. The competition between these factions is intense and frequently spills over into politics. Even the emperors declare their support for one faction or another. Dioskoros himself writes a few lines of verse describing the emperor's "angelic face, traveling on gold coins," and his "radiant life so fully honoring the Greens."[19] We do not know which emperor he means.[20] He may be speaking abstractly, or revealing his own preference, calling for an emperor who would support the same chariot teams as he does.

A papyrus found at Antinoopolis over a hundred years ago gives a contemporary illustration of chariot captains (see Figure 11.2), one holding a whip, and all wearing their crash helmets. Along with the picture comes a fragmentary text with handwriting dating to around AD 500.[21] It is not clear what the charioteers are doing. "Are they preparing for the race, acting as a jury during the course of it or to hear complaints after it?"[22] Most of the original picture is missing, so we only catch a piece of the action, but what it does show is crucial. Curled up reading about the greatest chariot races in history, local bookworms have images such as this connecting their ancient literature to the dramatic races of their own hometown.[23]

As we move from the small town to a big city, we should imagine what this world sounds like. Most importantly, it is a multilingual world. Most

---

[18] *P.Cair.Masp.* 2.67188.v.6-10 = *AP* 9.357 (trans. Paton).   [19] *P.Cair.Masp.* 1.67097.F.
[20] Contra Baldwin 1981, 285–286. We have no positive evidence for Dioskoros surviving the reign of Justin II, so Maurice cannot be proven.
[21] Turner 1973, 194.   [22] Turner 1973, 194.
[23] From a book accompanying related literature: Turner 1973, 194–195.

Figure 11.2 An illustration of charioteers from an Antinoopolis papyrus, AD c. 500

of the population in Roman Egypt speaks Egyptian, in most cases as their first language. A smaller group speaks the standard Greek of the eastern Mediterranean, thanks either to birth or education. This smaller group tends to dominate the elite levels of Egyptian society, and generates much of its official paperwork.

Most of the evidence we read in this book is written in Greek by Greek speakers, who can make sense of Greek sounds. But most people in that evidence cannot do so. Greek might sound like nonsense to them. We must always remember this when we read their stories. At the start of this book, when Maria testified about her husband's murder, we read an English translation of a Greek court document and this makes it sound familiar to our ears. But Maria herself may not speak Greek, may not be able to make sense of the judge's words without a translator, and may have no idea what is going on around her when she steps outside her own Egyptian-speaking circles.[24] People like her are more typical in the villages and small towns. Native Greek speakers are probably rare in those places, and few people have the need for a classical education.

Anyone in southern Egypt wanting this kind of education goes to a big city to get it. Antinoopolis is by no means a university town. In Egypt, only Alexandria earns that distinction, and stands out among the empire's best options. But few make it to Alexandria to study: Dioskoros may have, decades ago, but we are not sure.[25] Aphrodito may have a schoolhouse of sorts, a large room or set of rooms, or a miniature theater, with space for seats around the edges and room for copying exercises on the walls. However, to receive a more advanced education than this small town can provide, Aphrodito's elite go to Antinoopolis.

This includes the family of Dioskoros. Given the importance of education to Dioskoros's career, he probably puts plenty of thought into educating his own children. Unfortunately the evidence on the subject is thin, and his children barely visible. He names his sons Victor, Theodosios, and Petros. Only the first is a family name, the rest apparently new choices, possibly from his wife's side. Petros appears in a receipt the boy's teacher gives to Dioskoros in 567 "for wages for teaching your son."[26]

The receipt is damaged, and the teacher's full name is missing. But his family is from Lycopolis, and the date of the agreement suggests that Dioskoros meets him in Antinoopolis and that his son is being educated there. We might even guess that Dioskoros has moved to Antinoopolis to see to his son's education, but the damage to the receipt hides any discussion of what Petros is supposed to learn.

---

[24] In fact, I make no claims about Maria's linguistic position, but merely use her as an example of what might be true linguistically of any given person in Aphrodito.
[25] See page 190, on Dioskoros's legal education.   [26] Petros 16; date: Fournet 2008a, 331.

Structurally, the receipt is a contract of apprenticeship, in which Dioskoros pays the anonymous teacher to take on his son as an apprentice. There is no mention of any larger institution with a more wide-ranging faculty: the education of Petros is a matter of individual relations, subject to private contract law. The teacher will receive three gold carats for his work, but for how much work we cannot tell.

We do not know much about the city's other educational options. One loan agreement from Antinoopolis introduces Flavius Ioannes the *psêphistês*.[27] This word may mean mathematics professor.[28] But since Ioannes also works as an assistant in the city's municipal offices, the term probably just means that he is a "calculator" or accountant of some kind. If an advanced education in math could be had in Antinoopolis, there is no evidence for it. As we will see, Dioskoros's own math is not very accurate.

The Aphrodito papyri "testify that Dioskoros fulfilled a teaching role at various levels."[29] Dioskoros is perhaps "the teacher of his own children" for a time in Antinoopolis or "on return to his hometown, he taught some children of the elite of Aphroditopolis: as a man of culture he might have naturally fulfilled that role."[30] Dioskoros's own papers include verbal conjugation tables "notable for their accuracy." These exercises may have been produced in response to Dioskoros's own dictation, even by his own children.[31] The backbone of this basic education is intense study of Homer's *Iliad*. Here again, the Aphrodito archives hint at Dioskoros's role as a teacher. His copies of the *Iliad* and the *Scholia* or commentaries to it include "notes, lectional signs, and corrections ... added in Books 10 and 11 by one or more readers, probably his students."[32]

Basic mathematics is also part of this education. Students learn how to multiply and divide, how to manipulate fractions, and how to put these skills to a practical use in real-world situations. For Dioskoros, this appears most clearly in a series of measuring tables written in his own hand.[33] The tables begin with a long list of ratios between different units of measure. "The *modios xystos* is to the artaba as 3 is to 10," we read in the opening line, and "the artaba is to the *modios xystos* as 10 is to 3." Later entries compare the artaba to the *modios koumoulatos*, the *modios koumoulatos* to the *modios xystos*, and so on for seventy lines of ratios.

Dioskoros's tables also include instructions on how to measure the storage capacity of a wide range of structures. To determine the capacity

---

[27] Ioannes 230: see page 153. [28] Vanderheyden 2012, 798. [29] Cribiore 2001, 40.
[30] Cribiore 2001, 40. [31] Whitby 2001, 28; see page 190. [32] Cribiore 2001, 141, note 52.
[33] *P.Lond.* 5.1718.

of "a granary: measure the length multiplied by the breadth and again by the height, then multiply by 27 and divide by 8." (His unit of cubic storage held three and three-eighths of his units for measuring grain.[34]) "A canal: measure the length multiplied by the breadth and again by the height . . . A reservoir: measure the higher and the lower," the rest of the instructions largely illegible in the next two lines.[35]

The instructions for how to measure the size of a ship are also unclear in the surviving copy. The next entry explains how to calculate the number of bricks needed to finish a house wall. The text as a whole concludes with a series of equivalent measurements: twelve cubits to an *amma*, 400 cubits to a *stadion*, and so on – the ancient equivalent of a chart explaining the relationship between inches, feet, yards, and miles.

These tables have a number of problems.[36] In the earlier sections of the text, Dioskoros seems to combine two different sources, one giving measures of weight and another giving measures of storage capacity. This combination introduces a few errors, and "his table as a whole will often – and especially for the weight of wheat – have been misleading."[37] But his composite table "appears to be incomplete, it may have been a preliminary version, and perhaps Dioskoros realized and rectified his errors before composing the final copy."[38]

Once he has his final copy, it may serve educational purposes, but it has practical uses as well. The original editor of these tables wrote that since Dioskoros "was a landlord and a tax-payer . . . he must have had practical knowledge of weights and measures."[39] Dioskoros may draft the text for a client.[40] He may also provide measuring services for hire.[41] We can imagine a number of scenarios bringing texts like this to life.

A tenant paying rent in grain needs to know how a *modios* relates to an *artaba*, whether he should pile his *modios* high (*koumoulatos*) or level it off (*xystos*). In AD 532, Kuriakos the coppersmith leases a room in a farmhouse from Dioskoros's father Apollos.[42] When the room is walled off, Apollos – or whoever else has the work done – would need a way to calculate how many bricks he needs to finish the job. In AD 570, Pekusis the sailor leases a ship from Flavius Theodoros, and will probably want a way to verify that its carrying capacity is actually the 11,634 liters Theodoros claims it is.[43]

---

[34] Shelton 1981, 101.   [35] *P.Lond.* 5.1718.71–75 with *BL* 1.304.   [36] Rathbone 1983, 267–270.
[37] Rathbone 1983, 270.   [38] Rathbone 1983, 270.   [39] *P.Lond.* 5.1718 introduction, 160.
[40] Rathbone 1983, 270.
[41] A suggestion I owe to an anonymous reviewer of the initial proposal for this book.
[42] *P.Lond.* 5.1691.   [43] *P.Lond.* 5.1714; see also page 116.

(Theodoros works for the duke at the same time as Dioskoros lives in Antinoopolis, and Dioskoros himself writes this lease.)

It is hard to know how to judge Dioskoros's intellectual accomplishments. His legal education is good.[44] He may have gone to school in Alexandria.[45] It has been suggested that he studied under the well-known Christian philosopher John Philoponus.[46] But the claim that Dioskoros is "juridically up to date" may misunderstand the evidence.[47] Dioskoros "certainly kept and used notes from the lectures he attended," but the law as he studied it was most likely in a form codified before the great contemporary collections issued during the reign of Justinian.[48]

The evidence for his literary education is better. Homer is the basis of this education. The Homeric material in Dioskoros's library includes large portions of several hundred lines of the *Iliad*, along with the collection we have mentioned of *Scholia Minora* to the *Iliad*, glossaries or explanations of certain Homeric terms.[49] The fragments of the *Iliad* come from the second half of Book Two. They begin at the very start of that book's famous catalog of ships, the description of the forces sailing from the Greek world to Troy. This section of the *Iliad* is famous, widely studied for its political picture of early Greece. However, what a jumble it must seem to Dioskoros, a hodge-podge of strange names and unknown places. The first fragment, for the fifty ships of Boeotia, takes the reader through Hyria, Eleon, Medeon, Coroneia, Onchestos, Anthedon, and other places hundreds of miles and over 1,500 years away.

Alongside all of this material are the verbal conjugation tables which we have already mentioned.[50] These are, taken all together, hundreds and hundreds of lines giving all forms of the Greek verbs *boô*, *poiô*, and *chrusô*. The tables have some interesting problems: spelling errors, conjugation errors, additions, and accidental omissions. Some of these errors are caught at the time, and others go unnoticed. While the tables are good, they are not perfect.

Attic Greek – the language of classical Athenian literature – rose to importance a thousand years before the life of Dioskoros. This helps to put these conjugation tables in context. Some parts of Shakespearean English sound as strange to modern ears as Attic Greek would sound to those proficient in the Greek of late antiquity. The tables are on the reverse of documents, including a contract written in late 569, dating them to

---

[44] Urbanik 2013, 296.   [45] MacCoull 1988, 9.   [46] MacCoull 1986c.
[47] Urbanik 2008, 134 citing van Minnen 2003, 129.   [48] Urbanik 2008, 140.   [49] Fournet 1999.
[50] *P.Aphrod.Lit.* 3.1–4; see page 188.

Dioskoros's period in Antinoopolis.⁵¹ Two different styles of handwriting are apparent.⁵²

Imagine a notary somewhere outside of the native English world, maybe in India before independence from the British. Imagine finding among that notary's papers a list of the Shakespearean forms for the verbs to be, to have, and to do: "am; art; is; was; wast; wert. have; hast; hath; had; hadst; had. do; dost; doth; did; didst; didest," giving all singular forms of these three verbs in the present and past tenses. They are the school work of his students, perhaps his own children. The analogy is inexact, but the impression remains: we have imperial subjects struggling to improve, and using ancient forms of the imperial language to connect to a wider cultural world.

More important than Dioskoros's Homeric and grammatical material is his codex of Menander. We are rightly thankful that Dioskoros reads Menander, and "we may charitably hope that it was not he but an unworthy successor who used many of its leaves as waste paper."⁵³ The Menander codex was at the top of the broken jar holding the Aphrodito papyri found in 1905. Gustave Lefebvre, its discoverer, "noted that the Menandrian codex had been used as a sort of cork to close the jar and protect the papyri beneath, as though for the owner the latter had been more important."⁵⁴

As we have seen, this waste paper has the only surviving copy of the arbitration scene in Menander's *Epitrepontes*.⁵⁵ This scene

> must have been highly valued in late antiquity as reading material for all those involved in civil judication, *e.g.*, a notary such as Dioscorus ... because of the increased popularity of all forms of private arbitration and arbitration by (semi-)officials in late antique Egypt.⁵⁶

With this scene, Dioskoros's literary education and his legal work intersect.

A few other items appear in Dioskoros's collection. Short portions survive of the comedy *Demes*, written by Eupolis and produced in Athens in 412 BC.⁵⁷ Dioskoros may have owned some fragments of Aristophanes, now lost.⁵⁸ His papers also preserve not quite forty highly fragmentary lines from an otherwise unknown biography of the Attic orator Isocrates.⁵⁹ Dioskoros has scribbled little notes in the margin, *peithô, to sumpheron, to kalon, to dikaion*: "I persuade; the contributing;

---

⁵¹ Fournet 1999, 187.　⁵² Fournet 1999, 177.　⁵³ Bell and Crum 1925, 177.
⁵⁴ Kuehn 1995, 44.　⁵⁵ See page 53.　⁵⁶ van Minnen 1992, 94.
⁵⁷ Fournet 1999, 670. For Eupolis' *Demes*, see Storey 2003, 111–174.　⁵⁸ Fournet 1999, 677.
⁵⁹ P.Cair.Masp. 2.67175.

the good; the just." This is "not a bad outline of Dioscorus's career goals."⁶⁰ The library reflects the man.

Homer, Menander, and a biography of Isocrates may be a rather small literary collection. "He presumably did not personally own any other literature ... It is remarkable that in his poems Dioscorus himself explicitly refers only to the three authors mentioned." When he writes his poem of praise for Romanos while in Constantinople, he compares him to both Isocrates and Menander.⁶¹ As for Eupolis he "may not have been aware of this at all, and he presumably regarded it as another comedy by Menander."⁶²

These literary works draw well-deserved attention. We miss what is absent, what is missing from Dioskoros's literary world. We saw that Dioskoros keeps a headache remedy in his papers.⁶³ But he has nothing else on health or the body, and certainly no full-length medical texts. We know that people still read Galen in sixth-century Egypt, but not – as far as we can tell – in this small town.⁶⁴ We see no lives of the saints or any other writing from Egypt's great Christian figures, even though Shenoute and the White Monastery are not far from the town's mind. We see nothing from the Bible.

Maybe the people who inherit Dioskoros's papers put into storage only the things they no longer care about. They may keep the religious texts out for future use, or bring them to his father's monastery.⁶⁵ Alternatively, we can imagine the late antique literary canon as a hierarchy: the farther we get from the big cities and the fewer resources the local elite can summon to assemble their libraries, the fewer of the canon's top-tier works can we reasonably expect to find.

Outside of that canon, another notable absence in Dioskoros's library is magic. If Aphrodito ever had a library full of Coptic magic, we will never know. These texts may be quite rare, or they may be everywhere. Dioskoros himself writes a prayer that "betrays considerable familiarity" with Coptic ritual texts.⁶⁶

> Christ, I invoke you, Lord, ruler of everything, the first-begetter, the self-begetter, brought forth fully formed ... He who sees all things at once, you who is Eiao Sabao Brinthao, keep me as a son, protect me from all evil spirits and subdue for me all of the destructive spirits of the unclean, above ground and below, on the wet land and the dry, and all shadows. Christ!⁶⁷

---

⁶⁰ MacCoull 1988, 55.   ⁶¹ See page 178.   ⁶² Gagos and van Minnen 1994, 20.
⁶³ See page 145.   ⁶⁴ Sixth-century Galen: *P.Oxy.* 80.5227–5229.   ⁶⁵ van Minnen 2003, 128.
⁶⁶ Frankfurter 1998, 258.
⁶⁷ *P.Cair.Masp.* 2.67188.v = *PGM* 2.P 13A at page 202; see MacCoull 1987.

We see again the same evil spirits responsible for the collapse of several marriages in a previous chapter. Dioskoros "may have easily come to think that his financial troubles, often alluded to in his poems, were caused by a more than human agency."[68] More generally, his eye on both the wet land and the dry is a reminder: the power of the Nile is a constant threat, and a flood too great or too small spells ruin for the town.

Stranger to the modern eye than the evil spirits are the divine names for Christ: Eiao, Sabao, and Brinthao. The first two are common in magical texts, but written incorrectly: Iao and Sabaoth are standard divine names in Gnostic texts. But Brinthao appears to be unique to this Aphrodito prayer. Some people have wondered how Dioskoros comes across Gnostic writings.[69] This may be the wrong question to ask. If anything, this prayer shows the fuzziness of boundaries between theoretically distinct religious groups in late antiquity. Sabaoth is originally a combination of three figures: the God of the Old Testament, one of his leading angels, and an apocalyptic visionary.[70] He is a figure born in apocalyptic Judaism and adopted by Gnosticism in the early centuries after Christ. Gnostic texts speak of Sabaoth as an earthly figure repenting and being elevated into heaven, where he is enthroned.[71]

These texts from the famous Nag Hammadi finds come from a tradition quite apart from mainstream Christianity. Dioskoros is Christian, and would consider himself strictly orthodox. However, he lives in a world that takes spiritual strength wherever it can be found, and easily blurs the lines between one belief system and another. When he conjures Eiao, Sabao, and Brinthao, Dioskoros makes "his own deal with the unseen."[72]

Outside the literary and magical, Dioskoros also collects documents to serve as useful models for his own work. When Dioskoros lives in Antinoopolis, he has access to literary and documentary texts unlike anything he can get back home. Someone in this situation copies the things he likes and takes them back, even if he has to put a selection of unrelated texts onto the same papyrus. We have something like this among his papers – a three-page papyrus with copies of older texts.[73]

One of those texts is a letter addressed to a bishop named Kephalon, in which a public official named Ioannes repents of his violent past and at the same time blames his actions on his superior, a man named Victor. We met Kephalon in an earlier chapter.[74] It has been suggested that Dioskoros kept a copy of this letter because of its "pretentious style." But Dioskoros also

---

[68] MacCoull 1987, 97. [69] MacCoull 1987, 97. [70] Fallon 1978, 134. [71] Fallon 1978, 7.
[72] MacCoull 1987, 97. [73] P.Cair.Masp. 3.67295. [74] See page 125.

has an indirect family connection to Kephalon: the bishop Kephalon's son Christodoros is the intermediary in a rent payment to Dioskoros's father Apollos in the 540s.[75] From this small clue, we may imagine Dioskoros in Antinoopolis keeping company with the relatives of one of that city's former bishops.[76] He may keep the letter to the bishop not just for its style, but because it indirectly concerns a friend of the family.

Another text on this papyrus is a copy of a petition from Horapollon, the fifth-century author of a treatise on hieroglyphs.[77] Horapollon's study of hieroglyphs has had long appeal, despite his apparent confusion on some aspects of Egypt's sacred script. Even after Champollion had deciphered hieroglyphs in the 1800s, and Horapollon's work became obsolete, romantics who preferred a symbolic interpretation of their imagery continued to turn to Horapollon's work for support.[78]

It is doubtful that this part of Horapollon's history particularly interests Dioskoros. We know about Horapollon's interest in hieroglyphs only from other sources. His petition dates to the reign of Anastasius (AD 491–518). In it, Horapollon appeals to the policeman of the village of Phenebythis in the Panopolite nome, complaining that his wife has left him for another man and taken all of their movables. Here, a famous philosopher faces the same challenges facing dozens of common people in previous chapters. In a way, this is Dioskoros studying history, rummaging through official archives in search of useful models. Horapollon's petition "looks more like a piece of literature, a kind of novel."[79] This is how Dioskoros tries to write, too. He sees in his own work the direct continuation of styles and forms from decades, even centuries past.

We have already seen the condemnation Dioskoros's poems received from the first people to study them.[80] Scholars criticize him for his difficulty with the classical metrics of iambic poetry, but these criticisms are hardly fair. By his time, Greek had changed considerably from the classical period, and "the differences of length in Greek vowels were scarcely discernible."[81]

---

[75] *P.Cair.Masp.* 3.67326.
[76] Maspero's introduction to *P.Cair.Masp.* 367295 connects Kephalon to Antaiopolis, apparently because he believes that the Kuros dealing with Kephalon's son in *P.Cair.Masp.* 3.67326 is the same as Kuros the city councilman of Antaiopolis. But see Kuros 12 and Kuros 16 in Ruffini 2011. Nothing requires Kephalon to be bishop of Antaiopolis.
[77] See Maspero 1914, 170–174 for a French translation. For Horapollon generally, see Geen 2014, 269–270, 345 and 380–385.
[78] See Masson and Fournet 1992, 234 on the Greek forger Constantin Simonides.
[79] Geen 2014, 345.   [80] See page 19.   [81] Viljamaa 1968, 87.

Still, Dioskoros's poetry is hard reading, and would have been hard even for a native Greek speaker 1,500 years ago. His poems are heavily influenced by dramatic poetry and are full of wordplay.[82] They are dense, they rely on unusual word choices, and in one case unleash a "blizzard of uncommon words."[83] When the rare words fail him, Dioskoros coins words of his own.[84] He swaps a word he does not like with an analog or alternative definition, as if he were a student using a thesaurus or consulting his Homeric glossary. He calls someone "wide-minded" when "broad-minded" might be more easily understood.[85] Sometimes these twists and turns are clever, at other times they obscure his meaning and weaken his poetry.

However, all judgment of the quality of his poetry misses the point.[86] It makes no sense to compare Dioskoros to other literary authors, because he is not trying to be one. His literary output comes bundled with his documentary petitions. His poems are literary pleas to political authority, not works of art. Everything he writes in this gray area between poetry and petition reveals a moment of tension, in which his society's normal face-to-face rules falter and he needs to lay claim to someone's power and patronage.

One fascinating glimpse into Dioskoros's literary education comes in the form of a Greek-Coptic glossary he writes himself.[87] Dioskoros is bilingual, proficient in writing both Greek and Coptic. He needs Greek to thrive among the empire's Hellenized elite. His bilinguality probably comes from having a classical Greek education grafted onto a Coptic-speaking native milieu, and not the other way around. (His great-grandfather's name, Psimanobet, is clearly Coptic.[88]) If Dioskoros grows up speaking native Egyptian as his first language, this is necessarily true for nearly everyone in Aphrodito.

The impact of this linguistic and culture binarity is almost invisible now. We cannot tell if Dioskoros and others like him move back and forth between the two cultures with ease or great difficulty. The Coptic language is rich in Greek loanwords, "like raisins in a pudding."[89] It is possible that the Coptic elite do not see Egyptian culture and classical culture as particularly distinct.[90] And yet Coptic linguistic categories are so different

---

[82] Viljamaa 1968, 86–91 and 83.   [83] Schwendner 2008, 58–64 with quote at 62.
[84] See page 115, on one piece of Dioskoros's religious poetry.   [85] Schwendner 2008, 60.
[86] See generally Fournet 1999 and specific remarks at Fournet 2004, 70–71.
[87] *P.Lond.* 5.1821, the verso of *P.Lond.* 5.1674 in Bell and Crum 1925.
[88] MacCoull 1988, 149 raises the possibility that he was a "monoglot Copt."
[89] MacCoull 1988, 154.   [90] MacCoull 1988, 152.

from those of Indo-European languages that the shift from one to another must be tangible.[91] If we had all of Aphrodito's Coptic documents and none of its Greek documents, would its world look much different in shape and in values? Aphrodito would look even more local, no doubt, even less touched by the empire outside it. But Dioskoros would probably display the same values on one side of his bilinguality as he does on the other.

His glossary gives a glimpse into what that bilinguality feels like. Dioskoros does not worry about putting his own words into Greek, but worries instead about running into Greek that means nothing to him. His glossary is an emergency guide to refresh his memory on obscure Greek, translated into handy Coptic equivalents. We find some odd items in this glossary: for example, the Coptic word for a sparrow or ostrich, but used as slang, translating a Greek word which may mean penis. We find another Coptic word for genitals, translating a Greek word for a sea-bird, but used to describe airheads, or, in the words of one scholar, "scatterbrained persons."[92] The next entry gives yet another slang word for penis, *sarakoitin* or wanderer.[93] Some of these entries may seem strange choices for penis-slang, but remember that an ostrich is an animal that hides its head.[94]

We find this glossary on the back of a petition drafted around AD 570, during Dioskoros's time in Antinoopolis. This is late in life, long after his formal education is over. It is possible to imagine Dioskoros drafting this glossary after he has gone back home to Aphrodito, enjoying a retirement of sorts, "doing some serious work on his Greek poetic vocabulary."[95] But it makes more sense for him to worry about the quality of his Greek when he is living in the big city. The glossary's modern editors noted that several of the Greek words are poetical, concluding that Dioskoros's "principal object was to extend his knowledge of the Greek language."[96] So many of Dioskoros's petitions date from his period in Antinoopolis, and these petitions are exactly the situation in which Dioskoros needs to impress people with the quality of his education.

The first three entries in the glossary are the Greek words *anthrôpos*, *zôion*, and *thanatos* (man, animal, and death). After these entries, and no others, Dioskoros adds excerpts apparently based on the work of Secundus the Silent, a second-century philosopher. The anonymous *Life* of Secundus describes his vow of silence, which he took after causing his own mother's suicide. The *Life* also includes the written answers Secundus agreed to give

---

[91] MacCoull 1988, 156–157 for these categories.
[92] See Baldwin 1982, 80 on entries 161–162 with MacCoull 1986a. [93] MacCoull 1986a, 254.
[94] MacCoull 1986a, 254. [95] MacCoull 1986a, 256–257. [96] Bell and Crum 1925, 181.

to twenty questions posed to him by the emperor Hadrian. Dioskoros's versions of these questions and answers are "unrecorded variants" so different "that it is perhaps doubtful" whether the passage "is to be regarded as an excerpt from 'Secundus' at all and not rather as a different text partly derived from the known one."[97]

Here, Dioskoros copies Secundus-like questions and answers defining the glossary's first entries. This part of the text is fragmentary, and the answer to the question, "What is man?" is almost entirely lost. But comparing other versions of the text suggests that the answer Dioskoros wrote was *zôion logimon*, a talking animal.[98] Three lines down, one part of his answer still survives to the question, "What is death?" – *aperaton diastêma*, a boundless separation.[99]

As much as we remember Dioskoros as a poet with a purpose, sending petitions to the powerful, his work in the big city is just as much dominated by the practice of law. These two interests are not as far apart for him as they might be for a poet or a lawyer today. Dioskoros's literary bent and his legal work converge, in some cases on the same papyrus. One of his poems is written on the back of a contract to buy two slaves.[100]

Dioskoros's legal training is a marketable commodity in the big city. Several cases survive in which residents of Antinoopolis, and in some cases people from even farther away, have him arbitrate their disputes. Binding arbitration must have been as stressful then as it is now, the participants uncertain whether they would walk away from their dispute with the satisfaction they deserve. Nothing explains how people approach Dioskoros for his services, whether they come to him as strangers or through friends of friends. We can only assume that his reputation and social capital outweigh his small-town background and relative newcomer status in the city.

One fragmentary case from circa AD 570 is a classic example of arbitration as an attempt to solve the difficulties of remarriage.[101] A deacon named John has two children by his first wife, a daughter named Viktorine and a son named Phoibammon the weak. When their mother died, John had remarried and had another daughter named Philadelphia. Viktorine and Phoibammon come to Dioskoros to arbitrate their lawsuit against Philadelphia and her mother Amanias. Their father John has died without leaving a written will. But Viktorine and Phoibammon claim that while

---

[97] Bell and Crum 1925, 203. [98] Bell and Crum 1925, 204. [99] MacCoull 1986a, 256.
[100] Urbanik 2010, 220 and *P.Cair.Masp.* 1.67120.
[101] *P.Lond.* 5.1709 with trans. in MacCoull 2009.

still alive, he had said, "in the presence of witnesses, 'My children are to divide among them all that is mine: and I order that they divide it up among themselves, one-third to each, in accordance with my poverty'."

Amanias, with an eye on her daughter's financial well-being, has allegedly seized the entirety of the inheritance, and refuses to divide any of it until her daughter comes of age. In the colorful language of the day, Viktorine and Phoibammon complain that their relatives mock them, "saying, 'We will throw you out of the inheritance of your father,' in such a way as if we were children of a whore." Viktorine's own marital stability is at stake. While she is already married, to a man named Aphous – we saw their marriage contract in an earlier chapter – her dowry is locked up in her father's property, now in the hands of her step-mother and half-sister, who are keeping it for themselves.[102]

This is only one case, and we do not know how Dioskoros handles it. Living in Antinoopolis gives him many opportunities to put his knowledge of the law to work.[103] But think about this case: nothing in it is particular to life in a big city. So many of the legal disputes Dioskoros sees could just as easily take place back home in Aphrodito. What is particular about Antinoopolis – or at least, what marks the move from a town to a city – is the elevated level of culture. To tap into the Hellenistic cultural milieu, you have to move to a big city.

The education Dioskoros receives is an elite education. He does not share it with the vast majority of the people in his town. He may indeed be alone, we have no way of knowing. We can speculate, and ask whether any of the classical Greek mythology Dioskoros values so highly might ever trickle down to the popular culture of the village. Writing about the poets of late antique Egypt, Alan Cameron observes that

> this sort of culture is above all an elite phenomenon. Take mythological themes on the silver plate of the age, or the mythological textiles that have survived in such numbers thanks to the dry Egyptian climate. A cultivated person would at once identify, with some satisfaction, a Dionysiac procession, or Andromeda chained to the rock, or Meleager killing his boar. But a peasant or a monk would see only naked bodies, monsters, and demons. Similarly, if a peasant or monk heard or read the names Zeus, Leda, or Danaë, he would think demons, not an elegant mythological allusion.[104]

---

[102] For Viktorine and Aphous, see page 134.
[103] For a brief survey, see MacCoull 1988, 12–13 and Ruffini 2011, Dioskoros 3.
[104] Cameron 2007, 39.

With this in mind, we might imagine that some of his fellow townsfolk view Dioskoros's learning with suspicion, and even, potentially, hostility. Bear in mind that in the previous century, Shenoute and his monks at the White Monastery attack people who share Dioskoros's literary tastes.[105] Put another way, men with big-city culture may be the enemy to men back home in the village.

---

[105] Cameron 2007, 40–41.

CHAPTER 12

Conclusion

At the start of this book, I claimed that the Aphrodito records are unique, an unparalleled opportunity to live ancient life from the inside. They are also unique in another way: in the degree to which they give us a before and after picture of a single place seen at two different times. This book focuses on one of Aphrodito's archives, from the middle of the sixth century, but Aphrodito's second archive tempts us too. As we will see later in this conclusion, the view from the eighth century is quite a bit different. It leads us to wonder what has changed, and why, and how quickly. This in turn leads us to wonder about Aphrodito before the sixth century, and how it came to look like it does throughout this book.

I tend to think that the men and women of the ancient world had deeper ties to their history than we do to ours. But even today, the strength of these ties varies from person to person, place to place. In Aphrodito, the names of people long gone are embedded in the landscape and provide a constant reminder of generations past. Our journey through everyday life in Aphrodito has focused on the two generations of Apollos and his son Dioskoros, two of Aphrodito's big men from the 520s to the 570s. However, the town's surviving records also give us a way to learn about the shape of life there in the generations both before and since.

Glimpses of dominant families from previous decades are barely visible.[1] The family of Philantinoos is one we have already met. Philantinoos must have been born by the 460s, and probably earlier.[2] His son Kornelios and his grandchildren, Anna and Ioannes, appear in Aphrodito's records from the 520s onward, when Anna and Ioannes are most likely already adults. When Dioskoros marries Ioannes's daughter Sophia, the two families had already been connected for years, in part through shared business dealings with the town patron, Count Ammonios.

---

[1] See Ruffini 2008b for further discussion and references.
[2] Assuming his grandchildren to be adults when they first appear in the records in the AD 520s.

The family of Surion goes back at least as far. Surion himself is from the same generation as Philantinoos, born by the 460s, if not earlier. His son Mousaios is one of Aphrodito's tax contributors, probably at some point in the early 500s. He has four children, two of them explicitly described as well-born: their status as members of Aphrodito's elite would be obvious to everyone in town at the start of the sixth century.[3] When our records document these children, they have family property in several places and Dioskoros's father Apollos handles the lease on one of their properties.

The family of Sourous must have been as important in Aphrodito in the fifth century as the family of Dioskoros is in the sixth. Sourous himself is a child of the first half of the fifth century, a century before the time of this book. His wealth supports the region's richest monastery in the 520s, and must have been in place in the second half of the fifth century. It is possible – although we will never know – that at least part of this wealth came to Sourous through inheritance, the efforts of ancestors even deeper in Aphrodito's past. When we meet his descendants, Mariam and Helene, in the 560s, it is only for a moment, but their family does not seem to have fallen on hard times.[4]

The family of Kostantios and Mariam includes some of Aphrodito's high office holders. Kostantios, himself probably born in or before the 440s, has three sons: Ioannes, Apollos, and Victor. The first of these sons, Ioannes, serves on Aphrodito's tax board at one point in his career. The third son, Victor, has two sons of his own, Isakos and Daueid. Daueid, once one of Aphrodito's village headmen, is out of office and in debt by 514. Dioskoros's father Apollos offers to pay that debt for him. This favor is a subtle sign of a power shift in local politics, from one generation to the next.

These families reveal the prehistory of Aphrodito, a century before some of the stories we have seen so far. Their lives – in some cases dating as far back in the fifth century as the reign of Theodosius II – shape Aphrodito in the sixth century. They show that Aphrodito's collective memory stretches back to that previous time. When they write about the emperor Leo's grant of *autopragia* to Aphrodito, they are not writing about the distant past, but a world still part of their shared memory.

None of these families seem unusual. That is partly the point. As far as we can tell, they act the same as anyone else in Aphrodito with some means. They accumulate and use their wealth in the same way as Apollos and Dioskoros might. In several cases, they do so in collaboration with them. If

---

[3] For two of these children, see the discussion of Sibulla and Heraïs on page 150.   [4] See page 96.

they no longer dominate Aphrodito's local politics as they once did, this is a natural part of social change. They have earned and spent their influence in Aphrodito's social market, and now others move up to take their places. Dioskoros's time at the top did not last forever either. We have already seen hints of challenge to his influence and authority.[5] After his stay in Antinoopolis, he returns to Aphrodito, and in the 570s he handles the affairs of his father's monastery. At some point in this period, he dies. In the words of his own glossary, he finally faces the boundless separation between him and all that he knows.

His archive continues without him, in the hands of his wife Sophia, now in charge of her family's business affairs. In the first chapter, we saw that Aphrodito's papyri are not a completely unified group.[6] The papyri of Apollos and Dioskoros provide most of the evidence. That cache from late Roman Aphrodito dwindles and disappears toward the end of the sixth century. Its first text is from AD 506 and its last from 587 or 588.[7] However, the later papyri of Phoibammon and Kollouthos have made appearances throughout our visit to Aphrodito. The very last of these papyri dates to 646/647.[8] This is the very dawn of Arab rule, in the generation after the Persian conquest and Roman reconquest of Egypt. It is much too soon for the patterns and social structures of Dioskoros's day to disappear.

The next group of Aphrodito papyri found by its modern inhabitants restarts the story fifty years later. These papyri describe Aphrodito as it survives in the late seventh and early eighth centuries – these fifty years of silence could be a single lifetime in Aphrodito. The Coptic papyri from the 640s show men and women whose children might still be alive in the eighth century papyri. Dioskoros's own descendants – perhaps his great-grandchildren – might be alive in those papyri. He might appear in their minds, in their memory, in much the same way that his great-grandfather, Psimanobet, appears in his.

In short, this is not enough time for great change to sweep the town. Throughout late antiquity, Aphrodito fights to defend its administrative rights, which are perhaps a distant vestige from the days when it had been a legally independent city. Evidence from the Muslim period suggests that Aphrodito becomes a fully-fledged regional capital.[9] When we next get a glimpse of town affairs, under Muslim rule, one of their own still collects its taxes. But this does not mean that they ultimately won their battle for *autopragia* and saved themselves from the dominance of overbearing

---

[5] See page 28. [6] See page 9. [7] Fournet 2008a, 22–24. [8] *SB Kopt.* 3.1369.
[9] Bell 1908, 100–106 and *P.Lond.* 4, xiii, followed by Abbott 1938, 6.

patrons.[10] It means only that an administrative restructuring preserved local control and placed Aphrodito under even greater scrutiny from the central authorities.

We saw in the first chapter how the 1905 discovery of Aphrodito's late antique papyri was the second such find. A few years before, the 1901 discovery produced a papyrus archive from Aphrodito's Muslim period. This archive covers the period from AD 698 to 722. This narrow time range shows that "they were the archive of a single person, almost certainly the pagarch Basilios."[11] Basil is a latter-day Dioskoros, the local big-man, a Christian, presumably a landowner, his town's public face to the outside world. He may have succeeded his brother in the job.[12] Bear in mind the circumstances of the papyrus find: the same homeowner renovating the same property led to the papyri of both Basil and Dioskoros.

While Basil is from Aphrodito, many of the papyri in his archive come originally from the Egyptian capital, and the Muslim governor there, Qurra ibn Sharīk. In some ways, this Aphrodito archive is a record of competition between Qurra and Basil, "with Qurra constantly making demands and never fully being satisfied."[13] One editor of large portions of this archive saw its letters as "a good illustration of the extraordinary centralization of Arab government in Egypt."[14] He noted that the central government wrote to Aphrodito no less than nine times in January AD 710, including three times on the 30th alone. And this is only from the papyri we have.

Somewhere in the sea of new names and faces from Arab-ruled Aphrodito are men and women we can imagine as descendants of Apollos, Dioskoros, Phoibammon, and the others. These men and women no doubt fight the same fights and seek the same small victories that define small-town life for their ancestors at the end of antiquity. With such detailed data for the sixth and eighth centuries, we naturally wonder what took place in between, and what continuities we can find.

At first glance, the Muslim-era papyri show that "both the largest local monastery of the sixth century and the Psimanobet family were still landowners in the tax lists of the eighth."[15] The second half of this claim is only a guess. Psimanobet, the name of Dioskoros's oldest ancestor, is rare, but not overly so: as many as a dozen men with that name appear in the sixth-century papyri. The Psimanobet appearing in the eighth century need not

---

[10] Indeed, some scholars have assumed that they lost: see Zuckerman 2004a, 213.
[11] Wickham 2005, 134.   [12] *P.Lond* 4, xlvi citing *P.Lond.* 4.1592.   [13] Wickham 2005, 134.
[14] Bell 1908, 100.   [15] Wickham 2005, 419, following MacCoull 1984, 73–75.

be a relative of Dioskoros generations later. The first half of the claim is on safer ground. Apa Sourous, the town's largest monastery in the sixth century, is one of the most common place-names in town in the eighth century.[16] The standing of other local institutions and other local landowners is less clear. The papyri from the Arab period appear to show that the wealth of Aphrodito landowners shrank.[17]

While much of the new Aphrodito looks familiar when compared to the old, a good deal has changed as well. One of the most striking differences between late antique Aphrodito and Arab-ruled Aphrodito is the role of the military. We read nothing of Roman military service by the men of Aphrodito. The only soldiers we find in their stories are invariably outsiders. We may see this as another feature of Egypt's special status in the Roman world. Before the arrival of Rome, Egypt's Greek rulers were hesitant to arm the native Egyptians, rightly fearing the revolts that soon followed when they did.

Early in the Roman era, the emperors went to great lengths to keep Egypt isolated from the rest of the empire, nervous lest its vast resources fall into the hands of a threat to the throne. Later, in the last centuries of Roman rule, the emperors typically relied on foreign barbarian troops to staff their armies. Egyptian soldiers might see service no more grueling than patrol duty in the forts of the eastern and western deserts, and the southern border with Nubia.

By the eighth century, this had changed. With the arrival of Arab rule, Egypt has a new place in the geopolitics of the Mediterranean region. With the rapid expansion of the Muslim empire, Egyptians are now recruited for overseas wars. The military draft reaches throughout Egypt, and into Aphrodito. In AD 710, records mention sailors from Aphrodito who had been sent out on a failed expedition to Sicily. Of those who never returned, some are dead, others missing, believed to have settled in Africa, presumably absent without leave.[18]

These missing sailors take a toll on the men and women back home. We can imagine the anxiety in sending local sons away to a foreign war, and perhaps even the resentment that the requirement to do so is coming from foreign rulers the people of Aphrodito would consider unbelievers, heretical, or worse. No less importantly, the leading citizens of the town have to stand as surety to those sent overseas. In the previous year, AD 709, Cyrus,

---

[16] See, e.g., *P.Lond.* 4 page 591 and discussion in Marthot 2013, 211–212.   [17] Wickham 2005, 253.
[18] *P.Lond.* 4.1350.

Apollo, David, and Phoibammon – described as inhabitants of the three fields west of Aphrodito – write to Qurra, the Arab governor of Egypt.[19]

"We declare," they write, "we guarantee ... and are liable for the persons of these sailors, being those of our fields." The personal information of three sailors: Pnei, Georgios, and Apollo, follows. "Them we send northward ... that they may fulfill their expedition ... But if any one of them shall turn aside, we are ready to undergo any fine that our lord the all-famous governor may decree for us." We can assume that this guarantee was only one among many drafted in these years. The sailors of Aphrodito who stay in Africa on the way back from Sicily probably leave their patrons back home in debt.

The response from Arab authorities to desertion by these sailors is frankly authoritarian.[20] Qurra writes to Basil, telling him to "write to us the number of the sailors who have arrived in your district." The exact number of returning soldiers is less important than the information they have. Basil is to ask them about "those who remained in the said Africa and for what reason they remained there ... [and to] shortly procure for us without wasting time full enlightenment" about their situation.

Think back to the thieves and informants in Aphrodito nearly two centuries before. Villagers turn informant then rather willingly, in their search for more powerful local protection. Qurra may be able to find people willing to make the same trade in 710. Nevertheless, his demand that fugitives and those who give them shelter be fined is a strict one. Still more so is his insistence that the fugitives themselves be given forty lashes and nailed into a wooden arm and neck collar for transportation to the central authorities.[21] Local informants would have to be confident that they could avoid local retribution.

Aphrodito under Justinian sees an increase in taxes payable in gold. This seems to be part of a long-term trend toward increasing gold circulation and the monetization of the state revenue system. However, the state's fixation with gold as a means of tax payment really begins under Muslim rule. By the end of the seventh century, Aphrodito pays ten times in gold what it had paid at the start of the reign of Justinian.[22] This suggests a major change in local levels of monetization to meet the needs of the state.

The papyri from this period reflect this preoccupation. A papyrus from Qurra written in Arabic, dated early in AD 709, addresses the *sahib* or governor of Ashkauh (Ishqaw, or Aphrodito) and instructs him to "Look

---

[19] P.Lond 4.1494. [20] P.Lond. 4.1350; trans. in Sel.Pap. 2.433. [21] Bell 1908, 109.
[22] Banaji 2001, 83 and App. 1 Table 7, citing Casson 1938's figures from P.Lond. 4.1412–1413.

up the balance due from the bishop of your district of the amount imposed upon him by Abd Allah ibn Abd al-Malik and collect the first (amount) and rush it to me by my messenger and the messenger of the bishop."[23] Later that same year, the pagarch Basil himself writes to the people with an eye toward the revenue due to the government in good times. "The irrigation by the Nile this year has been even with the best irrigation ever," he writes. "Hence order the people of your land to undertake cultivation ... for when the land is cultivated, it prospers."

Behind this exhortation is a clear-cut vision of mankind's role on earth. "Cultivation by the people of the land is their chief duty," he writes, "after their duty to God."[24] Basil's interest is presumably not simply in the welfare of the people, but in their ability to render unto Caesar. But Basil and the local officials in this period are not to blame for the fiscal oppression of their own people. The message comes from above, and is handed down under threat of mortal violence. In AD 710 – the same year he writes demanding information about deserting sailors – Qurra writes to Basil about Aphrodito's gold tax. Claiming that Basil's payments are inadequate, Qurra chastises him: "we did not send you to pass your time in gluttony."[25] Qurra claims that the harvests have been good, the price of grain profitable, and that Basil has no excuse for payment arrears. "Do not therefore act in that way and give us cause to threaten your life."

This is not an isolated example, but part of a larger pattern of interaction between the Arab state and the native village in this period. In another letter, about someone he plans to punish, Qurra writes to Basil, "if you do not find him, send me his son or sons, and if he does not have sons, send me his wife, and if he does not have anyone to stand guarantor for him, send me his village headman."[26] A letter to the village from the central administration, perhaps in late AD 709, states, "You still owe a large amount of revenue ... I really used to think your administration more successful and better than what I have seen ... Beware of excuses, for I am not of those who believe in excuses or accept them."[27]

Nor are the threats limited to matters of regular taxation. The state makes other demands without hint of recourse. One text requires Aphrodito's men to perform maintenance work on the riverbanks with no suggestion of payment.[28] One Greek papyrus perhaps from Aphrodito in this period includes a requisition of just over a gold coin to support the

---

[23] *P.Qurra* 1. [24] *P.Qurra* 2.
[25] *P.Lond.* 4.1380; trans. in *Sel.Pap.* 2.434 (which offers "gormandizing," not "gluttony," for *phagonin*).
[26] Sijpesteijn 2013, 159 quoting *P.Heid.Arab.* 1.4.5–10. [27] *P.Qurra* 4.
[28] *P.Lond.* 4.1433, 1434; Sijpesteijn 2013, 173, note 309.

workers and artisans constructing the mosque in Damascus.²⁹ This sort of requisition is arbitrary and inherently irregular.

We have the makings of an interesting thought experiment. The scholarly vision of a servile state dominating Aphrodito seems to be accurate here, in the 700s, under Arab rule, but that may stem solely from the nature of the archives. We have the village voice in the 500s and that of the state in the 700s. True, the voice of the state in the 500s is also tremendously coercive, if we judge only by late Roman legislation. However, we do not see that legislation in the center turned into direct orders on the periphery. We do not see Roman officials in late antiquity demanding that Aphrodito's villagers inform on each other. We do not see them accuse Aphrodito's headmen of gluttony. We do not see them threaten villagers with kidnapping and death. We see the villagers accuse them of kidnapping, or, put more accurately, unlawful arrest.³⁰ But those cases are exceptional and deserve a judicial response. Qurra delivers his threats as a matter of course.

In Aphrodito's late antique legal disputes, the "outside world is kept out completely and the boundaries of the town are the confines of the settlement … The world of the settlements is carefully construed as a small world of local proportions."³¹ The long trips to Constantinople seem to be far and away the exception, and in those cases we see Aphrodito reaching out for help, not the government reaching in. In Islamic Aphrodito, we can no longer say the same. The outside world pushes against the town, and insists on the lives of the natives as the price for resistance.

In Roman late antiquity, ongoing social jostling – the never-ending search for a more powerful patron – ensures a dynamic equilibrium. No powerful provincial villain can push the village too hard without one day having a more powerful emperor push back. Can the natives in the Arab period fight back in the same way as their ancestors once did? Does that social marketplace still exist in this new world? Would Basil or any of his family take the long trip to Damascus to secure a reprieve from any of these demands? There is no suggestion that they do, and no likelihood that they would succeed if they did. The days of Apollos and Dioskoros are gone.

A generation ago, Peter Brown wrote about what he called the "new mood" of Roman late antiquity.³² He saw a world full of eccentrics, full of "vast and anxious" religious activity. A growing sense of self left late antique man wandering, severed from the bonds of traditional society.

---

²⁹ *CPR* 22.53.   ³⁰ See page 28.   ³¹ Gagos and van Minnen 1994, 46.   ³² Brown 1989, 49–59.

The great Christian organizers in this "puzzling age" were spiritual soldiers feeling the "revolutionary effects" of God's presence.

The timeline of Brown's discussion of this "new mood" is an early late antiquity, AD 170 to 300. In our later antiquity, in the 500s, this new mood has normalized. The late antique self, once severed from its classical moorings, becomes firmly docked once more. Aphrodito's constellation of churches and monasteries shows the religious enthusiasm of its people. The careful record-keeping of religious donations shows the know-how necessary to keep the forces of darkness at bay. The answers to the questions raised by the new mood are inscribed in the village landscape and on its papyri.

As one scholar once warned, late antiquity is "in danger of having become an exotic territory, populated by wild monks and excitable virgins and dominated by the clash of religions, mentalities and lifestyles."[33] Students drawn to this version of late antiquity should take Aphrodito as a cautionary tale. Much like Brown's new mood, this exotic territory seems normalized in Aphrodito's late antiquity. We see no clash of religions or mentalities, and the only holy men we meet are also the town's politicians and landlords.

One aspect of late antiquity seems even more central after our trip to Aphrodito: the role of patronage. Patronage is one part of the village's larger system of leverage and trust. In most situations, trust ensures that no guarantees are necessary. When they are, it is often enough to rely on peers, people whose status is less important than their ability to solve a problem. Only rarely do these people turn to the powerful and the elite for help. In Aphrodito, "there were at least two systems of patronage for peasants ... one focused on the danger – or protection – of the state, and one focused on the danger – or protection – of private landowners."[34]

But patronage is only one factor in Aphrodito's society. Social network analysis – a science that studies how all of us are connected – shows other sides to Aphrodito society. Adding up all social connections between all of the people in Aphrodito, and studying who seem to be the most central figures and how they relate to each other, shows that, measured quantitatively, Aphrodito's social networks appear to be relatively decentralized, with a low degree of hierarchy.[35] Another approach is to add up the social connections between all of the groups, the professions, the social classes, the town's Flavii and Aurelii.[36] Measured in this way, people in Aphrodito are more connected to people like themselves. Aphrodito's social ties are

[33] Cameron 1993, 6. [34] Wickham 2005, 528. [35] Ruffini 2008a, 198. [36] Ruffini unpublished.

not organized around Roman concepts of status or prestige. They are organized locally, with a preference for the man next door.

These approaches have not convinced everyone.[37] But the less mathematical, more impressionistic approach I take throughout this book arrives at more or less the same results. When people in Aphrodito search for patrons, rank and title matter, but they are not the only, or even the largest, determining factor. When they need legal guarantees that someone will not disappear, they do not obsess over status or rank. Power does not need status or rank, but it does need money. Put most simply, the men and women of Aphrodito care about pragmatics, about who has enough money to give a good guarantee. When they face theft or vandalism, they are less interested in the letter of the law than in who has the local knowledge to help them solve their problems. When they face murder, they just want to know where the bones are buried. When they do think about going to law, they work on the sidelines first, in the shadows of the court, to find informal solutions through the help of friends.

Aphrodito is not just an Egyptian story. It is also a late antique story, a story of the last generations of the Roman Empire in the east. Major events are afoot in the eastern Mediterranean region during this period. In the 530s, Justinian launches a major war of reconquest against Vandal North Africa. Its surprising success inspires an even greater war of reconquest against Gothic Italy. This venture lasts for decades. Before, during, and after these wars, Rome and Persia engage in an ongoing struggle for supremacy along the Roman Empire's eastern border.

The great health crisis of the day, the Plague of Justinian in the early 540s, leaves no direct trace in the papyrological record. Only a shadow of evidence, an increase in charitable donations by one aristocrat, hints at anything wrong.[38] Apollos and Dioskoros may have no reason to write about it. Maybe hundreds or even thousands of people in Aphrodito can die at once and sink from sight without a trace, but this seems unlikely. The view of the plague from the center, from the great cities and the literary elites, may be exaggerated.

Furthermore, what about the great religious controversies of the day? What about the heated debate within the Christian church over the nature of Jesus as both God and man? What about the final death throes of Egypt's traditional religion, the polytheism of the pharaohs? When Dioskoros describes Christ in a certain way, he may know how controversial others may find his words. Or he may find them to be second nature.

---

[37] Sarris 2009.   [38] See page 113.

When he describes backsliding pagan barbarians, he may really mean it, or he may be scoring an artistic rhetorical point. In Aphrodito, we see great religious change only in passing, in hints or obscure phrases.

The main intellectual movements of the sixth century also pass this town by. The great traditions of Neoplatonism – struggling and dying in Athens, growing and evolving in Alexandria – are a central part of our vision of sixth-century intellectual history. But they are absent from Aphrodito. Dioskoros may have studied under John Philoponus, one of Alexandria's great philosophers and theologians, but it is not likely that many people back home know or think that it matters.[39]

When the people of Aphrodito write the date in the name of Justinian or send a petition to Theodora, do they know anything of the human beings behind the names? Do they know the dark rumors circulating in the capital about Justinian the demon and Theodora the whore? These rumors survive today thanks to the bitter pen of Procopius and give a glimpse of the view from the corridors of power in the capital, but not the view from the periphery. When Justinian's long reign ends and his nephew Justin II takes power, does it make any difference at home in Aphrodito? When Justin begins his descent into madness, allegedly biting any courtier within reach, does it change Aphrodito's perception of his power, or its people's hope for satisfaction when they write to his officials?

Almost all of this world – almost all of the great narrative of the sixth century – is missing from the evidence of Aphrodito. No clue to most of these events appears in our papyri. You may ask why it would, and whether that silence proves anything. But then ask: how much of the great narrative of the sixth century matters to these people, or is even known to them? The Apions, aristocrats from another part of Egypt in this same period, are active at court and have relatives with property in Italy.[40] But they are exceptional.

My point is slightly insidious. Historians naturally go where the evidence takes them. Procopius and the sixth century's other great minds have left so very much. We want our work with these great minds to be important, and so we see the world the way they see it. We convince ourselves that we are right to dwell on the things on which they dwell. Aphrodito does not prove that these things are unimportant. But it is a reminder that for most people, much smaller things loom much larger.

---

[39] MacCoull 1986c, 164–166.
[40] With connections to Gregory the Great: Ruffini 2008a, 98, note 25.

Conclusion

Is Aphrodito typical? Could any villager in late antique Egypt arrive in Aphrodito and recognize its world? It is hard to see why not. On the one hand, we know that parts of Egypt are home to large estates owned by absentee members of the political elite. At a bureaucratic level, life might be different for a peasant living on the great estates of Oxyrhynchos. On the other hand, what makes Aphrodito so special? It has no characteristics that cannot be found in dozens of places throughout Egypt, and by extension throughout the Roman east. Its previous legal status as a city is not enough to make a difference: this distinguished past is completely absent from the worldview of the sixth-century present, except to the degree that it impacts who collects taxes from whom.

The apparent difference between the evidence from the large estates of Oxyrhynchos and the small landholders of Aphrodito is an illusion of scale, a distortion created by comparing region-wide data on the one hand and village-wide data on the other.[41] No one has made a persuasive case to the contrary. Great estates do exist in late antiquity. Those great estates do own entire villages. Aphrodito is not one of them. This difference matters, but only on the level of economic superstructures.

It makes relatively little difference on a day-to-day level. Think of life as one large puzzle, and one's social life as the steps one takes to solve it. Then compare one of the little men or women in a small village on a great estate to anyone we have met in Aphrodito. They confront the same puzzles and take the same steps to solve them as would anyone in any village in this period. Aphrodito reveals a map of social life throughout the Roman world in late antiquity. Men and women in estate-owned villages may have fewer solutions to their puzzles available to them, but we have no reason to think that they see the world at all differently from the men and women of Aphrodito.

Nevertheless, in so many ways, Aphrodito seems to stand outside the mainstream world of scholarly late antiquity. We are seeing things entirely backwards: that world of late antiquity is a scholarly construct. It exists at the rarefied heights of elite culture, in the glory of the Hagia Sophia and the last days of the Neoplatonists in Athens. This late antiquity has little to do

---

[41] Hickey 2012, 159–160 mentions Zuckerman's 2004 claim that the Ioulianos estate dominated Aphrodito, and my claim (Ruffini 2008a, 246–251), stated here, that Oxyrhynchos and Aphrodito can co-exist on two different levels of evidence. He writes that "the jury remains out, though I find myself skeptical." If Hickey thinks that Zuckerman and I are making similar or parallel claims, I disagree: I have rejected Zuckerman's claim in its entirety (see page 91). Nor do I think that my claim runs afoul of Hickey's argument regarding the Apions, which I support in its entirety.

with the everyday experiences of the vast majority of people in the Roman world.

The Roman world is sometimes described as a world of cities. In late antiquity, the great cities of the east – Alexandria, Antioch, Constantinople – monopolize our attention. However, for the average Egyptian peasant – and most likely, for the average Roman citizen more generally – the real late antiquity looks much more like Aphrodito than anything in Alexandria, Antioch, or Constantinople. Aphrodito may not be typical of the Roman world, but it is certainly comparable to vast portions of it, and may speak for the silent majority of the late Roman world, the world of villages.

Two visions of late antiquity have been most common over the last several decades. The first vision focuses on powerful bishops and charismatic holy men. The second vision focuses on rich aristocrats and the apparatus of state tax collection. The first vision is the product of successful late antique marketing for Simeon the Stylite and others like him. The second vision enjoys attention at least in part because of presentist concerns over class warfare. Both visions are true, but they labor over evidence produced by less than 1 percent of the population.

Another, and in my opinion far better, way to see late antiquity, to see how the rest of the population lived, is to look at the documents they generate. This late antiquity does not focus, with Procopius, on Justinian's great works of architecture. It calculates the number of mud bricks needed for a new separating wall. This late antiquity does not revolve around the rise of the holy man. It merely internalizes him, paying for his holy day at the same time as it makes payments to family and friends. This late antiquity does not produce widely read saints' lives or church chronicles. It struggles awkwardly to move from one language to the next, not quite sure what to call a Greek penis. And at the end, this late antiquity wonders, as we all do, about the answers to eternal questions. "What is death?" Dioskoros answers: *aperaton diastêma*, a boundless separation.[42]

This is a social claim. A rebuttal would insist on the role of economics in late antiquity, and insist that no one in Aphrodito could escape its eternal iron laws. This is true, but only up to a point. We are all moved by forces we do not see and cannot understand: in this way, Dioskoros and I have much in common. But this eternal commonality makes a focus on economic superstructures a less useful approach for studying village life in late antiquity.

---

[42] MacCoull 1986a, 256.

We should try to understand the world of villages in a way the villagers themselves would understand it. When critics of late antique economic structures condemn the commodification of wage labor and Dioskoros's role in its oppression of the Egyptian peasantry,[43] or claim that the Egyptian aristocrats spread "the poison of class animosity,"[44] they are speaking a language of their own – one the people of Aphrodito would not understand.

So many people using the Aphrodito evidence focus on the role of the state. But the state appears only at exceptional moments. Remember the murder mystery at the start of this book. The state appears to levy a fine on the killers, but this is a unique moment in the evidence. Nor do the relatives of the victims really expect any recourse from the state, which offers none. Maria wants only to find her husband's bones. The state is not the only vehicle for analyzing Aphrodito and towns like it. Another unit of analysis, perhaps a better one, is the individual and the individual's personal ties to others. We cannot understand anyone's life as they do if we insist on seeing it from the macro-level of the Roman Empire in its moment of crisis and transition. We must instead see it at the level of the crowd in the marketplace, full of faces known and unknown, friends and strangers jostling with each other in full view of others. At this level there is no state, there are only greater and lesser patrons, and this is for the best for almost everyone involved.

This is a world we dare not simplify. This is not purely a world of vibrancy and cultural creativity. Nor is this a world of decadence, of oppression, of decline and fall. This is not a world driven purely by status and hierarchy. Above all else, this is not a world of class struggle. It is a world of every kind of struggle: husband against wife, mother against son, brother against sister, client against patron, farmer against shepherd, neighbor against stranger, high man against low. Behind these struggles, behind the written moments of chaos and control, are a thousand moments more, invisible and quiet, built on trust between men and women who do not need to put pen to paper.

---

[43] See my response to Banaji's critique of Dioskoros on page 91.   [44] Sarris 2006, 199.

Bibliography

Abbott, N. (1938) *The Kurrah Papyri from Aphrodito in the Oriental Institute.* Chicago, IL.
Allinson, F. G., ed. (1964) *Menander: The Principal Fragments.* Cambridge, MA.
Alston, R. (2002) *The City in Roman and Byzantine Egypt.* London.
Amelotti, M. and G. I. Luzzatto (1972) *Le costituzioni giustinianee nei papiri e nelle epigrafi: Legum Iustiniani Imperatoris Vocabularium* 1. Milan.
Arnaoutoglou, I. (1995) "Marital Disputes in Greco-Roman Egypt." *Journal of Juristic Papyrology* 25: 11–28.
Azzarello, G. (2012) *Il dossier della "domus divina" in Egitto.* Berlin.
Bagnall, R. S. (1982) "Religious Conversion and Onomastic Change in Early Byzantine Egypt." *Bulletin of the American Society of Papyrologists* 19: 105–124.
  (1986) "Two Byzantine Legal Papyri in a Private Collection." In R. S. Bagnall and W. V. Harris, eds., *Studies in Roman Law: In Memory of A. Arthur Schiller.* Leiden: 1–9.
  (1987) "Church, State and Divorce in Late Roman Egypt." In K.-L. Selig and R. Somerville, eds., *Florilegium Columbianum: Essays in Honor of Paul Oskar Kristeller.* New York, NY: 41–61.
  (1989) "Official and Private Violence in Roman Egypt." *Bulletin of the American Society of Papyrologists* 26: 201–216.
  (1992) "Landholding in Late Roman Egypt: The Distribution of Wealth." *Journal of Roman Studies* 82: 128–149.
  (1993) *Egypt in Late Antiquity.* Princeton, NJ.
  (1995a) "Review: T. Gagos and P. van Minnen, Settling a Dispute: Towards a Legal Anthropology of Late Antique Egypt." *Bryn Mawr Classical Review* (http://bmcr.brynmawr.edu/1995/95.10.11.html).
  (1995b) "Women, Law, and Social Realities in Late Antiquity: A Review Article." *Bulletin of the American Society of Papyrologists* 32: 65–86.
  (2005) "Village and City: Geographies of Power in Byzantine Egypt." In J. Lefort, C. Morrisson and J.-P. Sodini, eds., *Les Villages dans l'Empire byzantine (IVe – Xve siècle).* Paris: 553–565.
  ed. (2007) *Egypt in the Byzantine World: 300–700.* Cambridge.
  (2008) "Village Landholding at Aphrodito in Comparative Perspective." In J.-L. Fournet, ed., *Les archives de Dioscore d'Aphrodité cent ans après leur découverte: histoire et culture dans l'Égypte byzantine.* Paris: 181–190.

Bagnall, R. S. and B. W. Frier (1994) *The Demography of Roman Egypt*. Cambridge.
Bagnall, R. S., N. Aravecchia, R. Cribiore et al. (2015) *An Oasis City*. New York, NY.
Baldwin, B. (1981) "Dioscorus of Aphrodito and the Circus Factions." *Zeitschrift für Papyrologie und Epigraphik* 42: 285–286.
  (1982) "Notes on the Greek-Coptic Glossary of Dioscorus of Aphrodito." *Glotta* 60: 79–81.
  (1984) "Dioscorus of Aphrodito: The Worst Poet of Antiquity?" *Atti del XVII Congresso Internazionale di Papirologia* 2: 327–331.
Banaji, J. (1998) "Discounts, Weight Standards, and the Exchange-Rate between Gold and Copper: Insights into the Monetary Process of the Sixth Century." In G. Crifo and S. Giglio, eds., *Atti dell'Accademia romanistica costantiniana: XII Convegno Internazionale in onore di Manilo Sargenti*. Naples: 183–202.
  (2001) *Agrarian Change in Late Antiquity: Gold, Labour, and Aristocratic Dominance*. Oxford.
Barnard, H. (2005) "Sire, il n'y a pas de Blemmyes: A Re-Evaluation of Historical and Archaeological Data." In J. C. M. Starkey, ed., *People of the Red Sea*. Oxford: 23–40.
Barns, J. W. B. (1976) "Loan of Money with Hypotheke: PCairo Maspero 67023 + PFitzhugh." In A. E. Hanson, ed., *Collectanea Papyrologica. Texts Published in Honor of H. C. Youtie*. Bonn. 2: 589–594.
Beaucamp, J. (1998) "Les filles et la transmission du patrimoine à Byzance: dot et part successorale." In J. Beaucamp and G. Dagron, eds., *La transmission du patrimoine: Byzance et l'aire méditerranéenne*. Paris: 11–34.
  (2000) "Donne, patrimonio, chiesa (Bisanzio, IV-VII secolo)." In G. Lanata, ed., *Il Tardoantico alle soglie del duemila*. Pisa: 249–266.
  (2007) "Byzantine Egypt and Imperial Law." In R. S. Bagnall, ed., *Egypt in the Byzantine World: 300–700*. Cambridge: 271–287.
Bell, H. I. (1908) "The Aphrodito Papyri." *Journal of Hellenic Studies* 28: 97–120.
  (1917) "The Byzantine Servile State in Egypt." *Journal of Egyptian Archaeology* 4: 86–106.
  (1940) "Antinoopolis: A Hadrianic Foundation in Egypt." *Journal of Roman Studies* 30: 133–147.
  (1944) "An Egyptian Village in the Age of Justinian." *Journal of Hellenic Studies* 64: 21–36.
Bell, H. I. and W. E. Crum (1925) "A Greek-Coptic Glossary." *Aegyptus* 6: 177–226.
Bell, P. N. (2013) *Social Conflict in the Age of Justinian: Its Nature, Management, and Mediation*. Oxford and New York, NY.
Bjornlie, M. S. (2007) "Review: P. Sarris, Economy and Society in the Age of Justinian." *Bryn Mawr Classical Review* (http://bmcr.brynmawr.edu/2007/2007-06-04.html).
Blanchard, A. (2012) "Le papyrus Bodmer et la reception de Ménandre à l'époque byzantine." In P. Schubert, ed., *Actes du 26e Congrès international de papyrologie*. Geneva: 77–82.

Boud'hors, A. (2008) "Du copte dans les archives d'Apollôs." In J.-L. Fournet *Les archives de Dioscore d'Aphrodité cent ans après leur découverte: histoire et culture dans l'Égypte byzantine*. Paris: 67–76.
Bowman, A. and A. Wilson, eds. (2013) *The Roman Agricultural Economy: Organization, Investment, and Production*. Oxford.
Bransbourg, G. (2015) "The Later Roman Empire." In A. Monson and W. Scheidel, eds., *Fiscal Regimes and the Political Economy of Premodern States*. Cambridge: 258–281.
Brown, P. (1971) "The Rise and Function of the Holy Man in Late Antiquity." *Journal of Roman Studies* 61: 80–101.
  (1989) *The World of Late Antiquity*. New York, NY.
  (2016) *Treasure in Heaven: The Holy Poor in Early Christianity*. Charlottesville, VA and London.
Brubaker, L. (2005) "The Age of Justinian: Gender and Society." In M. Maas, ed., *The Cambridge Companion to the Age of Justinian*. Cambridge and New York, NY: 427–447.
Bryen, A. Z. (2013) *Violence in Roman Egypt: A Study in Legal Interpretation*. Philadelphia, PA.
Cadell, H. (1967) "Nouveaux fragments de la correspondance de Kurrah ben Sharik." *Recherches de Papyrologie* 4: 107–160.
Cameron, Alan (2007) "Poets and Pagans in Byzantine Egypt." In R. S. Bagnall, ed., *Egypt in the Byzantine World: 300–700*. Cambridge: 21–46.
Cameron, Averil (1993) *The Mediterranean World in Late Antiquity: AD 395–600*. London and New York, NY.
Capra, R. L. (2012) "On the Poetics of Dioscoros of Aphrodito: The Encomium on Duke Kallinikos (P. Cair. Masp. III 67315)." In D. Brakke, D. Deliyannis and E. Watts, eds., *Shifting Cultural Frontiers in Late Antiquity*. Farnham: 129–138.
Cartwright, D. and F. Harary (1956). "Structural Balance: A Generalization of Heider's Theory." *Psychological Review* 63: 277–293.
Casson, L. (1938) "Tax Collection Problems in Early Arab Egypt." *Transactions of the American Philological Association* 69: 274–291.
Castello, C. (1984) "La Novella 140 di Giuliano II e il malvagio demone divorzista." In A. Biscardi, J. Modrzrjewski and H. J. Wolff, eds., *MNHMH Georgiou A. Petropoulou (1897–1964)*. Athens. I: 295–315.
Cavero, L. M. (2008) *Poems in Context: Greek Poetry in the Egyptian Thebaid 200–600 AD*. Berlin and New York, NY.
Clarke, W. K. L. (1918) *The Lausiac History of Palladius*. London.
Cribiore, R. (2001) *Gymnastics of the Mind: Greek Education in Hellenistic and Roman Egypt*. Princeton, NJ.
Crislip, A. T. (2005) *From Monastery to Hospital: Christian Monasticism and the Transformation of Health Care in Late Antiquity*. Ann Arbor, MI.
Cromwell, J. (2014) "Managing a Year's Taxes: Tax Demands and Tax Payments in 724 CE." *Archiv für Papyrusforschung* 60: 229–239.

Decker, M. (2009) *Tilling the Hateful Earth: Agricultural Production and Trade in the Late Antique East.* Oxford.

Depauw, M. and W. Clarysse (2013) "How Christian Was Fourth Century Egypt? Onomastic Perspectives on Conversion." *Vigiliae Christianae* 67: 407–435.

Dickie, M. (1993) "Malice, Envy and Inquisitiveness in Catullus 5 and 7." In F. Cairns and M. Heath, eds., *Papers of the Leeds International Latin Seminar. Seventh Volume 1993. Roman Poetry and Prose. Greek Rhetoric and Poetry.* Leeds: 9–26.

Dijkstra, J. H. F. (2003) "A World Full of the Word: The Biblical Learning of Dioscorus." In A. A. MacDonald, G. J. Reinink and M. W. Twomey, eds., *Learned Antiquity: Scholarship and Society in the Near-East, the Greco-Roman World, and the Early Medieval West.* Leuven: 140–146.

(2004) "A Cult of Isis at Philae After Justinian? Reconsidering *P.Cair.Masp.* I 67004." *Zeitschrift für Papyrologie und Epigraphik* 146: 137–154.

(2008) *Philae and the End of Ancient Egyptian Religion: A Regional Study of Religious Transformation (298–642 CE).* Leuven.

Dossey, L. D. (2008) "Wife Beating and Manliness in Late Antiquity." *Past & Present* 199: 3–40.

Drescher, J. (1944) "A Widow's Petition: With Two Plates." *Bulletin de la Société d'Archéologie Copte* 10: 91–96.

Eke, T., S. Al-Husainy and M. K. Raynor (2000) "The Spectrum of Ocular Inflammation Caused by Euphorbia Plant Sap." *Archives of Ophthalmology* 118(1): 13–16.

Evans Grubb, J. (2005) "Parent-Child Conflict in the Roman Family: The Evidence of the Code of Justinian." In M. George, ed., *The Roman Family in the Empire: Rome, Italy, and Beyond.* Oxford: 93–128.

Fallon, F. T. (1978) *The Enthronement of Sabaoth.* Leiden.

Förster, H., J.-L. Fournet and T. S. Richter (2012) "Une *misthôsis* copte d'Aphroditê (P.Lond.inv. 2849): le plus ancien acte notarié en copte?" *Archiv für Papyrusforschung* 58: 344–359.

Fournet, J.-L. (1993) "À propos de *SB* XIV 11856 ou quand la poésie rencontre le document." *Bulletin de L'Institut Français d'Archéologie Orientale* 93: 223–235.

(1994) "Un papyrus médical byzantin de l'Académie des Inscriptions et Belles-Lettres." *Travaux et Mémoires* 12: 309–322.

(1997) "Du nouveau dans la bibliothèque de Dioscore d'Aphrodité." *Akten des 21. Internationalen Papyrologenkongresses, Berlin 1995. Archiv für Papyrusforschung Beiheft* 3: 297–301.

(1998) "Un nouvel épithalame de Dioscore d'Aphrodité adressé à un gouverneur civil de Thébaïde." *Antiquité Tardive* 6: 65–82.

(1999) *Hellénisme dans l'Egypte du VIe siècle: la bibliothèque et l'oeuvre de Dioscore d'Aphrodite.* Cairo.

(2000) "Le système des intermediaries dans les reçus fiscaux byzantins et ses implications chronologiques sur le dossier de Dioscore d'Aphrodité." *Archiv für Papyrusforschung* 46: 233–247.

(2001) "Du nouveau dans les archives de Dioscore d'Aphrodité." In I. Andorlini, ed., *Atti del XXII Congresso Internazionale di Papirologia*. Florence: 475–486.

(2002) "Un document inédit des archives de Dioscore d'Aphrodité au Musée Égyptien." In M. Eldamaty and M. Trad, eds., *Egyptian Museum Collections around the World: Studies for the Centennial of the Egyptian Museum, Cairo*. Cairo: 397–407.

(2004) "Entre document et littérature: la pétition dans l'antiquité tardive." In D. Feissel and J. Gascou, eds., *La pétition à Byzance*. Paris: 62–74.

(2008a) *Les archives de Dioscore d'Aphrodité cent ans après leur découverte: histoire et culture dans l'Égypte byzantine*. Paris.

(2008b) "Quittances de loyer du *topos* d'apa Michel d'Antaiopolis." *Bulletin of the American Society of Papyrologists* 45: 45–58.

(2010a) "Les tribulations d'un pétitionnaire égyptien à Constantinople: Révision de P.Cair.Masp. III 67352." In T. Gagos, ed., *Proceedings of the 25th International Congress of Papyrology, Ann Arbor 2007*. Ann Arbor, MI: 243–252.

(2010b) "Sur les premiers documents juridiques coptes." In A. Boud'hors and C. Louis, eds., *Études coptes XI. Troisième journée d'étude (Marseille, 7–9 juin 2007) (Cahiers de la Bibliothèque Copte 17)*. Paris: 125–137.

(2013a) "Notes d'onomastique aphroditéenne." In D. Lauritzen and M. Tardieu, eds., *Le voyage des légendes: Hommages à Pierre Chuvin*. Paris: 107–122.

(2013b) "Culture grecque et document dans l'Égypte de l'antiquité tardive." *Papyrology AD 2013: 27th International Congress of Papyrology. Journal of Juristic Papyrology* 43: 135–162.

(2016) "Sur les premiers documents juridiques coptes (2): Les archives de Phoibammôn et de Kollouthos." In Anne Boud'hors and Catherine Louis, eds., *Seiziemes journees d'etudes coptes*. Geneva: 115–141.

Frankfurter, D. (1998) *Religion in Roman Egypt: Assimilation and Resistance*. Princeton, NJ.

Frier, B. (1989) "A New Papyrology?" *Bulletin of the American Society of Papyrologists* 26: 217–226.

Gagos, T. and P. van Minnen (1994) *Settling a Dispute: Towards a Legal Anthropology of Late Antique Egypt*. Ann Arbor, MI.

Garnsey, P. (1970) *Social Status and Legal Privilege in the Roman Empire*. Oxford.

Gascou, J. (1976) "P. Fouad 87: Les monastères pachômiens et l'État byzantin." *Bulletin de L'Institut Français d'Archéologie Orientale* 76: 157–184.

(1977) "Review: P. J. Sijpesteijn, The Aphrodite Papyri in the University of Michigan Papyrus Collection (P. Mich. XIII)." *Chronique d'Egypte* 52: 360–368.

(1985) "Les grandes domaines, la cité et l'état en Égypte byzantine." *Travaux et Mémoires* 9: 1–89.

Gascou, J. and L. MacCoull (1987) "Le cadastre d'Aphroditô." *Travaux et Mémoires* 10: 103–158.

Gascou, J. and K. A. Worp (1990) "Les archives des huiliers d'Aphrodito." In M. Capasso, G. Messeri Savorelli and R. Pintaudi, eds., *Miscellanea papyrologica in occasione del bicentenario delVedizione délia Charta Borgiana*. Florence. 1: 217–244.

Geens, K. (2014) "Panopolis, a Nome Capital in Egypt in the Roman and Byzantine Period (ca. AD 200–600)." *Trismegistos Online Publications Special Series I* (www.trismegistos.org/top.php).

Gonis, N. (2009) "Reconsidering Some Fiscal Documents from Early Islamic Egypt III." *Zeitschrift für Papyrologie und Epigraphik* 169: 197–208.

Grey, C. (2011) *Constructing Communities in the Late Roman Countryside*. Cambridge.

(2012) "Concerning Rural Matters." In S. F. Johnson, ed., *The Oxford Handbook of Late Antiquity*. Oxford: 625–666.

Grossmann, P. (2010) "Antinoopolis October 2010: On the Church beside the Eastern Gate." *Aegyptus* 90: 165–181.

Grünewald, T. (2004) *Bandits in the Roman Empire: Myth and Reality*. Trans. J. Drinkwater. London.

Haldon, J. (2015) "Late Rome, Byzantium and Early Medieval Western Europe." In A. Monson and W. Scheidel, eds., *Fiscal Regimes and the Political Economy of Premodern States*. Cambridge: 345–389.

Hanafi, A. (1985) "Two Documents from the Archive of Dioscorus." *Bulletin of the Center of Papyrological Studies, Ain-Shams University* 1: 57–68.

(1988) "A Letter from the Archive of Dioscorus." In B. G. Mandilaras, ed., *Proceedings of the XVIII International Congress of Papyrology*. Athens. 2: 91–105.

Harper, K. (2011) *Slavery in the Late Roman World, AD 275–425*. Cambridge.

(2016) "People, Plagues, and Prices in the Roman World: The Evidence from Egypt." *Journal of Economic History* 76(3): 803–839.

Harries, J. (2001) "Resolving Disputes: The Frontiers of Law in Late Antiquity." In R. W. Mathisen, ed., *Law, Society and Authority in Late Antiquity*. Oxford: 68–82.

Hassanein, A. H. (1981) "Two Documents from Aphrodite." *Bulletin de L'Institut Français d'Archéologie Orientale* 81: 427–435.

Hickey, T. M. (2007) "Aristocratic Landholding and the Economy." In R. S. Bagnall, ed., *Egypt in the Byzantine World: 300–700*. Cambridge: 288–308.

(2012) *Wine, Wealth, and the State in Late Antique Egypt: The House of Apion at Oxyrhynchus*. Ann Arbor, MI.

Hillner, J. (2006) "Clerics, Property and Patronage: The Case of the Roman Titular Churches." *Antiquité Tardive* 14: 59–68.

Hobsbawm, E. J. (1969) *Bandits*. London.

Holleran, C. and A. Pudsey, eds. (2011) *Demography and the Graeco-Roman World: New Insights and Approaches*. Cambridge.

Hombert, M. (1923) "Un document nouveau d'Aphrodito." *Aegyptus* 4: 43–48.

Huebner, S. (2013) *The Family in Roman Egypt: A Comparative Approach to Intergenerational Solidarity and Conflict.* Cambridge.
Johnson, A. C. and L. C. West (1949) *Byzantine Egypt: Economic Studies.* Princeton, NJ.
Keenan, J. (1974) "The Names Flavius and Aurelius as Status Designations in Later Roman Egypt." *Zeitschrift für Papyrologie und Epigraphik* 13: 283–304.
  (1980) "Aurelius Phoibammon, Son of Triadelphus: A Byzantine Egyptian Land Entrepreneur." *Bulletin of the American Society of Papyrologists* 17: 145–54.
  (1984) "The Aphrodito Papyri and Village Life in Byzantine Egypt." *Bulletin de la Société d'Archéologie Copte* 26: 51–63.
  (1985a) "Village Shepherds and Social Tension in Byzantine Egypt." *Yale Classical Studies* 28: 245–260.
  (1985b) "Notes on Absentee Landlordism at Aphrodito." *Bulletin of the American Society of Papyrologists* 22: 137–169.
  (1988) "P. Cair. Masp. II 67135." *Bulletin of the American Society of Papyrologists* 25: 153–156.
  (1992) "A Constantinople Loan, AD 541." *Bulletin of the American Society of Papyrologists* 29: 175–182.
  (1995) "The Aphrodito Murder Mystery: A Return to the Scene of the Crimes." *Bulletin of the American Society of Papyrologists* 32: 57–63.
  (2001) "Egypt." In A. Cameron, B. Ward-Perkins and M. Whitby, eds., *The Cambridge Ancient History Volume 14: Late Antiquity: Empire and Successors, AD 425–600.* Cambridge: 612–637.
  (2005) "Review: C. Zuckerman, Du Village à l'Empire: Autour du register fiscal d'Aphroditô (525/526)." *Bulletin of the American Society of Papyrologists* 42: 285–297.
  (2007) "Byzantine Egyptian Villages." In R. S. Bagnall, ed., *Egypt in the Byzantine World: 300–700.* Cambridge: 226–243.
  (2008) "'Tormented Voices': P.Cair.Masp. I 67002." In J.-L. Fournet, ed., *Les archives de Dioscore d'Aphrodité cent ans après leur découverte: histoire et culture dans l'Égypte byzantine.* Paris: 171–180.
  (2014) "Law in the Byzantine Period." In J. Keenan, J. G. Manning and U. Yiftach-Firanko, eds., *Law and Legal Practice in Egypt from Alexander to the Arab Conflict.* Cambridge: 23–28.
Keenan, J., J. G. Manning and U. Yiftach-Firanko, eds. (2014) *Law and Legal Practice in Egypt from Alexander to the Arab Conquest.* Cambridge.
Kehoe, D. (2003) "Aristocratic Dominance in the Late Roman Agrarian Economy and the Question of Economic Growth. Review: J. Banaji, Agrarian Change in Late Antiquity." *Journal of Roman Archaeology* 16: 711–721.
Kelly, B. (2011) *Petitions, Litigation, and Social Control in Roman Egypt.* Oxford.
Kitzinger, E. (1977) *Byzantine Art in the Making: Main Lines of Stylistic Development in Mediterranean Art, 3rd–7th Century.* Cambridge, MA.
Kovelman, A. (1991) "From Logos to Myth: Egyptian Petitions of the 5th–7th Centuries." *Bulletin of the American Society of Papyrologists* 28: 135–152.

Kuehn, C. (1990) "Dioskoros of Aphrodito and Romanos the Melodist." *Bulletin of the American Society of Papyrologists* 27: 103–107.
  (1993) "A New Papyrus of a Dioscorian Poem and Marriage Contract: P.Berol. Inv. No. 21334." *Zeitschrift für Papyrologie und Epigraphik* 97: 103–115.
  (1995) *Channels of Imperishable Fire: The Beginnings of Christian Mystical Poetry and Dioscorus of Aphrodito*. New York, NY.
Laes, C., K. Mustakallio and V. Vuolanto, eds. (2014) *Children and Family in Late Antiquity: Life, Death and Interaction (Interdisciplinary Studies in Ancient Culture and Religion, 15)*. Leuven and Walpole, MA.
Lefebvre, G. (1907) *Fragments d'un manuscript de Ménandre*. Cairo.
Lemaire, F. (2010) "*Antimisthosis* in the Dioscorus Archive." In T. Gagos and A. Hyatt, eds., *Proceedings of the Twenty-Fifth International Congress of Papyrology, Ann Arbor, July 29–August 4, 2007*. Ann Arbor, MI: 397–408.
MacCoull, L. S. B. (1984) "Notes on the Social Structure of Late Antique Aphrodito." *Bulletin de la Société d'Archéologie Copte* 26: 65–77.
  (1986a) "Further Notes on the Greek-Coptic Glossary of Dioscorus of Aphrodito." *Glotta* 64: 253–257.
  (1986b) "An Isopsephistic Encomium on Saint Senas by Dioscorus of Aphrodito." *Zeitschrift für Papyrologie und Epigraphik* 62: 51–53.
  (1986c) "Dioscorus of Aphrodito and John Philoponus." *Studia Patristica* 18: 163–168.
  (1987) "P. Cair. Masp. II 67188 Verso 1–5: The *Gnostica* of Dioscorus of Aphrodito." *Tyche* 2: 95–97.
  (1988) *Dioscorus of Aphrodito: His Work and His World*. Berkeley, CA.
  (1990a) "Missing Pieces of the Dioscorus Archive." *Chronique d'Égypte* 65: 107–110.
  (1990b) "The Aphrodito Murder Mystery." *Journal of Juristic Papyrology* 20: 103–107.
  (1991) "'The Holy Trinity' at Aphrodito." *Tyche* 6: 109–111.
  (1992a) "A Cinderella Story from Byzantine Egypt: P.Cair.Masp. I 67089 and III 67294." *Byzantion* 62: 380–388.
  (1992b) "More Missing Pieces of the Dioscorus Archive." In M. Rassart-Debergh and J. Ries, eds., *Actes du IVe Congrès copte: Louvain-la-Neuve, 5–10 septembre 1988*. Louvain-la-Neuve: 104–110.
  (1993) "The Apa Apollos Monastery of Pharoou (Aphrodito) and Its Papyrus Archive." *Le Muséon* 106: 21–63.
  (2005) "The Antaiopolite Estate of Count Ammonios: Managing for This World and the Next in a Time of Plague." *Analecta Papyrologica* 16/17: 109–116.
  (2007) "More on Documentary Coptic at Aphrodito." *Chronique d'Égypte* 82: 381–390.
  (2009) *Coptic Legal Documents: Law as Vernacular Text and Experience in Late Antique Egypt*. Tempe, AZ.
  (2010) "Why and How Was the Aphrodito Cadaster Made?" *Greek, Roman, and Byzantine Studies* 50: 625–638.

(2011) "Monastic and Church Landholding in the Aphrodito Cadaster." *Zeitschrift für Papyrologie und Epigraphik* 178: 243–246.

Mandilaras, B. G. (1991) "The Feast of Thynis, Ἐν ἑορτῇ Θύνεως." *Tyche* 6: 113–116.

Marthot, I. (2013) Un village égyptien et sa campagne: Etude de la microtoponymie du territoire d'Aphroditê (VIe – VIIIe s.). Ph.D. thesis, École Pratiques des Hautes Études, Paris.

Martin, V. (1929) "A Letter from Constantinople." *Journal of Egyptian Archaeology* 15: 96–102.

Maspero, J. (1911) "Un dernier poète grec de l'Egypte, Dioscore, fils d'Apollos." *Revue des Etudes Grecques* 24: 426–481.

(1914) "Horapollon et la fin du paganisme." *Bulletin de L'Institut Français d'Archéologie Orientale* 11: 163–195.

Masson, O. and J.-L. Fournet (1992) "À propos d'Horapollon, l'auteur des Hieroglyphica." *Revue des Etudes Grecques* 105: 231–236.

McConnell, R. (2016) "More Land, More Production, or More Taxes? Revenue Growth on the Apion Estate." *Bulletin of the American Society of Papyrologists* 53: 355–366.

(2017) *Getting Rich in Late Antique Egypt*. Ann Arbor, MI.

McKim, R. (1996) "Philosophers and Cannibals: Juvenal's Fifteenth Satire." *Phoenix* 40: 58–71.

Messiha, H. (1983) *Fragments of Coptic and Greek Papyri from Kom Ishkaw. Annales du Service des Antiquités de l'Egypte*, Suppl. 29. Cairo.

Miller, T. S. (1997) *The Birth of the Hospital in the Byzantine Empire*. Baltimore, MD.

Mirković, M. (1996) "Autopragia and the Village Aphrodito." *Zeitschrift der Savigny-Stiftung für Rechtsgeschichte. Romanistische Abteilung* 113: 346–357.

(2010) "Count Ammonios and Paying Taxes in the Name of Somebody Else in the Cadastre from Aphrodito." In T. Gagos and A. Hyatt, eds., *Proceedings of the Twenty-Fifth International Congress of Papyrology, Ann Arbor, July 29–August 4, 2007*. Ann Arbor, MI: 565–572.

Monson, A. and W. Scheidel, eds. (2015) *Fiscal Regimes and the Political Economy of Premodern States*. Cambridge.

Montevecchi, O. (1950) *I contratti di lavoro e di servizio nell'Egitto greco romano e bizantino*. Milan.

Morelli, F. (2013) "Egitto Arabo: Papiri e Papirologia Greci." *Papyrology AD 2013: 27th International Congress of Papyrology. Journal of Juristic Papyrology* 43: 163–186.

Moss, D. (1979) "Bandits and Boundaries in Sardinia." *Man* New Series 14(3): 477–496.

Palme, B. (2007) "The Imperial Presence: Government and Army." In R. S. Bagnall, ed., *Egypt in the Byzantine World: 300–700*. Cambridge: 244–270.

(2014) "Emotional Strategies in Petitions of Dioscorus of Aphroditê." *Imperium and Officium Working Papers* (www.academia.edu/8252762/2014_Palme_Emotional_Strategies_in_Petitions_of_Dioscorus_of_Aphrodit%C3%AA).

Papaconstantinou, A. (2001) *Le culte des saints en Égypte: des Byzantins aux Abbassides. L'apport des inscriptions et des papyrus grecs et coptes*. Paris.

(2007) "The Cult of Saints: A Haven of Continuity in a Changing World?" In R. S. Bagnall, ed., *Egypt in the Byzantine World: 300–700*. Cambridge: 350–367.

Papathomas, A. (2004) "Vereinbarung über die Rückgabe eines Heirats – bzw. Verlobungsgeschenkes (*dôphurion*) als Schreibühung." *Eirene* 40: 137–145.

Peachin, M. (2011) *The Oxford Handbook of Social Relations in the Roman World*. Oxford and New York, NY.

Pestman, P. W. (1961) *Marriage and Matrimonial Property in Ancient Egypt: A Contribution to Establishing the Legal Position of the Woman*. Leiden.

Pudsey, A. (2011) "Nuptiality and the Demographic Life Cycle of the Family in Roman Egypt." In C. Holleran and A. Pudsey, eds., *Demography and the Graeco-Roman World: New Insights and Approaches*. Cambridge: 60–98.

Quibell, J. (1902) "Kom Ishgaw." *Annales du Service des Antiquités de l'Egypte* 3: 85–88.

Rathbone, D. (1983) "The Weight and Measurement of Egyptian Grains." *Zeitschrift für Papyrologie und Epigraphik* 53: 265–275.

(2008) "Villages and Patronage in Fourth-Century Egypt: The Case of *P.Ross. Georg.* 3.8." *Bulletin of the American Society of Papyrologists* 45: 189–208.

Rémondon, R. (1965) "*P.Hamb.* 56 et *P.Lond.* 1419 (notes sur les finances d'Aphrodito du VIe siècle au VIIIe)." *Chronique d'Egypte* 40: 401–430.

ed. (1971) *Studi in onore di Edoardo Volterra 5*. Milan.

Richter, T. S. (2013) "Coptic Papyri and Juristic Papyrology." *Papyrology AD 2013: 27th International Congress of Papyrology. Journal of Juristic Papyrology* 43: 405–431.

Rowlandson, J. (1996) *Landowners and Tenants in Roman Egypt: The Social Relations of Agriculture in the Oxyrhynchite Nome*. Oxford.

ed. (1998) *Women and Society in Greek and Roman Egypt: A Sourcebook*. Cambridge.

Ruffini, G. (2006) "The Commonality of Rare Names in Byzantine Egypt." *Zeitschrift für Papyrologie und Epigraphik* 158: 213–225.

(2008a) *Social Networks in Byzantine Egypt*. Cambridge.

(2008b) "Aphrodito Before Dioskoros." *Bulletin of the American Society of Papyrologists* 45: 225–239.

(2008c) "Factions and Social Distance in Sixth-Century Aphrodito." In J.-L. Fournet, *Les archives de Dioscore d'Aphrodité cent ans après leur découverte: histoire et culture dans l'Égypte byzantine*. Paris: 157–170.

(2011) *A Prosopography of Byzantine Aphrodito (American Society of Papyrologists Monograph Series 50)*. Durham, NC.

(2012) *Medieval Nubia: A Social and Economic History*. Oxford.

(2013) "Review: B. Kelly, Petitions, Litigation, and Social Control in Roman Egypt." *Topoi* 18: 603–611.

(Unpublished) "Byzantine Aphrodito: Hierarchies and Network Analysis." A paper delivered at the Dumbarton Oaks in March, 2012, manuscript available from author.

Russo, S. (1998) "Il corredo dotale di una giovane antinoita." In L. Del Francia Barocas, ed., *Antinoe cent'anni dopo. Catalogo della mostra, Firenze, Palazzo Medici Riccardi 10 luglio-1° novembre 1998*. Florence: 149–153.

Sant Cassia, P. (1993) "Banditry, Myth, and Terror in Cyprus and Other Mediterranean Societies." *Comparative Studies in Society and History* 35(4): 773–795.

Sarris, P. (2006) *Economy and Society in the Age of Justinian*. Cambridge.

(2009) "Review: Ruffini, Social Networks in Byzantine Egypt." *American Historical Review* 114: 1571–1572.

Sauneron, S. (1983) *Villes et légendes d'Égypte*. Cairo.

Scheidel, W. (2009) "Real Wages in Early Economies: Evidence for Living Standards from 1800 BCE to 1300 CE." *Princeton/Stanford Working Papers in Classics*. Version 4.0 (www.princeton.edu/~pswpc/pdfs/scheidel/090904.pdf).

ed. (2012) *The Cambridge Companion to the Roman Economy*. Cambridge.

Schwendner, G. W. (2008) "An Applied Linguistics Approach to Dioscorus' Homeric Glossary & Poetic Corpus." In J.-L. Fournet, *Les archives de Dioscore d'Aphrodité cent ans après leur découverte: histoire et culture dans l'Égypte byzantine*. Paris: 55–66.

Shaw, B. D. (1984) "Bandits in the Roman Empire." *Past and Present* 105: 3–52.

Shelton, J. (1981) "Two Notes on the Artab." *Zeitschrift für Papyrologie und Epigraphik* 42: 99–106.

Sijpesteijn, P. M. (2013) *Shaping a Muslim State: The World of a Mid-Eighth-Century Egyptian Official*. Oxford.

Storey, I. C. (2003) *Eupolis: Poet of Old Comedy*. Oxford.

Tawfik, Z. (1997) "Wet-Nursing Stipulations in Greek Papyri and Arabic Sources." In B. Kramer et al., eds., *Akten des 21. Internationaler Papyrologenkongress, Berlin, 13.-19.8.1995*. Stuttgart and Leipzig. 2: 939–953.

Thomas, J. P. (1987) *Private Religious Foundations in the Byzantine Empire*. Washington, DC.

Totelin, L. (2012) "Botanizing Rulers and Their Herbal Subjects: Plants and Political Power in Greek and Roman Literature." *Phoenix* 66: 122–144.

Turner, E. G. (1973) "The Charioteers from Antinoe." *Journal of Hellenic Studies* 93: 192–195.

Urbanik, J. (2005) "A Priestly Divorce in the Seventh Century Palestine." In Z. Służewska and J. Urbanik, eds., *Marriage, Ideal – Law – Practice: Proceedings of a Conference Held in Memory of Henryk Kupiszewski*. Warsaw: 199–218.

(2008) "Dioskoros and the Law (on Succession): Lex Falcidia Revisited." In J.-L. Fournet, *Les archives de Dioscore d'Aphrodité cent ans après leur découverte: histoire et culture dans l'Égypte byzantine.* Paris: 117–142.

(2010) "*P. Cair. Masp.* I 67120 *Recto* and the Liability for Latent Defects in the Late Antique Slave Sales or Back to *Epaphe*." *Journal of Juristic Papyrology* 40: 219–247.

(2011) "A Broken Marriage Promise and Justinian as a Lover of Chastity: On Novela 74 and P.Cair.Masp. I 67092 (553)." *Journal of Juristic Papyrology* 41: 123–151.

(2013) "Diligent Carpenters in Dioscoros' Papyri and the Justinianic (?) Standard of Diligence: On P. Cairo Masp. ii 67158 and 67159." In J. Urbanik, ed., *Culpa. Facets of Liability in Ancient Legal Theory and Practice: Proceedings of the Seminar Held in Warsaw 17–19 February 2011. (Journal of Juristic Papyrology Suppl. xix)*. Warsaw: 273–296.

(2013) "Tapia's Banquet Hall and Eulogios' Cell." In P. J. du Plessis, ed., *New Frontiers: Law and Society in the Roman World.* Edinburgh: 151–174.

(2014) "Divorce." In J. Keenan, J. G. Manning and U. Yiftach-Firanko, eds., *Law and Legal Practice in Egypt from Alexander to the Arab Conquest.* Cambridge: 154–175.

van Minnen, P. (1992) "Isocrates and Menander in Late Antique Perspective." *Greek, Roman, and Byzantine Studies* 30: 87–98.

(1993) "Notes on Texts from Graeco-Roman Egypt." *Zeitschrift für Papyrologie und Epigraphik* 96: 117–122.

(1997) "Patronage in Fourth-Century Egypt: A Note on P. Ross. Georg. III 8." *Journal of Juristic Papyrology* 27: 67–73.

(2000) "Agriculture and the 'Taxes-and-Trade' Model in Roman Egypt." *Zeitschrift für Papyrologie und Epigraphik* 133: 205–220.

(2003) "Dioscorus and the Law." In A. A. MacDonald, M. W. Twomey and G. J. Reinink, eds., *Learned Antiquity: Scholarship and Society in the Near East, the Greco-Roman World, and the Early Medieval West.* Leuven: 115–135.

(2007) "The Other Cities in Later Roman Egypt." In R. S. Bagnall, ed., *Egypt in the Byzantine World: 300–700.* Cambridge: 207–225.

Vanderheyden, L. (2012) "Les letters coptes des archives de Dioscore d'Aphrodité." In P. Schubert, ed., *Actes du 26e Congrès international de papyrology.* Geneva: 793–800.

Venticinque, P. F. (2016) *Honor Among Thieves.* Ann Arbor, MI.

Viljamaa, T. (1968) *Studies in Greek Encomiastic Poetry of the Early Byzantine Period (Commentationes Humanarum Litterarum 42.4).* Helsinki.

Watts, E. (2006) *City and School in Late Antique Athens and Alexandria.* Berkeley, CA.

Whitby, M. (2001) "A Hellenist in Late-Antique Aphrodito." *Classical Review* 51: 27–28.

Wickham, C. (2005) *Framing the Early Middle Ages: Europe and the Mediterranean 400–800.* Oxford.

Wilfong, T. (2007) "Gender and Society in Byzantine Egypt." In R. S. Bagnall, ed., *Egypt in the Byzantine World: 300–700*. Cambridge: 309–327.

Wipszycka, E. (2007) "The Institutional Church." In R. S. Bagnall, ed., *Egypt in the Byzantine World: 300–700*. Cambridge: 331–349.

(2008) "Le monastère d'Apa Apollôs: un cas typique ou un cas exceptionnel?" In J.-L. Fournet, *Les archives de Dioscore d'Aphrodité cent ans après leur découverte: histoire et culture dans l'Égypte byzantine*. Paris: 261–273.

Worp, K. (2008) "Witness Subscriptions in Documents from the Dioscorus Archive." In J.-L. Fournet, *Les archives de Dioscore d'Aphrodité cent ans après leur découverte: histoire et culture dans l'Égypte byzantine*. Paris: 143–153.

(2014) "Nauklêroi, Kybernêtai and Nauklêrokybernêtai and Their Ships in Roman and Byzantine Egypt." *Analecta Papyrologica* 26: 261–278.

Yiftach-Firanko, U. (2006) "Spouses in Wills: A Diachronic Survey (III BC–IV AD)." *Journal of Juristic Papyrology* 36: 153–166.

Zuckerman, C. (2004a) *Du village à l'Empire: Autour du registre fiscal d'Aphroditô (525/526)*. Paris.

(2004b) "Les deux Dioscore d'Aphroditè ou les limites de la pétition." In D. Feissel and J. Gascou, eds., *La pétition à Byzance*. Paris: 75–92.

General Index

abigeatus, 70
abortion, 131
absentee landlords, 76, 82, 211
accounts, 78, 80, 124, 145
Ama Rachel, 149, 157
Ammonios, 20, 79, 102, 103, 112, 113, 114, 125, 151, 164
   accounts of, 77, 78, 113, 124
   and village headmen, 47, 49, 50
   and village taxes, 47
   estates of, 77, 78, 80, 85, 93, 104
   patronage of, 92, 102, 113, 164, 200
Antaiopolis
   Aphrodito's relationship with, 182
   bishops of, 125
   fiscal apparatus of, 85
   land of, 16, 92
   small claims cases in, 52
   violence in, 38, 119
Antinoopolis
   Aphrodito lawsuits in, 54
   craftsmen of, 103
   Dioskoros in, 159, 168, 184, 193, 196, 198
   education at, 187
   excavations of, 183
   history of, 182
   hospital of, 140, 144
   marriages in, 137
   minorities in, 184
   occupations of, 107
   slavery in, 108
   stylite of, 129
Antonine Itinerary, 10
Apa Romanos, 114
Apa Sourous monastery, 61, 113, 123
Aphrodito
   Christianization of, 112
   churches of, 120
   government of, 47, 50
   houses of, 11
   in the fifth century, 201
   occupations of people in, 21, 95, 105
   saints of, 123
   size of, 16
   tax register of, 24, 87, 89, 90, 92, 112, 117
   topography of, vi, 13, 15, 16, 17, 18, 94, 95
   typicality of, 18, 105, 211
   under Arab rule, 207
Apions, 77, 210
Apollos
   Life of, 129
   monastery of, 72, 114, 115, 117, 118, 119
Arabic texts from Aphrodito, 1, 8, 205
Arabs, war with, 22
arbitration, 53, 54, 57, 83, 116, 172, 191, 197
Athanasios, 165, 166, 168, 173, 179, 180
athletics, 185
Attic Greek, 191
autopragia, 23, 50, 51, 59
   benefits of, 51
   future of, 202
   loss of, 46, 92
   origins of, 46, 201
   payments for, 43, 84

Baldwin, Barry, 19
Banaji, Jairus, 23, 24, 25
banditry, 41, 68, 71, 72, 164
Basil, archive of, 8, 203
beatings, 30, 32
beekeepers, 99
Bell, Harold Idris, 23
bishops, 125, 126, 127, 130
Blemmyes, 38, 129, 169, 170, 171
blindness, 146, 147
Brown, Peter, 207

calendar, religious, 124
carpenters, 97
Chalcedon, 3
chariot racing, 185
charity, 27, 113, 144, 146, 154

General Index

child mortality, 131
children, 131
circus factions, 185
class warfare, 22, 212
Constantinople
  Apollos in, 173, 174, 175, 176
  Dioskoros in, 68, 126, 127, 175, 177, 178, 179
contracts, 52, 55, 84, 139, 180
Coptic
  documents, 8, 9, 83, 116, 202
  glossary, 100, 131, 147, 195, 197
  language, 116, 196
  speakers, 187, 195

demography, 46
demons, 136, 137, 138
Dioskoros
  and pasture land, 66
  and shepherds, 60, 61
  and the law, 69, 71, 72, 140, 190, 197
  archive of, 9
  as a teacher, 188
  education of, 190, 198
  family of, 21
  pasture land of, 62
  piety of, 116
  poetry of, 19, 23, 25, 115, 162, 179, 194, 195
  theft from, 63, 64, 65, 118
  titles of, 19
disability, 146, 147
disowning, 142, 143
disputes
  arbitration of, 54, 56, 116, 135
  government involvement in, 52, 207
  in public, 57, 143
  informal resolution of, 53, 59
divorce, 136, 137, 138, 139, 147
doctors, 143, 144
donatio mortis causa, 139

education, 184, 187, 188
Egypt, administration of, 43
engineers, 97
envy, 172, 173
estates, size of, 81
eugenestatai. See women, well-born
Eupolis, 191, 192
evil eye, 137, 173

factionalism, 30, 46, 68, 74, 100
feudalism, 23, 77
Flavius, rank of, 175
Fournet, Jean-Luc, 9, 20, 25

funerals, 140
furtum, 70

gender, 160
Gnosticism, 193
gold coinage, 23
goldsmiths, 99
golf. *See* Keenan, James
gross marketed surplus, 83, 89
guarantees, 110
guilds, 26, 64, 95, 96, 98, 100, 101, 104

Hathor, 10
Herakleios, party of, 50, 67, 68
hieroglyphs, 194
holy men, 27, 111, 128, 129, 130, 163, 208, 212
Homer, 188, 190
Horapollon, 194
hospitals, 143, 144
hunters, 101, 102, 103

inequality, wealth, 88
informants, 30, 64, 66, 67, 68, 69, 70, 146, 205
inheritance, 108, 141, 171
  and disowning, 142
  debts against, 31
  denial of, 31, 198
  disputes over, 135, 136, 152, 172
  laws of, 69
  selling of, 178
Ioulianos, 20, 24, 44, 84, 92, 161, 162, 172, 211
  accusations against, 20, 34, 44, 176
  and tax increases, 84, 166
  decree against, 177
  defense of, 35
  estates of, 91
Isocrates, 179, 191, 192

Jkow, 10, 12
Justinian, 3, 42, 46, 69, 171, 190, 209

Karanis, 4, 168
Keenan, James, 25
Kollouthos, archive of, 9
Kom Ishqaw
  excavations of, 5, 8, 9
  modern description of, 12
Kostantios, family of, 201
Kovelman, Arkady, 20
Kuehn, Clement, 20

labor, specialization of, 106
land
  monastic and church ownership of, 124
  transfer of, 86, 87

General Index

lawsuits, vexatious, 63
leases
   reverse, 83
   terms of, 76, 81, 82, 107
Lefebvre, Gustav, 8, 191
lex falcidia, 140
literacy, 133, 134, 151
loans, 76
love, 148

MacCoull, Leslie, 9, 13, 20, 24
magic, 193
Maria the wine seller, 149
marriage, 104, 148
   contracts for, 132, 134, 135, 151, 152
   gifts for, 132
Marthot, Isabelle, 25
math, 188, 189, 190
medicine, 145, 192
Menander, 8, 53, 54, 179, 191, 192
Menas the pagarch, 34, 61
Mirrit Boutros Ghali. *See* MacCoull, Leslie
miscarriage, 131
monasticism, 111
monetization, 24, 98, 205
Montaillou, 5
murder, 2, 28, 31
Muslim Egypt, 8

Nag Hammadi, 193
Neoplatonism, 210
network analysis, 209
Nikantinoos, 54, 55, 56, 59, 184
nuns, 37, 155, 156
nurses, 144

oil makers, 98
ostraca, 6, 98
Oxyrhynchos, 4, 77, 90, 102, 118, 211

Panopolis, 31, 32, 98, 182
Patrikia, 84, 161, 162, 163, 172
patronage, 164, 176
   imperial, 35, 47, 175
   in modern historiography, 23, 208
   of local officials, 31, 59, 92, 113, 164, 165, 200
   searching for, 32, 34, 154, 168, 207
peasant agency, 91
perilusis, 136
Persians, war with, 22, 202
Philantinoos, family of, 200
Phoibammon
   and Nikantinoos, 54

and Samuel, 76, 77
archive of, 9
as a land entrepreneur, 25
as a model career, 88
Phthla
   shepherds of, 61, 62, 167, 170
   village of, 10, 18
pillaging, 34, 35, 37, 41, 51, 167
plague, 24, 44, 113, 170, 209
Pliny the Elder, 10
police, 9, 36, 73, 99, 138, 183
pottery production, 97
prison, 31, 36, 37, 166
Procopius, 210, 212
profit, 89
Ptolemy, 10

Quibell, James, 5, 6
Qurra ibn Sharik, 8, 203, 205, 206, 207

rape, 37, 38, 138, 167
rental markets, 86, 91
rent-seeking, 51, 52, 86, 171
repenting, 126
Roman Empire, fall of, 22
Romanos, 178

sailors, 205
Sardinia, 68
Sarris, Peter, 24
Secundus the Silent, 196
Shenoute, 123, 127, 129, 157, 171, 182, 192, 199
shipbuilders, 101
Sicily, 71, 204
Simeon the Stylite, 111, 128, 129, 212
slander, 36, 171, 172, 173
slavery, 108, 154, 155, 156
Sohag, 182
soldiers, 53, 204
   as landlords, 75
   discharged, 39
   violence by, 119
Sophia, wife of Dioskoros, 150, 151, 202
Sourous, family of, 201
stylite, 129
sublets, 82
Surion, family of, 201

taxes, 43, 47
   and slander, 172
   and the *suntelestria*, 19, 150
   as plunder, 51
   collection of, 84, 85, 127

taxes (cont.)
    double collection of, 176
    female collectors of, 162
    petitions about, 165, 166, 169
    rates of, 84, 167, 205
    records for, 85, 86, 177
    remission of, 84
    transfer of, 141
    under Arab administration, 206
teachers, 187, 188
Temseu Skordon, 86, 88, 117
theft, 34
Theodora, 47, 134, 151
    patronage of, 46, 47
    petition to, 44, 51, 95, 97, 122
Theodosian Code, 71
Thynis, 166, 181
trade associations. *See* Guilds
trespass, 60, 61, 62, 63, 66, 67
Trinity, Holy, 127
trust, hierarchies of, 110

violence, 4, 166
virginity, 135

White Monastery, 123, 127, 128, 182, 192, 199
    and land ownership at Aphrodito, 157
    donations to, 157, 171
widows, 141, 157, 158, 159
wills, 141
witnesses, 53, 55, 56, 104, 133, 198
women, 22
    and poverty, 156, 157
    as land managers, 150
    in business, 149
    in village elite, 153
    missing, 159
    names of, 160
    well-born, 150, 151, 152
    without men, 156
work agreements, 101, 103, 104

Zuckerman, Constantin, 24

Index Locorum

CPR 22.53, 207
CPR 30.3, 172

P.Coll.Youtie 2.92, 153
P.Aphrod.Lit 4.39–40, 115
P.Aphrod.Lit. 3.1–4, 190
P.Aphrod.Lit. 4.1, 126
P.Aphrod.Lit. 4.11, 167, 170
P.Aphrod.Lit. 4.17, 173
P.Aphrod.Lit. 4.3, 167
P.Aphrod.Lit. 4.32, 160, 161
P.Aphrod.Lit. 4.34, 161, 173
P.Aphrod.Lit. 4.35, 162
P.Aphrod.Lit. 4.4, 172, 178
P.Aphrod.Lit. 4.48, 120
P.Aphrod.Lit. 4.5, 126, 175
P.Aphrod.Reg. 90, 97
P.Brem. 42, 10
P.Cair.inv. SR 3733 (2), 47
P.Cair.inv. SR 37333, 9
P.Cair.Masp. 1.67001, 53
P.Cair.Masp. 1.67002, 11, 37, 62, 65, 127, 165, 166
P.Cair.Masp. 1.67003, 119
P.Cair.Masp. 1.67004, 168
P.Cair.Masp. 1.67005, 31, 32
P.Cair.Masp. 1.67006.r, 157
P.Cair.Masp. 1.67006.v, 134
P.Cair.Masp. 1.67009, 38, 39
P.Cair.Masp. 1.67019, 46
P.Cair.Masp. 1.67020, 146
P.Cair.Masp. 1.67023, 153
P.Cair.Masp. 1.67024, 21, 46, 176
P.Cair.Masp. 1.67026, 35, 178
P.Cair.Masp. 1.67028, 69, 178
P.Cair.Masp. 1.67029, 175
P.Cair.Masp. 1.67032, 50, 68, 178
P.Cair.Masp. 1.67062, 79
P.Cair.Masp. 1.67077, 144
P.Cair.Masp. 1.67078, 36
P.Cair.Masp. 1.67087, 60

P.Cair.Masp. 1.67090, 164
P.Cair.Masp. 1.67091, 35
P.Cair.Masp. 1.67092, 138
P.Cair.Masp. 1.67093, 36
P.Cair.Masp. 1.67094, 109
P.Cair.Masp. 1.67095, 91, 109
P.Cair.Masp. 1.67096, 117, 143
P.Cair.Masp. 1.67097.F, 185
P.Cair.Masp. 1.67097.v.D, 142
P.Cair.Masp. 1.67097.v.F, 115
P.Cair.Masp. 1.67104, 81
P.Cair.Masp. 1.67109, 97
P.Cair.Masp. 1.67110, 96
P.Cair.Masp. 1.67116, 106
P.Cair.Masp. 1.67120, 108, 197
P.Cair.Masp. 1.67121, 136
P.Cair.Masp. 2.67126, 57
P.Cair.Masp. 2.67130, 67
P.Cair.Masp. 2.67133, 114
P.Cair.Masp. 2.67138, 77
P.Cair.Masp. 2.67139, 77, 78,
P.Cair.Masp. 2.67141, 79, 80, 105, 124, 145, 146, 159
P.Cair.Masp. 2.67143, 63, 64, 65, 99, 107, 146
P.Cair.Masp. 2.67144, 65, 66
P.Cair.Masp. 2.67146, 149
P.Cair.Masp. 2.67147, 100
P.Cair.Masp. 2.67151, 140
P.Cair.Masp. 2.67153, 20, 137
P.Cair.Masp. 2.67154.v, 139
P.Cair.Masp. 2.67155, 106, 137
P.Cair.Masp. 2.67156, 141
P.Cair.Masp. 2.67158, 103
P.Cair.Masp. 2.67159, 53, 104
P.Cair.Masp. 2.67163, 106
P.Cair.Masp. 2.67164, 107
P.Cair.Masp. 2.67168, 126
P.Cair.Masp. 2.67169, 89
P.Cair.Masp. 2.67175, 191
P.Cair.Masp. 2.67176.r + P.Alex.inv. 689, 116
P.Cair.Masp. 2.67188.v, 185, 192

232 *Index Locorum*

P.Cair.Masp. 2.67200, 50
P.Cair.Masp. 2.67202, 37, 172
P.Cair.Masp. 2.67234, 122
P.Cair.Masp. 2.67242, 122
P.Cair.Masp. 2.67253, 137
P.Cair.Masp. 3.67283, 44, 46, 125
P.Cair.Masp. 3.67287, 105
P.Cair.Masp. 3.67290, 52
P.Cair.Masp. 3.67295, 126, 193
P.Cair.Masp. 3.67296, 99
P.Cair.Masp. 3.67297 + P.Flor. 3.287, 65
P.Cair.Masp. 3.67300, 151
P.Cair.Masp. 3.67303, 80, 110
P.Cair.Masp. 3.67306, 150
P.Cair.Masp. 3.67309, 152
P.Cair.Masp. 3.67310, 133, 148
P.Cair.Masp. 3.67312, 108, 144, 171
P.Cair.Masp. 3.67314, 151
P.Cair.Masp. 3.67319, 50, 62, 65, 66, 67
P.Cair.Masp. 3.67323, 21, 47
P.Cair.Masp. 3.67324, 139, 141
P.Cair.Masp. 3.67325.r.IV, 150, 157
P.Cair.Masp. 3.67326, 125, 194
P.Cair.Masp. 3.67328, 109
P.Cair.Masp. 3.67329, 52, 87
P.Cair.Masp. 3.67330, 101
P.Cair.Masp. 3.67338, 127
P.Cair.Masp. 3.67352, 178
P.Cair.Masp. 3.67353, 69, 116, 142
P.Cair.Masp. 367295, 194
P.Cair.Masp. 1.67064, 19
P.Cair.Masp. 2.67147, 95
P.Col. 8.235, 10, 112
P.Coll.Youtie 2.92, 106, 107
P.Flor. 3.285, 98
P.Flor. 3.294, 134
P.Flor. 3.295 + P.Lond. 5.1678 + P.Lond.inv. 01607, 39,
P.Flor. 3.296, 167
P.Flor. 3.342, 174
P.Haun. 3.58, 168
P.Heid.Arab. 1.4, 206
P.Herm. 32, 89
P.Kell. 2.32, 10
P.Lond 4.1494, 205
P.Lond. 4.1350, 204, 205
P.Lond. 4.1380, 206
P.Lond. 4.1433, 206
P.Lond. 4.1592, 203
P.Lond. 5.1660, 84, 161, 162, 172
P.Lond. 5.1674, 11, 37, 83, 84, 165, 172, 184, 195
P.Lond. 5.1676, 135, 141, 145
P.Lond. 5.1677, 34, 49, 62, 172
P.Lond. 5.1681, 49, 51
P.Lond. 5.1687, 151

P.Lond. 5.1691, 189
P.Lond. 5.1694, 82
P.Lond. 5.1695, 150
P.Lond. 5.1699, 97
P.Lond. 5.1705, 82
P.Lond. 5.1706, 53
P.Lond. 5.1708, 136, 144, 172
P.Lond. 5.1709, 197
P.Lond. 5.1710, 134
P.Lond. 5.1711, 133, 148, 151
P.Lond. 5.1712, 137
P.Lond. 5.1713, 137
P.Lond. 5.1714, 116, 189
P.Lond. 5.1718, 188, 189
P.Lond. 5.1821, 195
P.Lond. 5.1894, 139
P.Lond.Herm, 86, 117
P.Mich. 13.659, 56
P.Mich. 13.660, 1, 30
P.Mich. 13.661, 29, 30
P.Mich. 13.670, 76
P.Mich.Aphrod. 54, 55
P.Michael. 41, 125
P.Michael. 42.A, 133
P.Michael. 42.B, 133, 147
P.Michael. 43, 81
P.Michael. 45, 77
P.Michael. 53, 139
P.Oxy. 16.2058, 64
P.Oxy. 80.5227–5229, 192
P.Qurra 1, 206
P.Qurra 2, 206
P.Qurra 4, 206
P.Ross.Georg. 3.16, 172
P.Ross.Georg. 3.38, 184
P.Ross.Georg. 5.32, 106
P.Stras. 1.40, 107
P.Stras. 1.46, 106
P.Turner 54, 129
P.Vat.Aphrod. 1, 81
P.Vat.Copti Doresse, 80, 158
PGM 2.P 13A, 192
PSI 7.815, 10

SB 1.4661, 89
SB 14.11357, 168
SB 16.12371, 32
SB 16.12542.7, 64
SB 18.13274, 154
SB 18.13320, 95, 182
SB 20.14626, 72, 118, 144
SB 20.14669, 79, 87, 97, 144, 170
SB 20.14670, 79, 144
SB 20.14699, 80
SB 20.15018, 50

SB 22.15522, 53
SB 22.15633, 133, 134, 151
SB 3.6704, 101
SB 4.7438, 175
SB 5.8938, 11
SB 6.9102, 175

SB Kopt. 3.1369, 202
Sel.Pap. 2.218, 21, 46, 176
Sel.Pap. 2.363, 50, 68
Sel.Pap. 2.431, 175
Sel.Pap. 2.434, 206
Sel.Pap. 1.87, 142